# HITLER'S LAST WEAPONS

# HITLER'S LAST WEAPONS

## The underground war against the V1 and V2

## Józef Garliński

Times
BOOKS

First published in Great Britain in 1978 by
Julian Friedmann Publishers Ltd.


**Library of Congress Cataloging in Publication Data**

Garlinski, Józef.
  Hitler's last weapons.

  Bibliography:  p.
  Includes indexes.
  1.  World War, 1939-1945—Aerial operations,
German.  2.  V-1 bomb.  3.  V-2 rocket.  4.  World
War, 1939-1945—Technology.  5.  World War, 1939-
1945—Underground movements—Europe.  6.  World
War, 1939-1945—Germany.  I.  Title.
D787.G36  1978       940.4′49′43        78-9784
ISBN 0-8129-0787-6

# CONTENTS

# PREFACE

The first time that I heard about the German secret weapons was in June 1944. I was then a political prisoner in a small concentration camp in Wittenberge, in the heart of Germany, where we were building a factory together with civilian workmen. It was the middle of the month and we had all been cheered up by the great days of invasion of the Continent, which could not be kept hidden from us. During work one of the labourers, a Pole, whispered to me: 'Very bad news, the Germans are bombing England with a secret weapon, the *Wunderwaffe*.'

In the evening, in the barracks, we passed on this information in whispers and our hearts were constricted by fear. Fragmentary news had reached us of a wonderful weapon in German hands which would change the fortunes of the war, but we had taken it for propaganda, not worth closer attention. Now it turned out to be true. We dreaded the thought of this new weapon, and the danger to the Allied armies on the French coast.

All prisoners, of every nationality, lived through the military build-up and the Allied landings on the Continent in a fever, for to each one this meant that the day of freedom was approaching; but the French and the Poles reacted in a specific way. Among the French were those whose towns or villages had already been liberated, and these had gone mad with joy, seeing themselves at home within a few weeks. Now, at the news that a new German secret weapon had been brought into action, their faces fell. For us Poles, the news had even more serious implications. Soviet armies were already on Polish soil, but we were clinging to the hope that the western Allies would advance quickly, overthrow the Germans and reach our western frontiers before the Red Army occupied the whole of Poland. In the camp we knew nothing of the secret Allied decisions to hand over our country to the Russians. If the Germans brought a new weapon into action at this stage, this might hold up the Allies' forward march and leave Poland at the mercy of her Eastern neighbour.

After the war I returned in thought many times to that June day which had frightened us so, and I tried to find out more about the secret German missiles. I learned that they were flying bombs, V-1, and rockets, V-2; I became acquainted with the technical details; I was interested in the fact that the matter was connected with the Polish Underground Movement, but my historical studies were concentrated on other subjects. I considered that it was still too early, that this subject required a greater distance in order to approach it objectively and without the understandable rancour of the first post-war years. It was therefore only recently that I decided to research this subject in depth.

The first serious reading in several languages showed that in the search for and the fight against the German experiments, which chiefly concerned the V-1 and the V-2, the underground movements not only in Poland but in the other occupied countries, Belgium, Denmark, France, Holland, Luxembourg and Norway, took part. I also discovered that the danger had been greater than is generally supposed and that the Germans were well ahead in the scientific world, especially in rocketry. I learnt that on both sides of the front dividing Hitler from the west an enormous amount of intelligence work was carried out, and that many surprising errors were committed, errors which today seem difficult to believe.

In spite of the numerous books which have appeared on this subject none has taken in the whole question: the German side, the Allies, and the underground efforts in the occupied countries. Studying documents, statements and books already published, I came upon other secret German weapons, but I have concentrated solely on the flying bombs and rockets, for only they were finally brought into operation.

As always in historical studies there stood before me the problem of assessing the events described; it was necessary to adopt a definite position, above all on who was responsible for starting the war and on the manner in which it was conducted. I had not and I have not any doubt that war of aggression is a crime, and from this point of view the leaders of the Third *Reich* were responsible. Theirs also is the guilt of violating international laws regulating armed conflicts, and the guilt of mass genocide. However, this responsibility cannot be extended to the whole nation. I reject the accusation that all German scientists working on the secret weapons are war criminals. They were after all subjects of their country; the war was no fault of theirs; they were bound to work for the national war effort. Morally there is no difference between the maker of a bayonet and the maker of an atomic bomb. This must be said clearly, for post-war propaganda has caused confusion on this subject. Opinions coming from the east, for instance, maintained that the German scientists who worked on the rockets and went to the United States after the war should stand trial: but there is not a single word about the German brain-drain to Moscow.

Every war brings with it death, conflagration, suffering and hatred; but it also produces in people physical and moral strength, it creates conditions in which great, sometimes heroic deeds are done. The intensification of effort also brings about technical progres which contributes to human development. So it was with the German rockets. Built with the thought of overthrowing the enemy and designed for mass destruction, with the passing of the post-war years these same missiles have helped man to reach interplanetary space.

In my work I have relied on archival sources, on published material and on statements from the participants of the events described. For help shown to me I am grateful to the Museet for Danmarks Frihedkamp in Copenhagen, the Rijksinstituut voor Oorlogsdocumentatie in Amsterdam, the Comité d'Histoire de la 2e Guerre Mondiale, the Public Record Office and two Polish Institutes in London: the General Sikorski Historical Institute and the Polish Underground Movement (1939-45) Study Trust.

I am indebted to the individual help of many people, above all to Professor R.V. Jones of the University of Aberdeen, J. Helme and B. Maurer of Copenhagen, J.C. van Winkelen and Z. Hornung of Holland, R. Gheysens of Belgium, J.B. Krokowski and Col. M. Protesewicz of France. I would also like to thank Col. K. Iranek-Osmecki, Lt-Colonel T. Lisicki and Lt-Colonel B. Zieliński, with whom I had many conversations in London.

For financial assistance towards my research, I am indebted to the Kosciuszko Foundation in New York.

London, November 1977                                              J.G.

# ILLUSTRATIONS AND MAPS

Photographs by courtesy of: Associated Press Photos, Bundesarchiv (Koblenz), Wacław Czarnecki, David Floyd, Wincenty Hein, Imperial War Museum, Reginald V. Jones, William Kimber and Co. Ltd, G.J.I. Kokhuis (Holland), Libraire Jules Tallandier (Paris), C. Lindemann, Tadeusz Lisicki, Museet for Danmarks Frihedkamp (Copenhagen), Thomas Nelson and Sons Ltd, Radio Times Hulton Picture Library, Michał Wojewódski, Zygmunt Zonik.

# GLOSSARY OF NAMES

*A-1, A-2, A-3, A-4* — prototypes of V-2
*Agence Immobilière* — French underground organization connected with General de Gaulle
*Agir* — French intelligence network organized by Captain Hollard
*AK* — *Armia Krajowa* (Home Army)
*Akcja Kontynentalna* — Continental Action: the initiative of the Polish Government in London to activate the Polish communities in France and Belgium
*Alliance* — French underground organization set up in co-operation with the British
*Alsos* — American mission to check German progress with the atomic bomb
*Arka* — Bureau of Economic Studies of *ZWZ*
*Bałtyk* — a cell of the intelligence network *Lombard*
*Bardsea* — plan to mobilize Poles in France during invasion
*BCRA* — *Bureau Central de Renseignements et d'Action* (de Gaulle)
*Black Plan* — plan for evacuation of London under threat by V-1 and V-2
*Bodyline Committee* — British Committee of scientists to investigate V-1 and V-2.
*Boucle* — Belgian intelligence network
*Bug* — American prototype of V-1
*CIU* — Central Interpretation Unit
*Crossbow Committee* — British committee of scientists which took over from the Bodyline Committee
*Die Rote Kapelle* — German Communist underground

|                        |                                                                                                                                            |
| ---------------------- | ------------------------------------------------------------------------------------------------------------------------------------------ |
|                        | intelligence network                                                                                                                        |
| *Eclipse*              | — Allied postwar plan for administration of Germany                                                                                          |
| *Eleuthère*            | — French underground organization connected with General de Gaulle                                                                          |
| *Enigma*               | — German cipher machine                                                                                                                      |
| *Equipe Z*             | — group of Polish cryptologists in France                                                                                                   |
| *EU/P*                 | — sub-section of the Polish section of SOE, dealing with the Polish minority in Northern France                                             |
| *F*                    | — SOE independent French section                                                                                                            |
| *F2*                   | — Polish intelligence organization in France                                                                                                |
| *Famille Martin*       | — underground group in Northern France                                                                                                      |
| *Gestapo*              | — *Geheime Staatspolizei*                                                                                                                    |
| *Hydra*                | — bombing operation on Peenemünde, 17-18 September 1943                                                                                      |
| *Iodoform*             | — system of secret signals sent, in connection with dropping and landing operations, by the Polish Radio in Britain through the BBC         |
| *Kedyw*                | — *Komenda Dywersji* (Diversion and Sabotage Command of the Home Army)                                                                       |
| *Lombard*              | — intelligence group of the Home Army                                                                                                        |
| *Monika*               | — Polish underground organization in Northern France set up in connection with Continental Action                                           |
| *Most*                 | — 'bridge': two-way operation with a plane landing in Poland and returning to its base in Allied territory                                   |
| *Motyl*                | — secret landing-ground in Poland                                                                                                           |
| *NKWD*                 | — *Narodny Komissariat Vnutrennich Dyel* (People's Commissariat of Internal Affairs: used for Soviet secret police)                          |
| *Noball*               | — air-operations against the launching-pads of V-1                                                                                          |
| *ORA*                  | — *Organisation de Résistance de l'Armée* (connected with General de Gaulle)                                                                 |
| *Operation Paperclip*  | — revised American plan for using German rocket specialists                                                                                  |

Europe on 1.1.1941

| | |
|---|---|
| *Overcast* | — American plan for using German rocket specialists |
| *Overlord* | — the invasion of the continent |
| *P.C. Bruno* | — unit of French cryptologists |
| *PIU* | — Photo Interpretation Unit |
| *POWN* | — *Polska Organizacja Walki o Niepodległość* (Polish Organization of Fight for Freedom) |
| *PRU* | — Photo Reconnaissance Unit |
| *RF* | — SOE section working directly with de Gaulle's BCRA |
| *RSHA* | — *Reichssicherheitshauptamt* |
| *Rumpelkammer* | — German V-1 offensive against Great Britain |
| *RWD* | — Polish pre-war light aircraft |
| *'S'* | — Polish liaison outpost in Switzerland |
| *SD* | — *Sicherheitsdienst* |
| *SHAEF* | — Supreme Headquarters, Allied Expeditionary Force |
| *SOE* | — Special Operations Executive |
| *SS* | — *Schutzstaffel* |
| *Safehaven* | — control of German scientists connected with armaments |
| *Sealion* | — German plan for invasion of Great Britain |
| *Seeräuber* | — 'Corsair': German monitoring station in Paris |
| *Service Clarence* | — Belgian underground group |
| *Ultra* | — British secret unit for distributing deciphered German messages |
| *V-1* | — *Vergeltungswaffe I* (flying bomb) |
| *V-2* | — *Vergeltungswaffe II* (rocket) |
| *WVHA* | — *Wirtschafts-und Verwaltungshauptamt* |
| *Werwolf* | — secret Nazi organization |
| *Wild Boar* | — special German night-fighter unit |
| *Wildhorn* | — secret landing in Poland |
| *ZWZ* | — *Związek Walki Zbrojnej* (Union for Armed Struggle) |

# HITLER'S
# LAST
# WEAPONS

# CHAPTER ONE
## The Beginning

1

Early in the morning of 17 October 1939 Vice-Admiral Hector Boyes, the naval attaché at the British embassy in Oslo, decided not to use his car but walked the short distance to his office. There was a slight frost although the day promised to be sunny.

The Vice-Admiral, a slim good-looking man with a reputation for decisive energy, to-day walked slowly and hesitantly. His thoughts kept returning to the telegram he had received three days earlier. During the night of 13-14 October, at the British naval base of Scapa Flow in the north of Scotland, in the safest place in the world for her, a narrow sea-passage, the mighty battleship *Royal Oak* had been hit by two torpedoes and had gone to the bottom within thirteen minutes, taking more than 800 seamen with her.[1]

The news seemed unbelievable, on the fringe of utter absurdity, impossible. But it was true and it brought the darkest thoughts to mind. The Admiral had seen service in the First World War; he knew the Germans and their fighting qualities; but he never imagined they could be more dangerous than they were in 1914-18. It was obvious now, however, that they were, since their U-boat had undertaken the crazy enterprise of attacking a British battleship in the very heart of what had appeared to be an impregnable base.

Until then British public opinion had made little of the German dictator; caricatures of him had appeared frequently in newspapers with his outstretched arm and the lock of hair falling on his forehead; his shrieks, given out over the radio, had produced shrugs. Yet he must have something, since the German nation acknowledged his leadership and had put its whole future into his hands. Over sixty million people looked up to him in admiration and fascination. The exploit of the German U-boat was a sign of fanaticism, and for soldiers like the Germans fanatical leadership could take them a long way.

The embassy building loomed ahead and within a few minutes the attaché was in his room. He lit a cigarette and looked at the correspondence lying on his desk, fearing more news of German successes at sea and sunken British ships.

His secretary came in and handed him a large white envelope, already opened and bearing no address. She explained that it had been passed on by the ambassador's office and that it had been put anonymously into the embassy letter-box.

The admiral looked inside it and took out a long letter in German. He knew the language fairly well and started to read; but he had to reach for the dictionary. Several minutes later he put the letter aside, shut his eyes and, deep in thought, sat back in his chair. Was this from a secret informer? The letter described German missiles equipped with wings; it mentioned rockets, warned against poison-gas, and drew attention to a study by the *Wehrmacht* concerning radio measurements of distance.[2] It was all so unexpected, so extraordinary, that the attaché had an interpreter brought in and together they began to work their way through the complicated text.

It was impossible to be certain about the value or authenticity of the document at this stage: was it material of exceptional value, or a German attempt at misinformation? But the naval attaché couldn't take the risk in case it was accurate. The document must be passed on to London with the utmost speed.


2


The German nation had never come to terms with its defeat in 1918, or with the decisions of the peace conference, which it called the 'Versailles dictum'. It was generally held that the army had not been 'defeated' but had been forced to surrender by the breakdown of the domestic front, and by the lack of special weapons which would have taken the enemy by surprise. Revenge was constantly in the thoughts of many prominent Germans, and from the immediate post-war years scientists had begun work on new inventions.

Experiments were carried out in various fields, some of them openly, perhaps to stress that the scientists were not so much preparing for war as concerned with general, peace-time development and progress. The clauses of the Versailles treaty, limiting the production of conventional weapons, had to be taken into account; they had to be circumvented and new types of military armament discovered.

In 1933 when Hitler came to power, the situation changed immediately. Rearmament began on a vast scale, obvious to all, not only to intelligence agents.

Tanks and guns were built, the infantry was motorized, the number of divisions increased; the limitations imposed on building the navy, decided in Versailles, were ignored; Hermann Göring promised the German people the best and the largest air force in the world, within a few years. He declared that no enemy aircraft would ever again penetrate the territory of the Third *Reich*.

So far, however, these preparations consisted only of conventional weapons, and the defeat in the last war had proved that these would not be proof against the opposition, who would probably once more form an alliance and create a common front against any attempt by Germany to ignore the terms of Versailles. New weapons were needed and all the decisions, experiments and tests connected with them must be kept secret. The enemy was clever. Complete surprise was what counted. During the First World War gas had been used: it was nothing new now, and many countries were preparing for it, but it could not be excluded from the list of new weapons because it was possible that new chemical elements might be employed. As well as gas there was talk of bacterial warfare, of death rays, of aerial torpedoes and pilotless aircraft, of long-range guns, of rockets, of magnetic mines.

By now, below the surface of outward peace a full intelligence war was being waged. British agents were trying to penetrate the screen of German military preparations, and naturally they were most interested in the new inventions, the first report on which reached London in June 1934 and concerned bacterial warfare. Later reports constantly referred to this same threat. Others mentioned gases which could penetrate civilian gas-masks.[3] No more was heard of other new weapons.

In the meantime Hitler began his bloodless conquest of Europe.

He occupied the demilitarized Rhineland in October 1936, using none of these weapons and therefore revealing no military secrets.

### 3

Wernher von Braun was born in 1912 in Pomerania, which at that time belonged to Germany. Six years later, when Pomerania became part of the revived Polish state,* his family moved to Germany. The small boy proved to be an exceptionally clever child with an interest in physics and chemistry. He was a good scholar, displaying an uncompromising drive towards the aims which he set himself. At seventeen he became a student at the Higher Technical School in Zürich.

At this time, work on jet-propelled missiles was already fairly advanced in Germany. The young Wernher was so interested in the subject (he was in touch with the leading scientific researchers on rocket technology—engineers Karl Wahmke, Rudolf Nebel and Klaus Riedel) that he transferred to the University of Berlin, where he studied under a friend of his father, Professor Karl Emil Becker. Professor Becker, however, was not only a university lecturer but also a colonel in the army and head of its Weapons Office. Seeing how gifted his new student was, and having complete trust in him because of the family connection, he proposed that the young man should join his department where he would find excellent conditions for work on liquid-fuelled rockets. Von Braun accepted this proposal without hesitation, quickly losing touch with his previous scientific contacts[4] and joining the special department working on military rockets, at the head of which stood a thirty-five-year-old captain of the *Reichswehr*,** engineer Walter

* Towards the end of the 18th century Poland lost her independence and her territory was partitioned between three annexers: Austria, Prussia and Russia. As a result of the First World War and the many years of struggle by the Polish nation, Poland regained political independence and part of the territory lost at that time.
** The German regular army. It was limited by the decrees of the Treaty of Versailles to 100,000 soldiers, without an air force and with a reduced navy. In 1935 Hitler, rejecting the decisions of Versailles, replaced it by the *Wehrmacht*.

Dornberger.

This step influenced the whole later career of the young scientist and was to expose him to accusations not only of abandoning the men with whom he had worked until then, but even of using their secrets and ideas.

It would seem that these accusations were not justified. Von Braun had an exceptionally precise mind; he was sober, cold and pragmatic and his decision to work with the army probably arose from his desire to find the best conditions for his work. It is true that in 1932 the Germans were not yet re-arming openly and that Hitler was not yet in power; but the centuries-old German tradition pointed to the army as the factor which would play the most important part. Anyone who was offered work by the army could expect privileges. Although there is no proof that von Braun did make use of the ideas of others, one thing is certain: he displayed amazing ability, determination and diligence.

In 1934, when he was 22, von Braun presented his doctoral thesis to the University of Berlin. It was entitled 'Constructional, theoretical and experimental contributions to the problem of rockets with liquid propulsion'. He was awarded the degree, but it is said that his work never reached the examiners because the military command had argued that the manuscript concerned top priority secrets.[5] What is more likely is that the thesis was read by Professor Becker.

There is a German saying that God is always on the side of the strongest battalions. So it was with von Braun. He worked hard, he made straight for his goal, he was exceptionally talented; but he had rivals, equally clever and determined, who had begun to work on rockets earlier.

The first rival, whom destiny eliminated, was engineer Reinhold Tiling, creator of a six-foot rocket. The rocket came out of several experiments with flying colours; it could, so its inventor claimed, cross the English Channel. On 11 October 1933 his laboratory blew up and he, fatally burnt, crawled to a near-by pond and died.[6]

Hardly nine months had passed before another potential rival had gone, a man who worked together with von Braun in the Weapons Office. This was another newly-fledged doctor, engineer Karl Wahmke, already well advanced in his research. On 16 July 1934, at the army proving-ground in Kummersdorf West, he was to give a demonstration before his superior officers of a small liquid-fuelled rocket. A group of officers and scientists gathered and Wahmke with two assistants shut themselves into a concrete emplacement from which the rocket was to be set off. The noise of the motor had reached those waiting, when a cloud of smoke and fire appeared above the building. An explosion followed which killed Wahmke and severely wounded his assistants.[7]

There was yet another rival, engineer Rudolf Nebel, who had already given several successful demonstrations of his rockets. Destiny also removed him from von Braun's path, for when Hitler came into power in 1933, the atmosphere around Nebel began to thicken. People began to call him the 'Jewish page-boy', for he had worked closely with Professor Albert Einstein, and his fiancée was a Jewess. She was arrested, passed through several prisons and finally died years later in Auschwitz. Nebel was dismissed from the Weapons Office and ordered not to carry out any further experiments. When he refused the Gestapo put him in prison in Berlin.[8] He did come out of it later, but he never returned to working exclusively on rockets. A few years later von Braun was instrumental in purchasing his patent for a rocket motor propelled by liquid fuel, but this was a gesture to appease an embittered rival.*

Another stumbling block in von Braun's career might have been Professor Hermann Oberth, a specialist in liquid-fuelled rockets, who had a number of successful experiments behind him and was greatly respected in the German scientific world. He was a German, but born in Rumania and not a German citizen. When the Nazis came to power this fact decided the professor's fate. Work on the rockets was carried out in the greatest secrecy; no foreigners were allowed to take part in it and Oberth had to return to Rumania. In 1938 he was invited to Vienna and given limited access to research facilities and also offered German nationality; but these were only pretexts to keep him within the orbit of German authority. He knew many technical secrets and it was necessary to ensure that his

---

* After the war there was an epilogue: in 1967 engineer Nebel appealed to the court of the German Federal Republic, demanding compensation and a pension, since he had invented the rocket, V-2. His case was rejected (Wojewódzki, op,cit., pp. 36-38).

knowledge should not be made available to enemies of the Third *Reich*.[9]

There was also Klaus Riedel, who had himself done valuable research on rockets; but he accepted von Braun's authority unreservedly and became his close associate.[10]

Enemies of the young scientist, and there was no lack of them, accused von Braun of 'assisting' in the removal of his most dangerous rivals, but there is no definite proof. One thing only is certain: great possibilities opened up before him and he made full use of them.

4

In the mid nineteen-thirties, when the Nazis came to power and began their preparations for war, it was not yet certain which area of research into secret weapons would bring the best results, and thus where the greatest and most urgent efforts should be directed. The choices were multiple, and theoretical studies and experiments had to be carried out at different centres and by many people. As each centre could not be fully appraised of what the others were doing, it was inevitable that there would be overlaps in the work.

The experiments on rockets were already well advanced. It was well known that the authorities were thinking of using them in the next war, although only the Army Weapons Office was responsible for research on them. This state of affairs annoyed the air force, who considered that anything which flew should be under its control. At the head of the air force was Marshal Hermann Göring, after Hitler the most powerful man in Germany at that time. Göring, puffed up with the ambition of a famous First World War air-ace, was enraged that the rocket experiments were not under his control. But the Army Weapons Office had powerful protectors, and the years of fame and achievement for the air force were still in the future. Infantry, supported by artillery and tanks, were still considered the main force for any future war. Rockets were, after all, not flying machines but ballistic missiles; it was logical to leave them within the competence of the army.

So, since they could not get hold of the rockets, the thoughts of air force command turned in another direction: they must begin looking for a new weapon of their own.

For some years Dr Paul Schmidt had been conducting experiments on a pulse-jet engine, jointly financed by the army and the air force. This engine could be used in the coming years for aeroplanes, eventually pilotless ones, and might have a great future. In 1934 the Army Weapons Office, fully occupied with its rockets, agreed to the control of the air force over all Dr Schmidt's experiments.[11]

From this moment the rivalry began in earnest. The army pushed on with its research on rockets; the *Luftwaffe* took up the idea of pilotless aircraft. Both these secret weapons should have been in the same hands and in the same laboratories, for they both depended on the principle of the jet engine. But this time German logic failed.

5

The pilotless aircraft, also called the flying bomb, was basically similar to the under-sea torpedo, widely used during the First and Second World Wars. The torpedo, once it has been fired, can no longer be steered: it is kept on its course by an automatic pilot and moved forward by its own impulsion. It is in reality a miniature submarine without a crew. The flying bomb was just such a piece of equipment, only in the air.

The earliest tests with this weapon were carried out during the First World War. In 1918 the American air force built its prototype, called the 'Bug', and was ready to put it into mass production when the war ended. After the war further experiments were carried out, but high costs caused them to be discontinued in 1925.[12]

In post-war Germany, in the search for new weapons, tests with the flying bomb were not overlooked. At first they concentrated on a low-explosive rocket, mounted on a glider and flown by a pilot. These tests were carried out during the years 1929-31 by Alexander Lippisch and Fritz von Opel. At the same time similar tests were being carried out separately by an Italian, Ettone Cattaneo, and an Austrian scientist, Dr Eugen Sänger. During the thirties Sänger carried out his experiments with a rocket motor in the Higher Technical College in Vienna. In 1934, after a number of successful tests, he put before the Austrian Ministry of Defence a research project on an aircraft which, powered by a rocket motor, could attain a speed of 600mph and a ceiling of 16km. The ministry threw out his proposals and the dean of the engineering faculty at the college forbade him to carry out further experiments. A few years later he was recruited by the Hermann Göring Institut, which belonged to the *Luftwaffe*, in Braunschweig-Völkenrode. Here his abilities and experience were directed above all to research on the engines.[13]

The experiments with rockets mounted on a glider or propelling an aircraft showed that it was an ineffective weapon, and that a more positive result could be expected from the use of a jet engine, working on the principle of pulsation and driven by petrol. So the *Luftwaffe* took up Dr Schmidt's experiments. Since 1929 he had been working on an engine called the *Strahlrohr*, which was successfully tested on an airfield in München-Wiesenfeld.[14] Schmidt had come to the Hermann Göring Institut and there collaborated with Sänger.

After many experiments, which took several years and were carried out in various places, the German air force finally came to the conclusion that its flying bomb would have to be a pilotless aircraft, the size of a small fighter, propelled by a jet engine. The Second World War had been raging for over two years when the Gerhard Fieseler aircraft factory in Kassel built the first fuselage of such a plane. On it was mounted a jet engine based on Dr Schmidt's model, the subject of intensive research by the Argus factory from March 1942. All this work was supervised by engineer Robert Lusser, the technical director of the Kassel factory,[15] who should be given recognition as the constructor of the flying bomb, although many other names, some of them already mentioned, are connected with this idea.

In June 1942 Air Field-Marshal Erhard Milch was convinced by the representatives of Argus and Fieseler that, since the prototype was already in existence, their models should be given high priority on the list of aircraft production. But military use of the new weapon was still a long way off. The flying bombs proved to have a number of constructional faults that required further experiments. Time and again after being fired they changed their flight-direction or fell back to earth, often dangerously near the launching-pad.

When these difficulties could not be connected or explained a remarkable test was carried out: Captain Hanna Reitsch, a famous test pilot, volunteered to fly in one of the bombs in the hope of finding the cause of their erratic behaviour. This courageous flight took place in the autumn of 1943, in a specially constructed bomb with a built-in cabin, and ended fortunately in a landing on a beach.* It was instrumental in establishing that the constructional faults concerned the casing and exterior instruments controlling the bomb.

Countless tests took place, further faults were ironed out, improvements made, and finally the flying bomb was ready for military use. The details of its construction were as follows: length of fuselage 8,40m; spread of wings 5,40m; total weight including explosives 2,160kg; maximum speed 500km per hour; maximum ceiling about 3,000m; range 250km; weight of explosives 1,000kg; tank for 80 octane petrol capacity 150 gallons; fuel consumption 1 mile to the gallon.** It was driven by a pulse-jet engine, pulsating at 200-300 beats per minute, and was kept on its course by an automatic pilot based on three gyroscopes. Two of them regulated the directional rudder and the altitude rudder, the third held the bomb on its course. When it reached its appointed target the automatic pilot cut out, the altitude rudder locked, the fuel ceased to flow, the characteristic putt-putt of the engine stopped, and the bomb went into a noiseless dive and exploded on impact. This pilotless aircraft could not start by itself and was catapulted from a ramp similar to a small ski-jump.[16]

On 24 December 1942 the first successful launch and flight of the new weapon took place. The bomb flew faultlessly over the short course and fell on target.[17] The long, exhausting road of ideas, experiments, tests and improvements had at last reached an end; the weapon could be put into mass production. The cost was about £125 per bomb.

During the several experimental phases the weapon was given

---

*   See Appendix I, item 1.
**  There were, in the course of time, certain small deviations from the above details, for the Germans made constant improvements and produced seven versions of the flying bomb.

various names, finally passing into the history of Second World War as the 'V-1'.*

6

The beginning of the very idea of constructing rockets must be sought in ancient China, many centuries before the birth of Christ; it was closely connected with the invention of gunpowder. But to go back so far would require too lengthy a historical dissertation. Very briefly it may be said that rockets were first of all used for military purposes; later the principle was employed for amusement, in the form of fireworks; once again they came back into use as weapons, and then again as entertainment, until finally, in the 1940s, they returned as long-range and highly destructive weapons.[18]

It was towards the end of the nineteenth century, after several thousand years of experiments, and after long centuries of complete neglect, that rockets found their way back to the laboratories as an object of dominant military interest. In 1890 the Swedish scientist Lieutenant-Colonel Baron Wilhelm von Unge asked engineer Alfred Nobel, the inventor of dynamite and famous founder of international prizes, among them a Peace Prize, if he would finance experiments into an 'aerial torpedo', designed for military purposes. Nobel accepted the proposal, for he himself had experimented a little with rockets, and for the six years until his death he financed Baron von Unge. Five years later a company called 'Mars' was set up in Stockholm, which financed further experiments. This resulted in the production of a rocket 75 centimetres long, 11 centimetres in diameter, weighing 35 kilograms, with a 2 kilogram warhead. The rocket was driven by solid fuel and could fly for about 5 kilometres at a speed of 300 metres per second.

In 1909 the German firm of Friedrich Krupp in Essen bought up von Unge's patents and began its own intensive experiments. Apparently they were unsuccessful, for during the First World War the German army did not use rockets. Only the French did, and

---

\* The symbol 'V' comes from the word *Vergeltungswaffe*—'retaliation' weapon.

then in a very limited way, against Zeppelins and stationary observation balloons.[19]

Then, after the war, the various experiments mentioned earlier took place in Germany. The same names which have been noted in connection with the building of the flying bomb, V-1, crop up again here.* There is nothing strange in this, for the propulsion of both weapons was based on the same principles.

Undoubtedly not all the scientsits were thinking of war and revenge; many were interested in purely scientific experiments, their minds literally on 'higher things';** but the interests of militarism prevailed and in practice almost all the outstanding German scientists interested in these problems were to be found in military laboratories. Their greatest efforts were directed towards producing a rocket propelled by liquid fuel; for solid fuel, burning unevenly and difficult to regulate, had proved impractical. Similar experiments were being carried out at the same time in other countries.

In 1932 a group of German scientists under Professor Becker constructed the first military liquid-fuelled rocket and began experiments with it. Two years later came the final division between the air force and the army. The *Luftwaffe* worked wholly on the V-1, the army on rockets. At this time the name of Wernher von Braun became inseparably connected with the latter. There now began feverish research and development activity, which lasted for a number of years. Here it is only necessary to describe the result of this activity and the appearance of the military rocket, the stream-lined fuselage of which was directed towards London.

The overall length of the rocket was 14,30m; the diameter of the body at the centre 1,51m; the diameter across the fins 3,56m; the weight including fuel and high explosive at the moment of take-off 12,805kg; the weight of the warhead including explosive (chiefly

---

*   A. Lippisch, F. von Opel, E. Cattaneo, E. Sänger, P. Schmidt, R. Lusser.
**  Amongst these was Professor Hermann Oberth, who in the early twenties published a work entitled, *Die Rakete zu den Planetenräumen* (The Rocket into Interplanetary Space).

amatol)* 1,000kg; the weight of the liquid fuel (alcohol and oxygen) 8,796kg; fuel consumption 125kg per second; range 290km; the highest ceiling in the stratosphere 97km; velocity 1,700 metres per second. The rocket was propelled by a jet engine burning ethyl alcohol mixed with water, bringing down its strength to 75%, uniting with liquid oxygen forced through by a special pump driven by hydrogen peroxide in an 80% concentration. The rocket was steered automatically by graphite rudders situated in the tail. It did not require a launching-pad and lifted itself from a special firing table standing on a concrete slab. Radio contact with the ground was maintained by a transmitter situated just behind the warhead. The rocket consisted of four main sections: in the nose was a warhead filled with high explosive; then the instrument section; below this was the bulkiest and heaviest section with a fuel tank for the liquid alcohol and a second tank for the liquid oxygen; and finally, in the tail section, the engine and the steering equipment. The cost of production of one rocket was about £12,000.[20]

It was an exceptionally complicated shell, consisting of several thousand parts, many sensitive to small external influences. It was built in the haste of a war-time race by a number of eminent scientists under von Braun. Before it could be used in a large-scale attack on London, about 56,000 alterations and improvements were made to it. In various phases of its development it was called A-1, A-2, A-3, A-4. This last model was the death-dealing weapon described above which became known as the 'V-2'.

It was fired for the first time on 13 June 1942, but it flew barely a few kilometres, fell into the sea, exploded and sank. The second flight, which took place on 16 August, was also a failure.

But on 3 October of that year it was a different story. Autumn sometimes provides lovely, sunny, faintly misty mornings, without the slightest breeze to move the tops of the trees. It was noon; numerous observers had gathered and the slim cone of the rocket, painted black and white, pointed upwards to the skies. The order

---

* This explosive proved to be suitable, for it was not oversensitive to high temperatures and shocks, and it was important to ensure that the rocket did not explode prematurely.

was given, flames showed at the base, and with a deafening roar the huge, glistening object began slowly to draw away from the earth. After a few seconds it began to gain speed; after 22 seconds it broke the sound barrier, rose to a height of 50 kilometers and glided away in a north-easterly direction. All the time its radio was giving out signals. It flew for 190 kilometres and fell into the Baltic.[21] When this great success was confirmed by fishing boats operating in the area a few hours later, von Braun commented that it was 'a pity that the rocket landed on the wrong planet'.[22]   The launching had taken place near a small village on the Baltic called Peenemünde.


7


Some years earlier, von Braun—not unusually for a young man—had been in the habit of spending short periods of leave from his work at his parents' home. By Christmas 1935 work on the building of rockets had gathered great impetus and the existing experimental stations, chiefly the proving-grounds in Reinickendorf and Kummersdorf West, not far from Berlin, had ceased to suffice. Research and tests had changed from purely scientific to military; the rockets were beginning to fly greater distances and scientists had to be assured of two basic conditions: space and safety. The German *Reich* was not at war, so it could not yet justify wholesale evacuation of parts of the country in order to establish extensive and secure proving-grounds. It was necessary to look for a suitable area on the sea coast, which meant in practice the Baltic, for the North Sea was too close to the countries of potential enemies.

Von Braun was sworn to complete secrecy about his work, but he regarded his parents as quite safe and in a conversation that Christmas with his mother he confided in her and told her what he was looking for. She, going back in memory, remembered that Wernher's grandfather used to shoot wild duck on an island in the Baltic called Usedom.* This island was situated not far from Szczecin at the mouth of the river Oder; from memoirs it appears that it was densely wooded, sparsely inhabited and far from larger settlements. Von Braun went there that same year, surveyed the

* See Appendix I, item 2.

whole island and decided that its northern promontory, on the west of which was the small village of Peenemünde, was admirably suited for experimental purposes.[23]

Some time later Walter Dornberger looked over the area and was of the same opinion, but this was not enough. The rocket had its critics: many of the highly-placed persons who determined budgets still believed that conventional weapons would be more effective. They had, therefore, to be convinced. In March 1936, on the proving-ground in Kummersdorf West, a demonstration firing of a rocket was prepared, to which the commander of the army, General Werner von Fritsch, was persuaded to come. The director of the experimental group of the air force, Lieutenant-Colonel Wolfram von Richthofen, came along too.

The demonstration, preceded by a lecture and figures, was a great success and von Fritsch was enthusiastic about the new weapon. He was an artillery man; it appealed to his imagination. The representative of the air force, which had already begun experiments with a pilotless aircraft, V-1, was similarly impressed. His report on the demonstration reached the Director of Aircraft Construction, General Albert Kesselring. In April a conference took place in his office, in which General Becker, Captain Dornberger, von Braun and Lieutenant-Colonel von Richthofen took part. In fact Kesselring had doubts as to whether the hopes of constructing a rocket that could fly over 300 kilometres could be realized, but he showed interest in the experiments. Since Peenemünde had already been found, only the decision of the authorities was necessary in order to take it over. At this point, as Dornberger put it later, the highest authorities 'virtually suffered an attack of acute generosity', for on the same day a representative of the Air Ministry travelled to the town of Wolgast, to which the required piece of land belonged, and immediately set about arranging the conditions of the sale. After negotiation the sum of 750,000 marks was agreed upon.[24] Although the money was provided by the air force, the place was given the name *Heeresversuchstelle* (army experimental station). It is probable that the *Luftwaffe* had had such trouble in finding a suitable proving-ground for the V-1 that it leapt at the chance of sharing with the army the area it had found.

The island of Usedom, (stretching from the south-east to the north-west) just off the mainland on the Baltic coast, at the mouth of the Oder, is about 50 kilometres long. Its width in some places does not exceed two kilometres; in one place it reaches 25 kilometres, and in the north-western corner, which interests us, it is about four kilometres. In the 1930s the greater part of the island was covered with pine woods; inland lie several lakes, and the coast is sandy. The island was once inhabited by Slav tribes, but in the twelfth century they were pushed back by the Germans. For seventy years from 1648 the Swedes interrupted German rule; during the Second World War it was a strictly-guarded experimental area for testing secret weapons; to-day it is an attractive tourist spot.[25]

Peenemünde was a small fishing-village and in its vicinity extensive work began in 1936 to change the island into a secret proving-ground and one of the most modern experimental stations.

Access to the place was extremely difficult, requiring appropriate communications facilities, so an airfield was built on the northern edge. An asphalt road was laid, which became the boundary cutting the northern part of the island into two parts. The western side was taken over by the air force experimental stations with the V-1, the eastern by the army with the V-2. In spite of the strict division between them, there were some common installations, such as the airfield and the asphalt road, and also the power station, set up in the west.

Since these were only experimental stations and proving-grounds, and not factories for mass production, the air force only built launching-pads for the V-1 and some comparatively small workshops for fitting and testing. Experiments on the V-2, however, were different. The rocket was much more complicated than the flying bomb; it had thousands of parts, and was constantly being improved and altered. A large staff of army scientists, engineers and technicians were working on it, with the result that the eastern part of the island was built up on a much grander scale. In the northern part there were numerous launching sites for the rockets, and a little lower down huge workshops for experiments, planning, tests and fitting, together with a wind tunnel. In the southern part there were production workshops, where test missiles were constructed; not far from that was an extensive settlement occupied by the scientists; a little further on, near the village of Karlshagen, were barracks for soldiers and workmen and, during the war, a prisoner-of-war and a concentration camp. The very important liquid-oxygen plant was on the western side of the headland, under the control of the *Luftwaffe*. The number of people employed there, scientists, technicians, office workers and workmen, grew from month to month; during the period of most intensive work it was over twenty thousand. The whole area was guarded by counter-espionage agents of the *Abwehr*.*

As well as the on-the-spot expertise gathered in Peenemünde, the stations there called upon the knowledge of many people who worked for scientific institutions in Germany generally. These included the *Deutsche Institut für Luftfahrforschung* (the German Institute for Air Research) in Berlin, the *Raketenflugtechnische Forschunginstitut* (Institute of Technical Research on Rockets) in Trauen, and the *Hermann Göring Institut* in Braunschweig-Völkenrode. Apart from such major scientific institutions, the experiments with the V-1 and the V-2 also depended on numerous factories and experimental stations scattered over the whole *Reich*, which assisted Peenemünde with their own inventions and improvements. The V-1 and V-2 needed electrical equipment, insulation, outer casings of a suitable thickness, signalling parts, propulsion materials and many other accessories and materials.

For the construction of the workshops and testing ground on the island of Usedom the sum of twenty million marks was earmarked, but this sum soon proved too small and the budget had constantly to be increased. This was no easy matter, since for some time the experiments were not considered as a priority. In the end, three hundred million marks were spent on the installations alone.[26]

8

Adolf Hitler, the fifty-year-old dictator of the Third *Reich*, in spite of an outward appearance of self-assurance and decisiveness, was a superstitious man, sensitive to outside influences beyond his control, totally absorbed in himself and in mysterious voices, which

* This was the name of the intelligence and counter-intelligence organization of the German armed forces, set up in 1925 after the Treaty of Versailles. (See Appendix I, item 3.)

only he heard. He was not governed by any morality; he was not
burdened with any 'middle-class' scruples; he recognized no
restraints nor arguments in the area of humanitarianism or respect
for the rights of others. And he never disregarded the opinion of
astrologers or his own intuition, to which he often paid more
attention than he did to knowledge and experience.

It was early one morning during the first half of March 1939.
Rain was falling, the biting cold went through every covering and
the dictator, wakened from sleep after only a few hours of rest, felt
unwell and bad-tempered. The evening before, as usual, he had
seen two films and later had talked uninterruptedly for several
hours. He had gone to his apartments in the new chancellery of the
*Reich* very late that night.[27]

And yet there was really no reason to be in a bad mood, for since
he had come to power six years earlier everything had gone
splendidly. He had checked inflation, beaten unemployment,
rejected the conditions of the Treaty of Versailles, created a new
powerful army and restored the German nation's faith in its own
strength. In 1937 his detachments had marched into the Rhine
Basin, demilitarized after the war, and nobody had hindered him.
In March of the following year German tanks had rolled into
Vienna, he had taken over Austria and again nobody had opposed
him. The *Anschluss,* the incorporation of the whole country into
the Third *Reich,* had followed. German nationalists had been
thinking of this since the end of the First World War, arguing that
the same language was spoken in Austria. Attempts were made to
give to this annexation the appearance of the free consent of the
Austrian nation.

The dictator's bad mood lightened for a moment as he
remembered his triumphal entry into Vienna, into his native
Austria, but the moment of joy passed at once as he looked at the
window streaming with rain. He had been wakened early because
he had to go to Kummersdorf West, not far away, where there was
an artillery testing ground and where for the first time he was to see
a rocket fired. He had already read the reports on it, enthusiasts
had informed him that the experiments with rockets were going
very well and that a new, lethal weapon, which would take his
enemies by surprise, would come out of it, but so far he had not
taken it seriously. He had at last agreed to watch a demonstration

but, as it turned out, they had chosen an appalling day for it.

In this very same month he was going to take another step: one which might lead to world-wide conflict. After the annexation of Austria he had turned his sights on Czechoslovakia, which for some years had been under pressure from the Nazis, who were demanding that the Sudetenland, inhabited by Germans, should be given up. The conference in Munich* had ended in complete victory; the Czechs, left on their own, had given them the territory, but this had not solved the problem. In spite of his own signature Hitler had decided to go farther, to take over the whole Czechoslovakian Republic. He had already made the decision to send his troops into hapless Prague in a few days' time.

He had no high opinion of the determination of France and England; his intelligence agents reported that they were unprepared for war both militarily and psychologically. But the attack on Czechoslovakia would be such an open violation of the Munich pact that the Western politicians might lose patience. What then? He was ready for any eventuality. He had built up a modern army; he had foreseen that Germany could not become a great power again without the use of force; but the prospect of another great war was not easy to accept. The horoscopes were optimistic, his advisers told him not to waver, but the final decision was his alone. And at just such a moment he had to go and look at some experiments.

The rain fell ceaselessly, but the demonstration was successful. Several rockets were fired and, with a deafening roar, rose up into the sky and disappeared into the low clouds. Von Braun gave explanations. Hitler's suite, among whom was the new army commander-in-chief, General Walter von Brauchitsch, were delighted; but the dictator remained silent. Later he was shown a model of the big A-3 rocket, so constructed as to show the internal

---

* On 30 September 1938 a meeting took place in Munich between the dictators of Germany and Italy, Hitler and Mussolini, and the Western leaders, Neville Chamberlain, Prime Minister of Great Britain, and Eduard Daladier, premier of France. As a result of this meeting an agreement was signed giving the Germans the Sudetenland which at that time belonged to Czechoslovakia. The Western powers, unprepared for war, expected in this way to put an end to further expansion by Hitler.

equipment. That did not interest him either. Normally at the demonstration of a new weapon, he was very lively, asked a lot of questions. This time he looked at the rocket with protruding eyes but it was obvious that his thoughts were far away.*

It was only during lunch in the neighbouring mess, eating his salad and drinking mineral water, that Hitler showed a little more interest. He talked to General Becker, asked a few questions and once even smiled. The engineers and technicians listened to his every word eagerly, putting all their hopes in him, but the dictator expressed no definite opinion. Even worse, he remarked that during his Munich days he had known a man who carried out experiments on rockets, and he had considered him to be a crank. Only at the very end of the meal did there fall from his lips the sentence: 'That was something powerful.' After lunch, just before his departure, the disappointed and anxious technicians heard a dry and enigmatic: 'Thank you.'[28]

A few days later, on 15 March 1939, Czechoslovakia ceased to exist; and it turned out that the dictator's fears were unfounded. The Czechs, so brutally treated at Munich, hoped that England and France, who had guaranteed their new frontiers, might yet help them; but they were utterly disappointed. Since 1935 they had had a pact of mutual assistance with the Soviet Union, but Stalin had quite different plans. He wanted to take the world by surprise a few months later, and had no intention of opposing Hitler. Deprived of all hope the Czechs did not take up arms. Hitler made their country a Czech and Moravian Protectorate, and Slovakia became a satellite state with Father Joseph Tiso at the head.**

The 'removal' of Czechoslovakia from the European map produced one result: on 31 March Great Britain gave a guarantee to Poland, promising assistance in the event of a German attack. This event absorbed Hitler much more than the problem of Czechoslovakia. Although self-educated he knew the history of

* A few weeks later Hermann Göring saw a similarly successful demonstration and was completely convinced. He apparently looked forward to the time when rockets were adapted to all vehicles, clearly not taking into account that this would be a very expensive form of transport, using up enormous quantities of liquid fuel.
** After the war he was tried in in Czechoslovakia, convicted and executed for collaboration.

Europe and was aware that relations between Germany and Poland
stretched back to the tenth century and had nearly always been bad.
Poland lay in the way of the German *Drang nach Osten* (Drive to
the East); for hundreds of years she had stood up to Germany when
she was a power, and it was only towards the end of the eighteenth
century that she had fallen. She had lost her independence to
Austria, Prussia and Russia, and the territory had been split
among the three. This partition of Poland, although facilitated by
her own internal chaos, was nonetheless an unprecedented act of
plunder and enlightened Germans knew this; but all the same it was
eaily forgotten which Polish territory had been appropriated at that
time. So when, after the First World War and more than a century
of Polish struggle for independence, Poland was once again to be
found on the map of Europe, containing within her frontiers part
of the provinces formerly lost in the West, German nationalists at
once raised their voices in protest. It was only to be expected that
having so recently regained their independence the Poles would
take up arms at the thought of a new slavery. The first attempts at
pressure, at Gdańsk,* had shown that the Poles would not give
way. Now the British guarantee would strengthen their defiance.

On 23 May, in the chancellery of the *Reich,* a secret discussion
took place with the most senior army commanders present, during
which Hitler informed them of his opinions about the near future:

> 'The national and political unification of Germans has taken
> place with a few exceptions. Further successes cannot be
> expected without loss of blood . . . Poland will always stand by
> the side of our enemies . . .
>
> Gdańsk is not the object of our concern. We are concerned
> with expanding our living space in the East and with
> safeguarding food supplies while settling the Baltic problem . . .
>
> If fate forces us to fight the West, then it will be well to have
> at our disposal greater territories in the East . . .
>
> By the same token the question whether to spare Poland
> becomes irrelevant and there remains the decision to attack

---

* After the First World War Gdańsk (in German, Danzig) had become a
free city, in which a High Commissioner of the League of Nations
officiated and Poland had the right to use the port facilities.

Poland at the first occasion that occurs. We cannot believe in a
repetition of Czechoslovakia. There will certainly be
fighting . . .

It is important that every method should be used
ruthlessly . . .'[29]

Exactly three months passed and an astounded world learnt that
a Soviet-German pact had been signed in Moscow.* It appeared
that fascism and communism could not only exist side by side, but
could even support each other. Two days later, on 25 August, the
Polish-British alliance was signed in London.

On 1 September, early in the morning, German armoured
columns crossed the frontiers of Poland in several places without a
declaration of war, everywhere meeting with opposition. After three
days of fighting and feverish diplomatic activity, Great Britain and
France informed the *Reich* that they were at war with her.

The Second World War had begun.

* See Appendix I, item 4.

# CHAPTER TWO
## The War

1

Antoni Kocjan, a slim, mild-looking man of about forty, could find no relief in the crowded goods-truck. Every muscle ached, the soles of his feet burned, his throat was so dry that it was hard to swallow, and as his empty stomach contracted with pain every few minutes, his head whirled with confused thoughts.

Two days earlier the German police had forced their way into his Warsaw flat in the early hours of the morning, dragged him out into the street, thrown him into a lorry with a number of other men and taken him to the covered riding-school of the First Regiment of Lancers. There, after their names had been taken, they had all been ordered to lie flat, face downwards on the wet sawdust, where they were kept for forty-eight hours. The SS-men from time to time walked over the prone bodies, beating those who were restless. Once the prisoners were given a morsel of bread, but although there were water taps it was forbidden to move. A score or so, reclaimed by German firms, were released; the rest, numbering over a thousand, were then transported to the railway station and loaded into goods trucks.

Kocjan found himself near the side of the truck; he had something therefore to lean against, but there was not enough air to breathe deeply. The mass of sweaty, wriggling bodies, thrown around by the rocking of the train, jostled him continuously and filled him with disgust; and yet these were men just like him, bewildered and unhappy. The iron fist of German terror had laid hold of them, dragging them from homes in which they had still felt safe, and thrown them into these trucks travelling to the unknown. Several half-insinuations from the SS-men suggested that they might be travelling in the worst of directions.

Kocjan was already a man of considerable achievement. At school he had not been one of the brightest scholars, but he was possessed of a stubborn ambition which had made him work harder and longer than his school-fellows. Thanks to this he had escaped from a small, provincial town and passed the competitive entrance examination for the Warsaw Technical University. There he had started to work with the well-known designers of light aircraft, Stanisław Rogalski, Stanisław Wigura and Jerzy Drzewiecki.* On completing his studies he moved to the Experimental Aircraft Workshops, where he was employed in the construction of gliders. His preliminary success encouraged him to set up glider workshops in Warsaw, producing excellent craft of various types. Kocjan also built motor-gliders, powered by a very economical small engine. The best known of them, called Bąk, had been well-received in Europe and had achieved two world records, for height and for distance, which remained unbeaten until 1947.[1]

In September 1939 came the sudden German attack and a short war on two fronts, for Stalin's divisions attacked from the east; there followed a new partition of Poland between aggressors, and a cruel taste of defeat—and now Kocjan found himself in an overcrowded truck, going quickly south. A year had passed since the Germans had marched in and he had not yet learned to adapt to the new order around him.

It was night when the train stopped, the doors were unbolted and they were ordered to jump out. German voices barked. Forming up in fives, surrounded by SS-men, driven along by the baying of dogs and curses and blows from rifle-butts, they moved off towards the countless electric lamps which flickered in long rows in the dark distance.

The march was almost at the run, and not all the prisoners, of various ages and in varying physical condition, could keep up the pace. One of the older men fell down and his neighbour stopped to help him up. The nearest SS-man, with a shout, tore the prisoner's cap off his head, flung it into the darkness and with his rifle-butt pointed in its direction. The prisoner took a few steps aside and

*    See Appendix I, item 5.

immediately a series of shots rang out. He fell to the loud laughter of the soldiers and the howling of the dogs, who, excited by the shots and the smell of blood, strained at their leashes to get to the prostrate body. A raucous command rang out and the column halted. From the front came an officer who lit his torch; he looked down at the prone body, exchanged a few words with the soldiers and turned to the prisoners. For a moment he stared at them in silence and then he began to light up the faces nearest to him and beckoning with his finger drew some of them out of the ranks. He stood them a little way off the road, once more flashed his torch and barked an order to the soldiers. Shots from automatic pistols rang out and ten bodies fell to the ground. 'That is for an attempt to escape', said the officer in pure Polish. Again several prisoners were drawn out of the ranks; they were ordered to take off their belts and braces, tie them to the feet of their murdered fellows and drag the corpses on to the road. There was another barked command and the column moved forward. The dogs, excited beyond control, broke away from the soldiers leading them, and threw themselves on the corpses, tearing and biting them. The young SS-men made no attempt to stop the animals; their loud laughter rang out again.[2]

Kocjan, hidden in the middle of the column, cowered down and made himself still smaller. He was breathing heavily, although he was not very tired. He could not understand, couldn't comprehend where he was, what was happening to him. He had travelled abroad, he had been in Germany, he had met engineers and designers, and they seemed to be normal, reasonable people. He had also seen them in Warsaw and had always been of the opinion that their level of civilization and culture was high. He himself had been brought up in Olkusz, situated in the south of Poland, not far from Cracow. His family was poor and modest, the town small, but its history reached back to the thirteenth century. He had grown up in the shadow of ancient walls, old churches, history and tradition. Where had these young soldiers come from, who could kill so easily and find in it a cause for merriment? Who had sent them here, who had trained them, who had reared them? He felt himself going hot all over: in his heart and soul his basic beliefs were undergoing a complete change, and instead of fear he began to feel anger and hatred.

2

September in England is usually mild and sunny, sometimes even very hot, but in 1940 it was wet and low clouds covered the skies and shut out the sun. Under different circumstances people would have grumbled at the cold, but in those days nobody thought about it, for the whole country had only one idea: to survive. Just a few months had passed since the front in France collapsed and since the dramatic evacuation of the British army from Dunkirk. A German invasion was now expected. Day after day waves of Nazi bombers, protected by fighters, flew over England, and on this air battle depended not only the fate of the British Isles, but the outcome of the whole war.

Flight-Sergeant Józef František manoeuvred the joystick, straightened out his plane, went down through the clouds and flew low over the waters of the Channel towards the air field at Northolt, to the north-west of London. As on every previous day, he had broken away from the formation of Polish 303 Squadron and flown over the Channel to lie in wait for the returning German bombers. He already had several kills to his credit on these sorties, and so far on this day he had put a Dornier into the water. Commanders forbade these solitary escapades, for they were bad for discipline and spoiled group tactical plans, but nobody could deny that the sergeant was an excellent and courageous pilot.[3]

Józef František served in one of the two Polish squadrons which took part in the protracted air battle, but he was not a Pole. He was a Czech, born in Prague, and he was eager to fight. He had had no chance to take up arms against the enemy when the Germans occupied his own country, and had crossed into Poland in the belief that the Poles would put up a fight. So it had happened, but the campaign was quickly over and the militant volunteer once again never reached the front. There were few aircraft and enough native airmen, so although the Czech was well-liked, he was not given a plane. When the Germans broke the Polish resistance and divided the conquered country with the Russians, the decision was taken by the Polish government to evacuate airmen to France and Great Britain. František got into a group which was sent to France where again he waited for a plane; but he had made friends with Polish airmen by then and felt at home among them, so he decided to stay with them. Together they crossed over to England, and although the Czechs had begun to build up their own squadrons, he stayed with the Poles.

The Polish fighter-pilots who found themselves in Great Britain were well trained and already had the September Campaign behind them. Some of them had also flown in France, but they had to get to know the different English equipment and also learn enough of the language to understand commands. They were trained in Hurricanes, and the slow, methodical routine of the British enabled them to master everything step by step, but the pace annoyed the Poles and they insisted that the best training would be a fighting mission. During one training flight, 303 Squadron met a formation of German bombers. Although no command had been given, Flying-officer Paszkiewicz attacked and, before the eyes of the astonished British commander, shot down a Dornier. The next day the authorities decided that the squadron was ready to go into battle.[4]

The German High Command had a precisely-worked-out plan for the invasion of the British Isles, under the code-name *Sea-lion,* but it could not set it in motion without supremacy in the air. The thirteen divisions earmarked for the invasion had to be ferried across the Channel in ships, and the British controlled the sea. So Grand Admiral Erich Raeder, commander of the German fleet, demanded supremacy in the skies so that at least his ships might not be threatened from above.[5] Hermann Göring had assured Hitler that he would easily dispose of the enemy pilots, and in July 1940 he commenced daily sorties over the Channel and the southern English ports and airfields, endeavouring at first to discover the strength of the British defences and engage the fighter planes, which were to be routed and shot down.

After this preliminary phase, on 8 August there began a major bombing attack on shipping around the southern coast of England, and fighter battles broke out which were to decide the issue finally. The Germans had a five-fold advantage in the air. At the beginning of July 1940 they possessed 1,880 bombers (1,305 ready for battle) and 1,444 fighters (1,163 ready for battle) against which the British had 672 fighters (504 ready for battle). The Germans, however, never used all their forces on a single day. At the highest point of the battle (15 September) only 1,097 planes (328 bombers and 769

fighters) flew over England, so German superiority was effectively
only two-fold*—so long as the British pilots fought almost without
resting.[6] Yet the Germans did not gain a victory and from 23
August Göring employed new tactics: he began a huge, daily
bombing of London, which lasted a full month. Beside the British
fought two Polish squadrons (302 and 303) and one Czech
squadron (310), as well as numerous pilots of these two
nationalities, and also Dutch, French, Canadians and Norwegians,
scattered throughout the British squadrons.

The world was able to listen to the noise of the bombs falling on
London, and to the din of the fighters battling over the city; the
course of the struggle was followed by radio eagerly and anxiously
in the occupied countries. The Germans had established in these
countries a network of garrisons, police stations, prisons and
camps; normal cultural development had been limited, and in
Poland the universities, theatres, museums, even the grammar
schools had been closed. The use of radios and the printing of
books and papers was forbidden. The aim of the Germans was to
break the spirit of the beaten nations and to deprive them of faith
in the future, and Nazi propaganda repeated ceaselessly that the
war was nearly over and that a new era of a thousand years of
German domination was beginning. The conquered had defended
themselves, formed underground armies, carried out acts of
sabotage, organized secret teaching-courses, and issued clandestine
newspapers. In spite of cruel punishments they also listened to the
radio and spread the news around, but all this only made sense if
there was basis for hope that the war would nevertheless be won. In
this they believed unreservedly and as long as all was quiet on the
Western front this belief had some foundation. But then came the
German attack: the Maginot Line broke, the allied coalition

---

\*    These are the figures put out by historians of the Allied camp and they
do not correspond with the German figures. According to Field-
Marshal Kesselring the *Luftwaffe* had only 900 fighters against 1,700
British. The same applies to the numbers of aircraft shot down on both
sides, exaggerated by war propaganda. For instance: on 15 September
the British shot down 52 aircraft, but their propaganda put it at 187;
the Germans shot down 27 planes, but they said it was 78. Both sides
exaggerated three-fold.

shattered and the *Blitzkrieg* announced by Hitler became fact. France surrendered, and the British Expeditionary Force, saved by a miracle from Dunkirk, without equipment, often without uniforms, caught their breath on the southern beaches.

The fall of France was such a great shock that in Poland, which was bound to her by strong historical and cultural ties, many people thought it was the end of all hope. There were suicides, the weaker withdrew from underground work, some even sought contact with the occupiers. And then the powerful voice of Winston Churchill rang out, and the most astonishing news of a great battle in the air and of the first German setbacks began to come in. Poland heard for the first time that Polish pilots were fighting and defeating Germans in the skies over England.

The German police had Poland firmly in their grasp, but there was not a single town, not a single village, in which this news was not passed on. It crossed every barrier, every obstacle and frontier; it reached everywhere, even sweeping through prison walls and over the death-charged wires of the camp at Auschwitz. The prisoners repeated it in whispers, exaggerating the number of Polish pilots and the number of the enemy shot down; into their eyes came a glimmer of hope. A small number of Polish boys in the English skies held the whole nation on their shoulders.*

Sergeant František circled London from the west and approached the airfield. He often thought about what was happening in Czechoslovakia, wondering how much news of this air-battle was reaching it. He presumed that they listened to radios and knew that Czech airmen were taking part, but he had no idea of the sensation it was causing at home. At this moment his thoughts turned to more immediate matters. He knew that at the airfield he would once again be reprimanded for wilfully leaving the formation, but he knew also that his latest success would weaken the commander's anger. He felt fine and had to release some of the energy that he had not used up. He swung slightly from

---

* The Battle of Britain lasted until 31 October and ended in a German defeat. The *Luftwaffe* lost about a half of its planes; British losses, in fighters only, were half of the German losses. 83 Polish pilots (13% of the fighter pilots of the RAF) took part in the battle, and 18 of them were killed.

his course, flew over Ruislip and performed a 'victory' roll over the house of his girl friend.*

3

The mysterious warning letter about German secret weapons, received a year earlier by the British naval attaché in Oslo, had been sent directly on to London, where it found its way to the centre of British intelligence on 4 November 1939. It was passed to Dr Reginald Jones, an expert on physics, ballistics and astronomy, and adviser to Naval Intelligence on these subjects; it was also passed on to other competent people. It aroused great interest and excitement among them, but also scepticism. So far, all that British intelligence had produced was news of preparation for bacterial and chemical warfare, and now some anonymous informer was warning of winged missiles, of radio-controlled rockets being tested in Peenemünde in the Baltic, and of experiments with radar, which the English considered to be their own exclusive secret. But the unknown writer's information suggested that he had extensive knowledge in several disciplines and great precision in presenting important and complicated details. Who was this man and how had he obtained access to what could be top-priority German secrets? Was this a German or a foreign agent who had managed to penetrate German security so deeply?

Dr Jones was also sceptical, but he felt instinctively that the information was worthy of belief or at least of very careful attention; other experts were, however, of a different opinion. According to them, the extent of the knowledge revealed in the secret report could not be obtained by one man alone, and who would have dared in Hitler's Germany to collect all the information for such a report? They therefore considered that the whole document was a fake and that it was a masterly German attempt at misinformation.[7] The details concerning Peenemünde and the experiments with rockets aroused particular astonishment and

* After 17 victories František killed himself on 8 October 1940, performing the same roll in the same place. He was promoted to Pilot Officer posthumously.

disbelief; so far only one intelligence report (17 October 1939) had touched on this problem, and then only very generally.

The *Oslo Report**, as it became known, was filed away, and three years passed before new reports concerning the German experiments caused it to be re-examined. In the meantime, however, in Great Britain a secret organization was being created which, in a relatively short time, would play an important role in the area of contacts with countries occupied by the Germans. As it turned out this role would be closely connected with the German experiments, the search for the place where they were being carried out, and with the sending of reports to London.

<br>

4

<br>

Winston Churchill was sixty-five years old when the Second World War broke out; but at an age when other men would be thinking of retirement he had to curb his temperament and energy. A burly, volatile man, with a round head and a strong jaw, he wore people down with his overwhelming personality and forced them to take a positive attitude towards his ideas, intentions and decisions. It was possible to admire him, respect him, like him; it was possible to hate him; it was possible to consider him an actor rather than a politician; but it was not possible to disregard or ignore him.

Great Britain entered the war under the premiership of Neville Chamberlain, but immediately after the German attack in the west, on 10 May 1940, he resigned, and he died shortly afterwards. The new Prime Minister was Churchill, who formed a coalition government and energetically set about rectifying his predecessor's errors. In contrast to Chamberlain he was a man of war; he did not believe in the efficacy of negotiation, and to treaties in the style of Munich he attached no importance. Churchill, naturally, was unable to change the course of events and hold the Germans in

---

\* J. Mader (op.cit., p.126) put forward the hypothesis that the author of the 'report' was Dr Hans Heinrich Kummerow, who was connected with the Communist spy ring in Germany, *Die Rote Kapelle*. He was arrested by the Gestapo and perished in the autumn of 1943. Nowhere is there any confirmation of this hypothesis.

France. He had to swallow the bitterness and shame of Dunkirk and the collapse of the Western coalition. But for him this was only the beginning.

The might of Germany on land was enormous; her strength in the air was also great, and any day an all-out attack on the south coast of England had to be expected. But on the sea the British fleet ruled and it was here that the new premier placed his hopes—the army of invasion would have to be brought by sea. Great preparations were made for resisting a German attempt to land on British soil, but Churchill, who detested a defensive position, was already considering how to turn to the attack and how to strike the enemy from the least expected side. His thoughts went to the countries ruled by the Nazis: to Austria, to Czechoslovakia, to Poland, Norway, Belgium, Denmark, Holland, Luxembourg and France. The Germans did not behave uniformly in all these countries; but everywhere where the Gestapo reigned they were hated, and anti-occupation, underground organizations were formed.

On 16 July 1940, during a German aerial attack, in Churchill's bomb-proof room under the Admiralty building a secret conference took place. Apart from the Prime Minister only two other people were present: the Secretary of State for War, Anthony Eden, and the Minister of Economic Warfare, Hugh Dalton. There, that night, the decision was taken to form a secret organization with the name *Special Operations Executive* (SOE), whose task would be to co-operate with the underground movements in the countries occupied by Germans. SOE was to start recruiting suitable people with a knowledge of Europe and European languages; it would provide training in sabotage and diversionary tactics, in radio liaison, in the use of modern weapons and in parachute jumping. It was to be a particularly difficult military service.[8]

Some of the countries occupied by the Germans, like Czechoslovakia, Belgium, Holland, Norway and Poland, had their governments in London; others, like France, had national committees there; Denmark, in which all the state institutions remained in place, had secret representatives in London. With all these SOE established secret liaison, creating special sections, and it laid the foundations for liaison with the underground movements, which were already operating under the German

occupation.* Everywhere attempts were being made to undermine
the Nazis and decrease their war potential; everywhere there were
acts of sabotage and diversion. But there was a lack of equipment
to carry them out efficiently, a lack of trained men and materials.
SOE was to take care of all this by dropping weapons and
parachutists, trained for special duties and equipped with
transmitters, weapons and money. As well as drops, submarines
under the cover of darkness carried agents to the French coast.
Some of these agents travelled by a roundabout route, through
Portugal, Spain and the Pyrenees and reached the south of France,
as yet unoccupied.

The Nazis strengthened their grasp on the occupied countries,
shot hundreds of men and women for 'collective responsibility' and
set up new concentration camps. Yet all this, instead of slowing it
down, only stepped up the underground struggle. The noise of
execution salvoes mingled more and more with the noise of railway
lines being blown up. For every prisoner sent to a concentration
camp another young person joined the ranks, eager to fight.
Europe was criss-crossed in every direction by secret paths of
communication, some of which reached far beyond the old
Continent and ran by safe ways across the burning heat of Africa,
or climbed far into the north to the arctic corners of Norway; but
they all led to the same destination: London, which was at that time
the centre of the freedom-fighting world.

SOE, which in the beginning had great difficulty in recruiting
suitable people, began to grow, and the flow of secretly contacted
volunteers increased.** Close co-operation was established between

---

* SOE had the following sections: Albanian, Belgian, Czech, Danish,
Dutch, French, the section of General de Gaulle's National Committee,
Greek, German, Iberian peninsula, Italian, Norwegian, Polish,
Yugoslav. Sabotage and diversion were also carried out in the Far East:
Borneo, Burma, Malay, (Józef Garliński, *Poland, SOE and the Allies*,
London, 1969, p.27).
** During the period of its greatest development, in 1944, SOE had at its
disposal almost 10,000 men and 3,200 women, with a very high
percentage of officers (1 to 4 among the men and 1 to 8 among the
women). The requirements for candidates were very high. (J. Garliński,
op.cit., p.27).

the SOE, the RAF and the Royal Navy. It opened workshops to make special equipment, and set up permanent lines of communication with the occupied Continent and the underground movements. The SOE were most interested in the German military experiments, for every new weapon in the hands of the Nazis meant the prolonging of the war and the occupation. It was thanks to the work of the European underground movements, and the help given them by SOE via the courier paths they had set up, that reports on the German secret weapons, including the V-1 and the V-2, began to arrive in London.

5

On 9 April 1940, as on every other morning, the inhabitants of Denmark were setting out to work. Suddenly, over the usual street noises, the clatter of trams and the clanking of horns, a strange new sound broke in, similar to the noise of car engines, but more powerful. Within a few minutes of these forbidding sounds, huge, dark-green trucks appeared on the streets of the small southern, frontier towns, loaded with burly figures in heavy steel helmets with dully-shining weapons. In Copenhagen, from a seemingly innocent merchant-ship, soldiers with fixed bayonets suddenly emerged and efficiently took control of the key points in the port. In the sky appeared the outlines of planes and on the astonished pedestrians fell a rain of white papers—German leaflets calling for calm and informing the inhabitants of Denmark that the 'Great German *Reich*' had decided to protect their country in order to preserve its neutrality and save it from an eventual, brutal attack by the western powers against Germany.

The Danish government gathered at a hastily-convened meeting with King Christian X to deliberate on the German ultimatum. The aggressors, who had crossed into Danish territory without any previous warning, were demanding that the country should be placed under their control and that they should have the right to use ports, airfields, railway lines and all machinery necessary for waging war. In return they promised peace and the right to retain all normal forms of state activity.

What was to be done? Denmark had no chance at all in a war

with a powerful opponent, who had moreover already crossed the frontier and occupied strategic positions. The sympathies of the Danish nation were on the side of the western allies, but this had no effect in face of the hopeless situation in which she found herself. The ultimatum was accepted.[9]

The German occupation of Denmark was, in comparison with what happened in Poland, very mild. The two nations were not divided by a bloody past, by wars, partitions, deportations and oppression; only Schleswig-Holstein had passed from hand to hand several times, but the last change of frontier in Denmark's favour had been carried out in 1920, peacefully by way of a plebiscite. The Germans not only permitted all institutions, such as universities, secondary schools, libraries, museums and theatres to stay open, they even accepted the continued existence of the Danish government, which did not cease to officiate and still—under German supervision—ruled the country. The royal family also remained and King Christian X continued as head of the state. It was, after all, only the beginning of the war and the country did not notice any scarcities nor view the military occupation as a special burden.

Denmark, a free country for many years, had no tradition of underground activities and so, at the beginning of the occupation, the resistance of the Danish nation was expressed by outward gestures, which were understood by everyone. One of them was the behaviour of King Christian X who, every day, as he always had done, rode round the capital on horseback. He was always greeted enthusiastically by his subjects, who often ran out into the road to shake his hand. The king did this willingly but he never took any notice of the German officers and soldiers who had been given strict orders to accord him the honours due to the head of state. But soon such demonstrations were not enough for the Danes, accustomed for so many centuries to political independence. In spite of the mild form of the German occupation and in spite of official orders and the warnings of the Danish government, some cautious resistance activity began. As usual the first signs of it were underground newspapers; after them came slogans written on the houses and walls, and later some, as yet small, acts of sabotage. The position of the underground workers was made more difficult since their activities were doubly illegal: in relation to the German occupying authorities and to their own government, which had forbidden resistance.[10] At that time, during the first months of the occupation, most of the population had accepted government policy and were opposed to anything that might annoy the Germans.

Military developments, however, made German behaviour deteriorate, and this changed the attitude of many Danes, who, up to then, had hoped to survive the war without being drawn into the conflict. But willy-nilly they were drawn into it, for the Faroe Islands, lying to the north of Scotland and belonging to Denmark, had been occupied, as a contingency, by the British, while the Americans kept a close watch on Greenland to make sure that the Germans could not establish themselves there. The collapse of the western front wiped out any hope of a speedy end to the worldwide conflict and the Danes came to see that they would have to take an unequivocal position at the side of the western allies against Hitler.

In November 1940 a representative of occupied Denmark made the first contact with an official from SOE, which had had a Danish section since September of that year. In Stockholm, Ebbe Munck met Sir Charles Hambro[11] to discuss the details of secret co-operation. It was not only a question of immediate activity, but of the whole attitude of the Danish nation. Up to that time Denmark had been neutral, even when occupied. About a year and a half after this first contact, in 1942, the Danish politician, Christmas Møller, came to London and spoke to his nation through a BBC World Service broadcast. In the same year the first eight parachutists were dropped into Denmark. Six of them were killed or fell into German hands, but a beginning had been made.[12]

In underground work, even of the most limited kind, one of the first things to be done, apart from propaganda, is to build up an intelligence network. Without access to information, action cannot be planned or co-ordinated; intelligence reports, often obtained by a mere handful of people and a small outlay of money, can be very important. SOE asked for information, so the Danes began to set up an intelligence network, taking in the coast of the Baltic Sea. The captains of coastal vessels and fishermen, operating chiefly near the Danish Island of Bornholm, lying due north of the mouth of the river Oder and also occupied by the Germans, were drawn into this work. The head of these operations was a major of the

Danish intelligence, V.L.U. Glyth.

In 1942 this network began to send in reports of mysterious flying objects, which appeared over the Baltic, glided to the north and the east and fell with a bang into the waves or exploded in the air. Since Denmark had by that time established liaison with Great Britain this information quickly reached London in the form of dispatches.[13]

This was the first, regularly repeated intelligence that the Germans were carrying out important experiments on the Baltic coast.*

6

The immediate effect of Germany's easy victory over Poland in 1939, and of the promising pact with Stalin, had been a lessening of interest in Peenemünde and the experiments. Hitler had little faith in the prototypes of new weapons produced there, and on 23 November 1939 he ordered the quota of steel allotted to them to be cut by half. The tempo of work decreased. But in June 1940, when the predicted *Blitzkrieg* became fact and the western front collapsed, the dictator went further; convinced that he would now win the war by conventional means, he struck Peenemünde off the previous priority list.[14] This led to an incident which might have been thought impossible in the Third *Reich,* especially after the German military triumphs: General Becker stood up to Hitler. There was almost a quarrel during which Hitler was told that he was making a mistake in underestimating the experiments being carried out at the secret base on the Baltic. This quarrel cost Becker his life, for he committed suicide a few days later; but it did not alter the critical situation of Peenemünde.

It is true that General von Brauchitsch came to its assistance by allowing, without Hitler's knowledge, 5,000 qualified specialists to be claimed from the army;[15] but this was still too small a number. Besides, the experiments also needed raw materials and many extra instruments and parts, and these were produced by various factories which had to be given specific orders to supply them.

* See Appendix 1, item 6.

German industry was working at full capacity, producing every kind of conventional weapon, and those who needed tanks, submarines, guns and aircraft had no intention of giving in to the demands of their rivals—certainly not to demands of some mysterious centre, carrying out secret experiments which did not enjoy Hitler's favour.

However, a few weeks after the collapse of the western front, the Battle of Britain began. Marshal Göring's air force was thrown back, and the threatened invasion was considerably deferred. Immediately things improved for neglected Peenemünde. In November, just after the first defeat, Hitler remembered the new weapons, and four months later he granted the experimental centre the right of an *SS*-category quota of raw and manufactured materials, which at last meant top priority.[16] Hitler's orders were law in the Third *Reich* and nobody dared to ignore them, but this did not mean that they were automatically carried out without difficulty or delay. Besides Hitler, many other influential people considered that the war would be won by the mass use of the most modern, but conventional, means of warfare. The defeat in the air over the British Isles and the strength of the British navy for the time being ruled out any chance of an invasion and an end to the war in west; the focus turned to the east.

The dictator had already entertained thoughts of war with Soviet Russia, where, in the huge open spaces, the use of very complicated and costly weapons would be an extravagance and a mistake. Therefore, he and many eminent and positive-thinking men had second thoughts about the experiments in Peenumünde. Nobody as yet knew what the value of the secret weapon would be in practical mass use; there were some actually vehemently opposed to it, only because it did not come within their competence; and finally there was the rivalry between the air force and the army. All this meant that even the granting of top *SS* priority did not achieve its desired effect.

Walter Dornberger, now promoted to colonel, did everything he could to gain allies for his beloved rocket, and to ensure that the work should not be held up. He went frequently to Berlin where he conferred with the influential people; he visited the factories which worked for Peenemünde; he cited Hitler's orders; but he kept coming up against difficulties and obstacles.

The quotas of raw materials and the co-operation of the factories which supplied many of the parts were a serious problem. An equally important problem was the quota of specialists and other, less skilled, but essential workers. The German *Reich* had mobilized an enormous army, air force and navy; every healthy male went around in uniform; many women had also donned it in the auxiliary services; and to these had to be added the various police formations, urgently needed in the occupied countries and also in the *Reich* itself. The lack of an adequate labour supply had at first been made up by volunteers from those countries forced by threat of invasion to work with the Nazis,* and from the conquered countries; but strident propaganda, promising good, well-paid work, had produced such poor results that more radical methods soon had to be employed. In Poland, round-ups were organized and young people were sent by force into the heart of Germany, where, despite the propaganda and promises, they were usually treated as slaves. They had to wear the letter 'P' sewn on to their clothes, they were not allowed to change their work or leave the place to which they had been deported, and sexual relationships with Germans were punishable by death. As the war went on the brutality of the recruitment methods increased and the number of foreign workers in the *Reich* grew quickly, reaching five millions of whom only 200,000 were volunteers.

A further source of manpower was the concentration camps. Besides the six camps already in existence before the war (Dachau, Oranienburg, Sachsenhausen, Flossenbürg, Mauthausen and Ravensbrück), new ones came into being, Auschwitz being the largest. The initially modest number of political prisoners began to increase with frightening speed and eventually reached a figure of several millions. Many found themselves behind barbed wire only because Himmler had hastily begun to build up the economic institutions of the *SS* and needed experts, whom he would not have been able to get from industry any other way.[17] During the first phase of the war when German victory seemed certain nobody had needed prisoners, so they had perished in their thousands; but the situation changed. In the second half of 1942 even Jews destined for extermination began to undergo selection, and the young and

* Bulgaria, Hungary, Rumania and Slovakia.

the strong were let into the camp at Auschwitz to work there for a while, instead of being sent straight to the gas chambers.[18] Near almost every camp or its branches was a newly-built munitions factory in which prisoners were employed.

This was happening throughout Germany and the conquered countries, but one might have expected that in Peenemünde, in a place so secret and well-guarded, with experiments so important that they might turn the scales of the war, only Germans would be allowed to work, and that even these would be carefully screened. All those in charge understood this; Hitler mentioned it in conversation with Speer;[19] and yet it turned out otherwise. Feelings of rivalry, unwillingness to co-operate, obstinate insistence on rights, inevitable jealousy, stupidity and pettiness combined to overrule this elementary principle of security, so important for the German war aims. Other industrial and production centres refused to give up their experts, and so to the workshops of these secret experiments were brought first prisoners-of-war, then workers of various nationalities, and finally (and most strangely), political prisoners.

The historian, studying the course of wars, often comes to the conclusion that war is, above all, a series of errors; of two more or less equal fighting sides, the one that makes fewer errors will win. Bringing foreigners into Peenemünde, men taken away from their own countries by force, was for the Germans a major error, and the consequences of it were not long in coming.

# CHAPTER THREE
## The German-Soviet War; the first information about Peenemünde

1

The dusk of the short, October day had fallen and over Moscow there hung a misty haze, reducing even more the already poor visibility. All the street lamps were turned out, the windows were tightly curtained, a few cars moved slowly, throwing only narrow streaks of light onto the road from their dark, blue-painted lamps. The steps of pedestrians rang out loudly in the thickening fog, and from time to time a patrol of armed soldiers loomed against the buildings. Every so often an underground tremor ran across the city and immediately after it came the heavy sigh of a near-by explosion.

In a small office, behind a desk covered with papers stood a thickset man. His drooping, round shoulders were draped in a military blouse, which was worn outside and pulled in by a belt; wide trousers disappeared into brown, Morocco leather boots, with soft soles. The thick, dark hair was brushed back, exposing a low forehead, and the long prominent nose and drooping moustaches gave a melancholy appearance to the whole face—but the eyes, although obviously weary, lit up from time to time with a gleam of authority.

This was Joseph Stalin, the all-powerful and absolute master of the Soviet empire, which now united within its extensive frontiers scores of nationalities and several countries until recently independent, which the rapacious hands of the dictator had reduced to subjection.

A few kilometres away, on the outskirts of the city, a great battle was being waged; the German tanks were pushing forward and only with the utmost difficulty was the Soviet infantry able to repair the breaks in the last line of defence guarding the capital of international Communism from the Nazis.

German bombers, marked with black crosses, appeared over Moscow day and night, sowing panic on the bridges, in the stations and on the roads running eastwards from the city, where crowds of evacuees seethed and floundered in the throng of cars carrying evacuated government departments, police and embassies.

Behind the thick walls of the Kremlin, with heavy curtains covering the door and windows, it was quiet and only the slight shaking of the whole building brought to mind what was happening outside. The dictator knew the situation his country was in. Two years earlier he had been convinced that his policy was correct. Against all the basic principles of the ideology he professed, against the hopes of all those who believed that in Russia new forms of mutual relations between countries and nations were being forged, against all the canons of Communism proclaimed for years, he had signed a pact with Hitler and helped him to start the war. The most glaring, the most brutal, repulsive and rapacious Fascism had gained the support of a country whose propaganda had proclaimed, to the point of tedium, the slogans of brotherhood and the freedom of all peoples. A second world madness was in prospect and the sly dictator had reckoned that once again the western front would hold out for years, that once again on the plains of France the young generation of the western democracies would fall and the German ally bleed to death. Europe, by her own hands, with her own weapons, would destroy the achievements of centuries, the fruits of her civilization and her culture; and then the untouched, well-equipped Red Army would advance and without a fight overrun the old Continent, fulfilling at last the former dreams of the white Russian Tsars. Therefore he not only gave Hitler political and moral support, but pledged himself to large supplies of raw materials.* He had sent them to the German *Reich* in countless trains, calculating that they would prolong the war in the

---

* In the treaty signed on 10 February 1940, Russia promised within twelve months to supply 900,000 tons of crude oil, 500,000 tons of phosphates, 500,000 tons of iron ore, 300,000 tons of pig-iron, 100,000 tons of chrome ore, 100,000 tons of cotton, and 1,000,000 tons of cattle feed (Aleksander Bregman, *Najlepszy sojusznik Hitlera* (Hitler's Best Ally), 4th edition, London, 1974, p.104).

west and make later Soviet conquest easier.

But he was mistaken. The war in the west lasted barely a few weeks; France asked for an armistice and Hitler, so recently just a needy ally, suddenly became the master of a large part of Europe. It was true that he had lost the Battle of Britain, but that in no way weakened his might on land and here the countless German divisions had suddenly found themselves without a worthy opponent. Stalin understood this. He sought a solution in political manoeuvres; he promised further, larger supplies; he agreed to various German proposals. But Hitler saw things differently. It was true that his chief enemy was Great Britain, but he could not attack her and he was afraid of British political tactics. He foresaw that sooner or later she would come to an understanding with Russia and push her against the *Reich*, so he decided that he would strike first at a moment chosen by himself. This was perfectly in the old German tradition of looking for living space in Eastern Europe.

During the night of 22 June 1941, along a huge front, over 1,500 kilometres long, from the Baltic to the Black Sea, more than 130 German divisions[1] advanced to invade the territories occupied by the Soviets. It immediately became apparent that the Red Army could not compare in arms, training, or (and this was most important) in determination to fight, with the German divisions. Within a few weeks Hitler's victorious army had advanced several hundred kilometres into Soviet territory, had taken a number of towns and over a million prisoners. The Soviet administration had also broken down, and the hatred of people for a political system that was maintained by force and terror had come into the open.

It was barely the middle of October when Hitler's tanks reached the outskirts of Moscow and only there did they come up against organized defence. Stalin, expecting that Japan would not take up arms against him, recalled in great haste the crack Siberian divisions and in a desperate appeal called on the patriotism of the Russian masses; and the early Russian winter, which more than once had been the last defence of the country when attacked, came on in the nick of time. All the same the situation was desperate and Stalin, who had himself decided to remain in Moscow, had to accept the evacuation of the government, the commissariats, the diplomatic corps and the factories. The city was in flames, German bombs hailed down on it daily, police reports brought bad news of the crowds on all the roads running east, of looting and of general panic, which even the NKVD was unable to control. Reports from outside confirmed a similar critical situation near Leningrad and on the southern front, where the Germans were taking town after town without any difficulty.

It was at this time of hopelessness that Stalin, in one of his speeches, said: 'We have lost for ever everything that Lenin created.'[2]

2

General Dornberger, meanwhile, had not for one moment let up in his efforts to secure maximum support for his missile experiments at Peenemünde, and in 1942 he suddenly gained a very influential ally. This was Albert Speer, a man barely thirty-seven years old, full of energy and ideas, who took over the important office of minister for Munitions and War Production on 8 February, after the death in a plane crash of the current minister, Dr Fritz Todt.[3]

Speer, an architect by profession, was on good terms with Hitler, who loved grandiose projects and had been planning with him a monumental reconstruction of Berlin, for which he himself drew up several plans. With the outbreak of war, of course, Hitler had more important matters on his mind, and his time became especially limited after the attack on the Soviet Union. In his strategy the dictator had expected that he would rout the Red Army in six weeks, and that six months would be enough to force the enemy to total capitulation;[4] but he underestimated. As the German tanks drove eastwards so Soviet resistance grew, and one of the reasons lay in the military and psychological mistakes made by Hitler himself. He attacked a huge country, inhabited by many nations who were waiting for help from outside to free them from Russian oppression; but he had no positive political plans in relation to them. The German divisions were greeted with great enthusiasm in the Ukraine, in the Baltic States and to some extent in Byelorussia, but the enthusiasm quickly faded when, behind the front-line troops, police units and the Nazi administration appeared. Instead of making use of the initial welcoming mood and promising the conquered countries their freedom, instead of breaking up the collective farms and restoring private property, the Nazis began a campaign of ruthless economic exploitation, and every demonstration of national feeling was met by terror. The attitude of the Germans is perhaps best characterized by the words of the head of the *SS*, Himmler, expressing their policy: 'The fate of Russians or Czechs is of absolutely no interest to me. Whether they flourish or die of hunger, concerns me only from the point of view of our need for their slave labour for the sake of our culture; I am quite indifferent to any other aspect.'[5]

In such a situation, where the arrival of the Germans brought suffering and death, the peoples inhabiting the Soviet Union turned to resistance. The attitude of the front-line divisions stiffened and in the occupied territories a partisan movement emerged, taking close interest in the lengthy German lines of communication. Before long the situation became so critical that the Germans cut down all trees for half a kilometre on either side of the railway lines, set up watch towers, and sent out constant patrols. But in the forests the partisans reigned. The optimistic attack on Russia turned out to have been madness, and a few months later Hitler took another, equally crazy, step, when on 11 December 1941 he declared war on the United States of America.

It is not surprising, therefore, that Speer, who attached great importance to the experiments in Peenemünde, found himself in a difficult situation. He was convinced that the rockets could assure Germany of victory and wanted, almost at any cost, to speed up completion of the tests with prototypes so that they could go over to mass production. But this required a specific decision by Hitler. The dictator, occupied by the war with Russia and the personal command of his armies, did not want to hear anything about rockets. On the boundless Russian steppes it was cars, guns, planes and tanks that were needed. The Minister of War Production was made responsible for the mass supply of these, not of rockets, the usefulness of which was not yet proven. The difficulty of Speer's situation was increased by the fact that, after taking up his important office, he came to the conclusion that the war must be won as speedily as possible, otherwise the economy of the Third *Reich* would be unable to support it. So it was difficult to argue for a weapon still in the experimental phase.[6]

In the early spring of 1942 the British carried out a heavy air-raid on Lübeck. Hitler, losing his patience and eager for revenge, then at last turned his attention to the rockets he had previously neglected; but now his attitude to the possibilities of the new weapon was quite unrealistic. At the briefing with Speer he gave the order for Dornberger to prepare a plan at once for the production of 3,000 rockets a month. If this were to prove impossible he wanted all the materials being supplied for the V-2 to be diverted to the navy.[7]

This threat, in the face of the utter impossibility of manufacturing such a large number of rockets monthly, strengthened the determination of the men who were doing all they could to bring about a successful firing of the V-2 and to pierce the indifference of the most important person in the country. But the first test ended in a fiasco. On 18 March 1942, in spite of several weeks of feverish preparations, the rocket exploded prematurely and did not even reach the firing state. Von Braun and Dornberger found themselves in an even worse position than before, since Hitler had by then raised his demands to 5,000 monthly. Putting aside the fact that such a complicated mechanism could not be mass-produced in haste, 5,000 rockets would have required 75,000 tons of liquid oxygen, and the yearly output at that time in Germany was only 26,000 tons.[8]

Again, a paradoxical situation arose. The ending of the experiments and the going over to mass-production of the V-2 constituted a very grave danger to Great Britain, although there no one was aware of it at the time. Any delays in rocket research were in British interests. Yet it was the British who had changed Hitler's changeable mind: he was primarily occupied with the eastern front, and would not have made the rockets a priority had it not been for the regular British air-raids which were destroying German factories, railway lines and towns, causing great losses in war production and reducing the force of resistance among the population. The dictator was driven to fury by the systematic British air attacks and wanted to pay back in kind; for this he needed long-range rockets to reach London.

Therefore, in spite of his obvious scepticism, Hitler listened to Speer's reports; under his influence, on 22 December 1942, he signed an order for the mass-production of this weapon, despite the fact that the experiments were not yet concluded and he himself had not even seen the film of the only successful firing.[9]

### 3

Some time earlier a quite extraordinary thing had happened: Antoni Kocjan had been released from Auschwitz.[10]

It is difficult to establish why. For some reason, against the accepted principle that there was to be no way out of a concentration camp, especially in time of war, the camp Commandant decided to release forty or fifty prisoners, caught in round-ups. There were no humanitarian motives; every step was designed to bring Nazism nearer to its goal: the conquest of Europe and the division of the world. Prisoners were destined to work and die in the camps, so the release of these young men must have had some object. It was probably intended to have a psychological effect on the Polish population, who knew of the existence of Auschwitz but in spite of the most fantastic reports did not realize what a death camp was really like. It was true that each of the released men was threatened with re-arrest and a return to the camp if he breathed a word of his experiences; but the Germans considered that this threat would have no effect. Whispered propaganda would carry the news of the frightfulness of life in the camp all over Poland. In this they were right; they were, however, mistaken if they thought this would weaken the determination of the resistance and eagerness for underground activity.

Kocjan, as soon as he returned to Warsaw, reported to his underground superiors and went back to his clandestine work. Normally, in the rare case of someone being released from a camp or prison, the person in question was required to observe an underground quarantine of several weeks' duration; in Kocjan's case this was not deemed necessary: he had been sent to the camp after a round-up and the Gestapo had nothing on him.

During the nine months that he had spent in Auschwitz, the underground movement in Poland had recovered from the depression caused by the collapse of France and had begun to operate again, but in a different way. Hopes for a speedy end of the war had vanished, so the mass recruiting of underground soldiers had been stopped and the system of cadres adopted.[11] The building up also began of agencies that might prove useful to Great Britain, which was at that time fighting almost alone. Important in this respect was an intelligence service reaching into the heart of Germany and bringing back reports on industrial production, on the location of factories and on lines of communication. These matters required specialist assessment and, therefore, in Warsaw, in the middle of 1941, a Bureau of Economic Studies had been set up, attached to the command of the underground intelligence of ZWZ.[12] It was given the code-name *Arka* and was led by Jerzy Chmielewski *(Jacek)*, an agronomist by profession. He looked for contacts among scientists and brought them into the secret bureau. Somewhat later it was decided to set up another similar body, the Economic Council, which was headed by Hipolit Gliwic. The Bureau and the Council worked side by side trying not to duplicate each other's efforts.[13]

Before his arrest Kocjan had served in a different capacity, but now his superiors considered that he would be of most use in working on the reports from Germany. He was therefore put in contact with Chmielewski, who made him head of the department concerned with German air production. The engineer took the codename *Korona* and got down to work, which particularly interested him as it was in line with his qualifications.

The military intelligence of the ZWZ, operating on the territory of the German *Reich*, carried out penetration in various ways and under various pretexts. Most often it made use of the recruiting of Poles for work in industry and on the land. The Nazi authorities, who in the west of Europe counted on the local populations and tried to give their recruiting at least the appearance of voluntary applications (in France and Denmark they even settled recruitment procedures with the governments), in the east simply organized blatant round-ups, which were like driving animals into the middle of the field. All the same there were still a number of bureaux accepting volunteers, even though they were there mainly for propaganda purposes. The Polish underground press and propaganda officially condemned volunteering for work in Germany, since this helped military production, and they branded the volunteers as collaborators; but for their own purposes volunteering was extremely useful, since those who went to Germany of their own free will usually had the right to choose their work and place of residence. The men and women who volunteered exposed themselves both to the scorn of their own people, which was sometimes expressed in assaults and could end in death, and to the risk of falling into the hands of the Gestapo, which meant torture and almost certain execution. But there was no lack of volunteers.

There was still another way of getting into German territory. This was volunteering for the Organization Todt, which built roads, airfields, defences and barracks; but from the moment of the outbreak of the German-Soviet war this ceased to be possible, for all volunteers were sent to the eastern territories behind the front. There also existed possibilities for individuals to travel under false papers, but these were used only by couriers and were not safe for more than a few days. After all, no help could be expected from the local inhabitants.

Hitler's *Reich* was a police state, only rivalled in this respect by the Soviet Union. On every work-floor and in every factory there operated both secret and open security systems, which employed a wide-spread network of informers. One had to be very careful of them, but cautious intelligence work could be carried on, largely because the factory workers were mostly foreigners. Among the many-tongued thousands it was relatively easy to hide and avoid spying eyes.

The Polish military intelligence, which sent trained people to the *Reich,* fairly soon began to obtain interesting and important information, which was sent by couriers to Warsaw and from there, once a month, by radio, to London. British intelligence was pleased with these reports, and demanded that their range should be widened and that they should be sent even daily.[14] Such hasty despatches could contain only bare facts, unverified and not supplemented by analysis, but copies remained in Warsaw and the Bureau of Economic Studies worked on them.*

Into Kocjan's hands came reports concerning the air force and the effects of the British bombings. Their contents embraced the types of aircraft, technical improvements, the level of production, the speed and range of fighters and bombers. Also important were

---

\* Intelligence reports were also sent to London concerning the German-Soviet war, but they are not connected with the subject of this book.

the details concerning the fuel they used.* The engineer worked on the information received and questions constantly came into his mind, which he sent on to the centre of intelligence. The questions went back to Germany, to the local network, and every time this meant further expansion and strenuous efforts to get into new places as yet unreached.


4


The day that Hitler attacked the Soviet Union was a decisive moment for Great Britain. For a year after the collapse of the front in France she had had to repel German attacks by sea and air almost alone. It is true that naval units and air and army formations of Poles, French, Norwegians, Dutch, Belgians and Czechs were fighting under British command; but they did not represent any great force numerically and, apart from ships, they did not possess their own equipment. The United States had shown much sympathy and given help, but it remained neutral. The war in the east was greeted with great relief, as a miracle, a gift from heaven; and Churchill, an experienced politician of long standing, was aroused by the mood of the moment to such an extent that within twenty-four hours of the attack on Russia, he had made a speech over the BBC, in which he offered the Soviet Union every assistance without any political conditions. This step was a few years later to have a fatal effect on Russia's neighbours, many of whom were handed over to the Russians.

The Germans' first great successes considerably weakened the hopes of the British for a long breathing-space, but Hitler's mistakes and the Russian winter and Soviet determination held up his offensive and stabilized the front. Assistance began to be organized for the new ally, and at the same time it was possible in Britain to think more quietly and freely of the campaign in North Africa and the threat to the homeland.

The *Oslo Report* had been put aside in the files, but it was not forgotten, and the German secret weapons had not been completely

---

\* The Germans flew on low-octane fuel, the British and Americans on high-octane.

# STOCK CONTROL

| QUAN. | DATE INV. NO. | D | PROT. EXP. s/o DATE |
|---|---|---|---|
| 2 | 29 Sept 18 1943 | c E | |
| | | | |
| | | | |
| | | | |
| | | | |
| | | | |
| | | | |
| | | | |
| | | | |
| | | | |
| | | | |
| | | | |
| | | | |
| | | | |
| | | | |
| | | | |
| | | | |
| | | | |
| | | | |
| | | | |
| | | | |
| | | | |
| | | | |

PRICE 12.95

PUB. & CAN. AGT. *Fee*

TITLE *Hitler near Weapons*

CLASS *War*

AUTHOR *Gartner*

TRITES BOOK SHOPS

dismissed as unrealistic. All the same, practically nothing had been heard of them for three years (in May 1940, a report came from the continent that Professor Oberth was working somewhere not far from Szczecin on a thirty-ton rocket with a range of over 300 kilometres). It was only in December 1942 that a Danish chemist (whose name is unknown), working in Germany, managed by some means (probably through SOE) to send the news to London that on the Baltic coast the Germans had recently successfully fired a large rocket which could fly a distance of about 300 kilometres. These details had been overheard in a Berlin restaurant where two German engineers had met.[15]

The new informant was not immediately believed, the more so as the circumstances in which he obtained his information might have been arranged to put the British on to a false trail; nevertheless London was alarmed and the people responsible for the matter became more alert.

Later the Danish informant sent two further reports on the same subject. In one of them he mentioned that the warhead of the rocket was supposed to contain five tons of explosives. Another informant reported that the German weapon was even more menacing and carried double that weight.[16] British intelligence was made very uneasy by this and started to reconstruct such a powerful rocket, coming to the conclusion that with that load of explosive it would have to be 120 feet tall.

But these were all suppositions and conjectures; they required confirmation. This came from a rather unexpected quarter. During the battle of El-Alamein the British took prisoner two German generals, Wilhelm von Thoma and Krugel.* After several months in solitary confinement in Great Britain, the two were put together alone for some hours in a room wired for sound. They already knew each other, so it was hard to imagine that they would not talk. This old intelligence trick was used without any thought of gaining news of the German secret weapons, rather of hearing future plans for the war in the desert. From a long conversation a number of small, insignificant facts were gathered, but Dr Jones's deputy, Dr Charles Frank, hit on something said by von Thoma, from which it became clear that a few months earlier, in the

---

* Christian name unknown.

company of Field-Marshal Walter von Brauchitsch, he had watched an experimental firing of the rocket and heard it said that it would be ready for military use in a year's time.[17]

British intelligence treated this information seriously, for General von Thoma was regarded as a competent general with technical training. But this was still only information at second hand, without any details as to where the experiments were being carried out. It could also be deliberate misinformation. So it was absolutely necessary to get details direct from Germany, from someone who had himself seen the tests with the secret weapon or was at least not far from them and knew where they were situated. There was no doubt now that it was necessary to search along the Baltic coast, and that the site would be guarded very strictly. The continental agents of the intelligence service, placed in German industry and even in the German armed forces, received appropriate instructions and their reports were awaited eagerly.[18]

As it happened the information came from another source.


5


At one of Hitler's briefings, after Speer had at last managed to convince him that the V-2 should be given top priority, the *Führer*, winding up the proceedings, had said: 'In this project we can use only Germans. God help us if the enemy finds out about the business.'[19]

This was a very proper opinion on an obvious problem, requiring no discussion, and yet, when Hitler said it, it was already too late. For some months already, foreign workers had been employed on the island of Usedom and although they were used for the heaviest, dirtiest tasks, without access to detailed information on the tests, nobody could blindfold them while they were working or stop them from moving around the area where they had to work.

As has been mentioned, the intelligence network of the Home Army*, operating on German territory, depended above all on Polish workers. Only a few of them before their deportation had

---

* On 14 February 1942 by order of General Sikorski, ZWZ had been renamed *Armia Krajowa* (AK), Home Army.

undergone 'intelligence training; the majority, numbering almost two million, had little idea of the nature of this work but were of immense service to the common cause. This usually happened by way of conversation and questions about what was going on in their region. Most frequently they reported insignificant details; sometimes, however, important news was obtained. It also happened that when someone saw something unusual or overheard an interesting German conversation, he would tell others in the hope that the information would be passed on. The Germans treated Poles very badly; it was no wonder that they were repaid with hate.

In the southern part of the island of Usedom, in a place called Trassenheide, there was a camp for foreign workers, among whom were Poles. Two of them, whose names remain unknown, were detailed to the dirtiest work of cleaning the latrines and drains, so that they moved around a fairly wide area with a cart and a pair of horses. The chains of guards and the constant searching did not surprise them since it was the same all over Germany, but they were interested in the noise of engines which came from the northern part of the island. This was not like any noise from the heaviest aeroplanes; it made the air vibrate. They could not get any closer, but they began to watch the sky to the north and several times, in the evening hours, they saw a small aircraft with short wings, as if docked, flying seawards.[20] They told what they had seen to another Pole, whom they met from time to time and who worked in the transport section, bringing food to the island. They did not even know that this man had an intelligence contact and that he sent the report through a network which passed it on to Warsaw.

It was the beginning of 1943* when the coded radio despatch reached London and came into the hands of Lt-Colonel Michał Protasewicz, who since April 1942 had been at the head of the VIth Bureau of the Polish General Staff. The main object of this bureau was secret liaison with occupied Poland and it was the only cell which had this function. It also maintained liaison with the Polish Section of SOE. Contact with the British intelligence service belonged to the IInd Bureau of the Polish General Staff and therefore the most urgent despatches from Poland went straight to

* See Appendix II, item 1.

it, via the VIth Bureau.

In accordance with the above principle the despatch received was sent immediately to the IInd Bureau, which at once passed it on to the intelligence service. It aroused great interest among the British, and Protasewicz received a number of requests for further details. He sent them by radio-telegram to Warsaw and a few weeks later received radio confirmation. This contained general details of the island of Usedom, stressing that the Germans had established a centre near Peenemünde for testing new weapons and that one of them was a small pilotless aircraft. One of the despatches said that a fuller report with a sketch map would be sent by courier.[21]

6

In the middle of the morning, after the inhabitants had gone to work, the streets of Vienna, like almost all cities under German occupation, gave the impression of lifelessness. It was the beginning of April 1943 and through the city a mild, southerly breeze was blowing, but except for a few hurrying passers-by and police patrols nobody seemed to be enjoying its pleasant touch.

A tram-car drew up at a stop on one of the main streets and a solitary woman got out of it. She looked round discreetly, crossed the road and went into one of the side streets. She found the address she required, looked at the list of tenants and pushed the appropriate bell. One short ring, then two considerably longer. The reply signal sounded and the door to the staircase opened automatically. The woman was no longer young so she looked for the lift, but seeing it was out of order she began to climb the stairs slowly. She finally stopped in front of one of the flats and again rang in the agreed manner. The door opened and before she could take a step, firm hands grabbed her and dragged her inside. In the dark hall several men with guns in their hands surrounded her.

The first feelings of courier *Sława** were of great shock; she thought that this was the end. But after a moment she felt some relief—a few days earlier she had delivered the secret mail, which she had brought from Warsaw, to another address.[22]

---

*   See Appendix I, item 7.

The Viennese Gestapo; knowing something about the woman they had arrested and aware that she was a Home Army courier, subjected her to cruel interrogation, demanding that she should reveal her contacts in Warsaw and the other addresses in Vienna. Although elderly, she was beaten with iron bars, hung upside down, boiling oil was poured into her nose, her fingers were broken. Not wishing to say anything and unable to stand the suffering, she bit through the veins of her wrist; but they kept her alive. To her physical sufferings was added fear about the mail which she had managed to deliver but of which she knew nothing further. The other contact address might also be under observation, and the important papers might be in German hands.

There was, in fact, someting to be afraid of, for the mail carried by *Sława* contained intelligence material concerning the German experiments in Peenemünde. They filled out the earlier despatches sent by radio, which had necessarily been laconic.

This valuable information of the Home Army Intelligence had as its source mainly the work of two men: Engineer Jan Szreder and an NCO of the *Wehrmacht*, Roman Träger. Szreder, in spite of his German-sounding name, was a Pole; working for a Home Army Intelligence group *(Lombard)*, he had volunteered for work in Germany, and at the beginning of 1943 found himself on the terrain of Swinoujście, in the near neighbourhood of Peenemünde. He was employed as a carter and rather thoughtlessly took the code-name *Furman**. He belonged to the transport unit supplying food to the area of the German experiments. He could not get near them, for the entrance was guarded by a tight security cordon, and the closest point he reached was the village of Zinnowitz in the narrowest part of Usedom; but he heard and observed a lot. It was to be seen that the Germans were conveying large amounts of industrial materials to the north headland and that something highly secret was going on, for everywhere there was very strict security. The local people knew that on the island there was a prisoner-of-war camp, and concentration and labour camps, inhabited by thousands of foreigners. Among the Germans,

* 'Carter' is *furman* in Polish. A good code-name should have no connection with the name, place of residence or employment of the person who takes it.

conversations were overheard about aerial torpedoes looking like small aeroplanes with stunted wings.[23]

Roman Träger was the son of an Austrian who lived in Bydgoszcz and who took German citizenship after the town was occupied by them in 1939. In spite of this he retained a feeling of loyalty to the Polish state, and contacted the Polish underground movement. The son was taken into the German army, given a signalling course and sent to Schleswig-Holstein with his unit. As a specialist he was detailed to various staff units to install and check the newest telecommunication equipment. In this way he arrived in Peenemünde. During his next leave he confided to his father the observations he had made during his service. He had seen small pilotless planes gliding, had heard the bang accompanying their start, at dusk had seen the streaks of fire trailing after them. His father told him in confidence that he was working for Polish intelligence and received his son's permission to use the information. Both of them, although Austrians by descent, regarded themselves as Poles, and since Austria and Poland were in the hands of the Nazis, they considered they were working for the right cause.

Young Träger during the years 1942-43, was sent several times to the island of Usedom, to Peenemünde and Karlshagen, so he found himself at the very centre of the experiments. He moved around freely, for his job was to check the portable telephonic equipment, and he was able to inform his father that the pilotless planes were ejected from steel rails and that they were steered from the ground by radio.* As well as this, experiments were being carried out there on several other types of new weapons. To these details he added a sketch-map of the whole terrain with explanatory comments.

The father, Augustyn Träger *(Tragarz)* then made contact with Bernard Kaczmarek *(Wrzos)* who, within the framework of *Lombard*, belonged to an intelligence cell called *Bałtyk* (Baltic). He had well-made false papers and was able to move around Germany fairly freely, collecting intelligence reports from agents hidden deep in enemy territory. To him came the information from engineer Szreder.

Within a few days the valuable intelligence material was in

* Erroneous information, see Chapter One, section 6.

Warsaw and in Kocjan's hands. It was very carefully examined and the locality mentioned was checked on the map. The report as a whole gave the impression of facts scrupulously collected. Put together, the two reports from sources quite independent of each other agreed on the salient points.[24] Kocjan prepared a short report which was sent quickly to London by radio. A second, more detailed report, with a sketch-map of Usedom, was sent off to England by courier.

This was carried on part of its route by the courier *Stawa*, and at the beginning of April 1943 she managed to deliver it to the contact address in Vienna a few days before her arrest. The report was on film and well hidden in the handle of an attaché case. Luckily the Germans never discovered this address. The case travelled on and, through trusted people who knew the frontier paths, was delivered to Switzerland where the Polish liaison network between the homeland and the west had an auxiliary outpost S.[25] In Switzerland diplomatic representatives of the western allies worked openly, as did the Polish legation, and residential agents of the intelligence service operated, so there was no difficulty in sending mail quickly to London.

This time the intelligence material which came into Lt-Colonel Protasewicz's hands exceeded in importance anything that had so far come from Poland on the subject of the German secret weapons. The sketch-map of Usedom with the territory of Peenemünde outlined in thick pencil, the description of the flying bombs, the manner of launching them, the great German security measures; all this confirmed fragmentary information, photographs, suppositions and guesses. The way was open for further important discoveries.

The whole report, after decoding, together with the sketch-map, was immediately passed on to the British authorities.[26]

The information arrived at the same time as similar reports sent to London from France and Belgium. These were both based on reports sent from the island of Usedom by workers from Luxembourg. There were about fifty of them and they were treated better than other foreigners, since the Germans considered them to be *Reichsdeutschen.**

* Pure Germans (by birth).

One of them, Pierre Ginter, working in the area of Peenemünde during the night shift as a telephone operator, managed to get hold of some plans of the secret weapons and the positions of the anti-aircraft guns. At the beginning of January 1943, after returning to Luxembourg, he handed over his trophies to Dr Fernand Schwachtgen, who under the code-name *Jean L'Aveugle* was head of the underground organization there. It had no direct contact with Great Britain, but was a part of the northern-France secret group, *Famille Martin*, which by four different routes sent the report to London, where it was put into Dr Jones's hands in June. It interested him greatly.[27]

The second informant was Henri Roth, who had also been directed to Peenemünde by the *Arbeitsdienst*.* As a *Reichsdeutsch* he had the right to write to his family, though his correspondence naturally went through the censor's hands. In his first letter the censors had cut out a whole page, and mention of the place where Roth worked was completely obliterated. So the young man's father, who was already in contact with the Belgian underground group, *Service Clarence*, drew their attention to it. The situation was exploited and Henri Roth later sent some very interesing information, which comprised not only details of the flying torpedoes, moving under their own impulsion, but also a sketch of the island of Usedom. The report drawn up from this, through a Belgian channel, reached London in June 1943.[28]

7

On a dark, rainy night, a British army car set out from Cardiff. It was heading for Aberporth in North Wales, where the first experimental anti-aircraft artillery regiment, equipped with small rockets propelled by solid fuel, was stationed. The driver, over-tired from long hours on duty, fell asleep at the wheel and the car crashed into a wall. The regimental commander, a young man of thirty-five, Lt-Colonel Duncan Sandys, sitting next to the driver, came out of the crash with broken legs and other injuries which put

---

*   Labour Service.

an end to his military career.

After three months in hospital, where he was in danger of having both feet amputated, Sandys returned to normal life, but this energetic and enterprising man had become an invalid for life. He was a member of Parliament, and feeling that he had enough mental resources to remain active, he returned to a life of politics. During a cabinet reshuffle he was appointed Joint Parliamentary Secretary to the Ministry of Supply and at once found himself at the heart of important military affairs, for the ministry was concerned not only with mass production, but also with experiments connected with armaments.

After the exceptionally important intelligence report had come from Poland, similar reports also arrived from Luxembourg. One of these reports contained a sketch of the large shed in which the V-2 was being erected.[29]

It is true that the experts were not agreed as to the importance of the information obtained or how to act on it, but it was decided that the danger was sufficiently grave for the highest authorities to be informed of it. Reports went to Prime Minister Churchill, to the Home Secretary, Herbert Morrison, and to the Imperial General Staff. After some days of discussion the suggestion was made that discovery of the German secret weapons, chiefly the rockets, required the nomination of one man, independent of the already existing intelligence cells and the various ministries and answerable directly to the War Cabinet, to co-ordinate information.[30]

When the decision had been taken, General Hastings Ismay, in the name of the chiefs of staff, recommended Duncan Sandys as the best candidate. He had the formal qualifications, for he had commanded the first experimental rocket regiment and, as secretary to the Ministry of Supply, he was in official contact with scientists and other experts. But this was not what counted most. Those who put his name forward considered that he had admirable qualities of mind and character, which suited him for this position. Prime Minister Churchill shared this opinion and on 20 April 1943 he accepted the proposal.[31] Sandys was to investigate the German long-range rocket development programme and would be responsible to the War Cabinet.

Sandys's appointment aroused great discontent among the experts already working on the problem of the German secret weapons. They were annoyed that he was a politician and an army man, not a scientist; that he had no experience in this field. Much was made of the fact that a few years earlier he had married Churchill's daughter. Dr Jones, although only a young man, may have felt bitterly disappointed, for he stood at the head of the scientific department of the Air Ministry Intelligence and was adviser to the security forces; but his feelings were nothing compared to the fury of Lord Cherwell. He held the office of Paymaster General and was an important figure in the government, for he enjoyed the trust and friendship of Churchill, who regarded him as his personal scientific adviser. Cherwell was of German descent,* a professor of Physics at Oxford. He was in middle age, with a high opinion of himself, and his reaction to Sandys's appointment was a mixture of hurt pride, resentment of young men, and sheer jealousy. For a long time he had made little of the experiments with rockets, contesting their existence with scientific arguments, and after Sandys had been promoted to an exposed and important office Cherwell became his inexorable opponent. Unfortunately this personal hostility blinded him to the importance of the German rocket threat.[32]

It soon appeared that the Sandys appointment was a good one. He took little heed of the envy of others and got down to work. He was to collect all important information from every available source, collating it and reporting the results to the Prime Minister himself. None of the eminent scientists or intelligence officers was formally responsible to him, but they were required to co-operate and make the results of their research available.

At that time there were a number of experts involved in research on weaponry: Professor Charles D. Ellis, for example, who was scientific adviser to the army, and Dr Alwyn D. Crow, a rocket expert, working for the Ministry of Supply. But the main burden of research into the German retaliatory weapons fell on Dr Jones. He was then barely 30 years old, but he already possessed great knowledge and exceptional intuition, which helped him when material proof for scientific conclusions was lacking. He was perhaps the only person in Great Britain to guess that the *Oslo Report* was not misinformation and that it contained data which

* His name had been Frederick Alexander Lindemann.

might be of great importance. He kept a copy of the report and as the war went on looked into it from time to time, finding on each occasion that the document had accurately foreseen what would happen.[33]

At the other extreme stood Lord Cherwell, under whom Jones had studied at Oxford and in whose laboratory he had carried out experiments. It is possible that Cherwell's antipathy to Sandys was not the only reason that he questioned the existence of the rockets and paid no heed to the reports which spoke of them. He was an eminent scientist, of great experience, but unlike Jones he lacked the vision which would have allowed him, perhaps, to see further than a scientific experiment. He had a pragmatic mind, relying only on figures, proven facts and known experiments. His position as a cabinet minister and personal adviser to Churchill was incomparably stronger than that of Dr Jones, who had no strong scientific background nor personal contacts. These two men joined issue on the development of the German rockets, on the outcome of which might depend the fate of London and perhaps even the war.

8

In the quiet village of Medmenham, not far from Henley, where every year the famous regatta takes place, fifty-odd kilometres to the west of London, a young girl sat by a table in a small room. She was wearing the uniform of a WAAF. In her hands was a magnifying glass and, bent over the table in concentration, she was studying a photograph in front of her. Long minutes later she straightened up, put down the glass and for a while sat still with closed eyes. Then she put aside the print she had been studying, picked up another photograph from a large pile and concentrated again.

Constance Babington-Smith belonged to the Cental Intelligence Unit (CIU), a special cell for interpreting photographs taken from the air. She was expert at her job and sharp-sighted enough to pick out objects photgraphed from a height of 10 kilometres. She also apparently had an inborn talent for correct interpretation, and it was therefore to her that the CIU gave anything doubtful and important enough to require quick and decisive action. That was why, in May 1943, a pile of photographs of Peenemünde had been brought to her tiny room with a request that they should be studied very carefully.[34] Alarming reports from the Continent about secret German preparations made the matter urgent.

The Second World War had brought about great changes in the air force, one of whose tasks was aerial intelligence, the photographing of enemy terrain from a great height, and the interpretation of the resulting pictures. Before September 1939 there already existed in Great Britain a special unit, the Photo Reconnaissance Unit (PRU), similar to the American Photo Interpretation Unit (PIU). When the United States entered the war towards the end of 1941, PRU was re-named Allied Central Interpretation Unit (usually referred to as CIU) and in certain respects came under the control of the Joint Chiefs of Staff.[35]

The information provided by this unit was very important and made an excellent supplement to the reports sent in by intelligence and the news obtained by prisoners of war. Every big bombing raid, every commando raid on the Continent, was preceded by photographs from the air. For short distances ordinary one-man fighters were used, for longer flights two-men Mosquitoes.

Although in 1942 not much was known of the German experiments with retaliatory weapons, flights were made over the sands of the northern coasts of Europe and from time to time photographs were taken. The island of Usedom was photographed for the first time on 15 May 1942, and this was repeated on 19 January of the following year at the request of the Americans (PIU). They had received information that long-range rockets were being built there.[36] Another flight was made on 19 March 1943 by order of the War Office. Flights for photographic purposes had to be camouflaged so that the Germans should not realize what was under scrutiny, so the aircraft went up and down the whole coast without dwelling over the island of Usedom.

Sandys had not been long in his new appointment when he turned to the RAF asking for new flights and new photographs of Peenemünde. Wing Commander Hugh Hamslow Thomas at Medmenham was ordered to set up a new photographic reconnaissance and to look out above all for long-range guns, rocket aircraft and rockets launched from underground, perhaps from a disused coal mine. The flight was carried out on 22 April.

Two days later the photgraphs found their way on to the desks at Medmenham for interpretation. The flights were repeated on 14 May and 21 and 25 June.[37]

All the photographs were enlarged in the Industrial Section under Flight Lieutenant E.J.A. Kenny. They were examined by experienced people but mistakes were often made, and this was what happened now. The launching-pad of the V-1 was taken for a mechanical pump to deepen the sea bed; a photograph of one of the most important buildings, in which liquid oxygen was manufactured, was wrongly interpreted. It was not yet surmised in London that the rockets were propelled by liquid fuel, for the British experiments employed solid fuel.

The enlarged photographs were nevertheless interpreted several times, and in May 1943 they appeared again on Miss Babington-Smith's desk. In this sort of work the principle was observed that the interpreter should be given no information, so that no clues or false leads were suggested. Among the many objects, easy to identify as houses and factory buildings, the sharp eyes of the young girl spotted, on several photographs, a dark, elongated shape, which resembled a railway ramp. A new packet of photographs was brought from a later reconnaissance flight and again this same dark shape was to be seen in them. This time, however, at one end, barely visible, was a small white dot. After long investigation and taking into account the light and shade thrown by this small object, the conclusion was reached that it must be an aircraft.

At this time in England the details of the flying bombs were not yet known and the name 'V-1' was not yet used, so the newly-discovered object was filed as 'Peenemünde 30'.[38]

# CHAPTER FOUR

## The development of Peenemünde; the even chances of the V-1 and V-2; Himmler and the experiments; Hitler convinced

1

In March 1943 Albert Speer returned to Berlin from Hitler's field head-quarters and immediately sent Colonel Dornberger some alarming information: the *Führer* has dreamed that no V-2 will ever reach England.[1]

In the Germany of those days it was not possible to ignore a dream like that, so the whole weapons-programme was immediately at risk. Even if Speer had invented this dream to cover himself for all eventualities,* this did not change the fact that all von Braun's and Dornberger's hopes were once again in great danger. Hitler was working under the dreadful pressure of failure on the eastern front and the bombing of Germany; he had not a moment's peace and was struggling like a trapped wolf trying to get out of a snare. He could at any moment capriciously decide on another scheme and, with one stroke of his hand, sweep the whole rocket project out of the war.

However, Speer knew Hitler too well and saw him too often not to know how to keep to a chosen path which he considered to be justified. It was a path of careful decisions and *faits accomplis*. Even before he sent Dornberger the information about the fateful dream, he had decided to extend the number of influential people who ought to know about Peenemünde and support its experiments.

* He was considered to be an extremely influential person in Hitler's suite and he did not want to lose this reputation. If Hitler were to insist on no longer giving the rocket experiments top priority, the dream was one way of telling von Braun and Dornberger (D. Irving, op. cit., pp. 26-7).

In February 1943 Professor Waldemar Petersen, the director of the great electrical firm, AEG (General Electric Company), was sent by Speer to the island of Usedom. He was a mature man who was not easily deceived by superficial impressions. He inspected the V-2 facilities at Peenemünde, examined everything carefully, listened to the explanations and returned to Berlin with a great deal of information. His report showed a high, almost enthusiastic, opinion of the rocket experiments. The following month a Long-Range Bombardments Development Committee, with Petersen in charge, was created at the Ministry of Armaments.[2]

At the beginning of May an even more influential person visited the eastern part of Peenemünde. This was Fritz Sauckel, in whose hands lay all labour affairs throughout Germany and the occupied countries. He, next to Himmler, was directly responsible for the dreadful plight of millions of people, who had been forcibly torn from their families and sent to Germany for heavy, almost slave, labour under the very worst conditions. He was received lavishly and shown a film of the first faultless firing of the rocket in October of the previous year. The following day he himself watched an exceptionally successful launching of the V-2 into the stratosphere. Sauckel was too experienced a member of the Nazi Party and of the inner ruling group to voice any great praise, although the excellent launch and flight of the rocket obviously impressed him. He knew that Hitler was not convinced of the value of the new weapon—perhaps he too had heard the rumour of the ominous dream—and he also remembered that Peenemünde had not been allocated top priority for resources or labour. He left saying nothing, but not long afterwards Dornberger's requirements for new workers began slowly to be met.[3]

Meanwhile Speer too had made some progress with the problems of mass production of the V-2, although the rocket was still in the experimental stage and required further improvements. Colonel Dornberger had already tackled this problem and had got in touch with Dr Eckener from the Zeppelin factory in Friedrichshafen, who had promised to put the plant at his disposal when the time was right. But Speer realized that such a great and difficult undertaking, requiring speed, must be directed by a single man with organizing ability and energy. As it happened Gerhard Degenkolb, who had managed most competently to put railway-engine production on its feet, was available, and he was entrusted with this new task. A special committee, with Degenkolb in charge, was set up in Berlin.

Hitherto it had been expected that the plan of Detmar Stahlknecht, a famous engineer from the Ministry of Transport, would be adopted. This plan had been drawn up in February 1943, just before Degenkolb's appointment, and it envisaged that from March 1943 to December 1944, 5,150 rockets would be produced, and that from September of that year production would reach 600 rockets a month. Degenkolb now convinced the Ministry that this plan was too modest and that he would present a new one. He anticipated that, by December 1943, production would reach 950 rockets a month and that three factories would be working on them: Peenemünde, the Zeppelin plant in Friedrichshafen and the Rax factory in Wiener Neustadt.[4] In addition hundreds of small firms received orders from Peenemünde for various complex parts. Naturally the Ministry accepted his suggestions, although his optimism exceeded anything that was technically possible then.

From the very first moment that Colonel Dornberger heard about Degenkolb from Speer and then met him, he felt an irresistible dislike of him (especially since he had apparently been involved in some way with General Becker's suicide).* Nor did von Braun show any great liking for the director of mass-production, although he officially supported him. Degenkolb was bursting with energy, but he was also dogmatic. A conflict developed very quickly between him and Dornberger on grounds of prestige, and although Speer tried to defuse the situation and, at briefing sessions, reiterated that the director of mass-production was subordinate to Dornberger,[5] Degenkolb didn't take this too seriously and the dislike between the two men grew.

Having achieved his aims for mass-production of the rockets, and remembering that Hitler needed to be convinced that they should be accorded top priority, since they would permit retaliatory bombardment of London and could even decide the result of the whole war, Speer accepted Dornberger's project of the construction of a great launching-bunker. It was to be built in northern France, near the town of Watten, with a very wide arc of

_____
* See Chapter Two, section 6.

fire directed towards the southern and eastern coasts of England. This gigantic structure would require 120,000 cubic metres of cement and would contain space for 108 V-2 rockets, fuel for three days, its own water supply and an excellent power system based on three independent electric circuits. It was also planned to install a liquid oxygen plant. In Peenemünde a plaster model was made of the bunker, together with essential graphs, figures and explanations, and Speer was ready for a critical discussion with the man on whom everything depended.

At that time Hitler was at Obersalzburg where he had gone from his field head-quarters in East Prussia for a short rest; it was there, on 29 March, that Speer reported with the plans for the great structure. Even the greatest exhaustion could not restrain the enthusiasm of the Leader of the Third *Reich*, who loved majestic plans and large-scale undertakings. He immediately accepted Speer's proposal and added his own ideas to it. Not one, but two and even three such bunkers should be built, so that, in the event of the failure of the rocket project, a large number of military units could be stationed there instead, ready for his defence of Western Europe. Furthermore, the roof of each bunker was to be twenty-three feet thick, and would thus fulfil another very important function: the enemy could not fail to find out about them and would undoubtedly attack them, and every bomb wasted there would be one bomb less dropped on German cities.[6]

As well as the Armaments Ministry, Speer was also in charge of the Todt Organization and thus had at his disposal building materials and foreign labour. It was planned that the first bunker would be constructed in four months and would be ready towards the end of July 1943. The tests with the V-2 were not yet completed, but that did not matter. Every effort to change the course of events and save the war, which was by then virtually lost, had to be carried out with the greatest haste, despite shortcomings, lateness or lack of materials.

2

At this point the rocket experiments attracted the most attention. But this did not change the fact that, right next door, on the same island, and with no less haste, work was being carried out on the V-1 flying bomb, and that the support of the leaders of the Third *Reich* was also being sought for this programme.*

Engineer Bree worked on the prototype. He spent some of his time at Peenemünde and the rest at the Ministry of Air Transport. On the spot, on the island of Usedom, in command of the test-firing range, was Major Stahms, while in charge of the technical side was Engineer Temme, who also had to deal with several private firms which produced specific components of the flying bomb. One of these factories belonged to Gerhard Fieseler in Kassel.[7]

Not only was there no close contact between the designers working on the V-1 and V-2; not only did they not exchange results from their experiments, which were after all closely related; there was distinct jealousy, and a determination to compete at whatever cost.

During the first years of the war the experiments with the rockets were more advanced, and the designers of the flying bomb listened to the roar of the rocket motors, and watched their fiery tails as they took off, in impotent rage. They themselves were still at the stage of early experiments, which did not allow them to launch the pilotless planes, and they had to content themselves with protests that the army was illegally taking to the air.[8]

Both sides were speeding up their experiments as fast as they could and, at the same time, wasting no opportunity to find out what their rivals were doing and how advanced they were. The authorities, both political and military, were not yet sure which project should be given priority, which of the two would be more deadly and which would be more cost-effective. Spying German eyes were collecting information and followed each move, rejoicing in each failure.

The airmen's exasperation reached its peak when, on 3 October 1942, the army had a great success. One of the rockets carried out its first faultless flight. The news of this achievement travelled immediately to the western side of Peenemünde, although the flight

---

* Works dealing with the German retaliation weapons usually concentrated on the V-2, which gives the impression that the Third *Reich's* leadership attached less importance to the flying bomb. This view is not borne out by the facts.

had been observed in any case, and it was known by the air force that their rivals had taken a great step forward.

This success had at all costs to be matched and so, at the beginning of December of the same year, Gerhard Fieseler, who was building the V-1, took off from the airfield at Peenemünde in a Condor bomber with an underslung flying bomb and launched it at the appropriate altitude. It carried no fuel, and the idea was to examine its aerodynamic qualities. It glided accurately over a set distance to the satisfaction of its designers. The same month, on Christmas Eve, a V-1 was launched for the first time from the pad and it covered the planned distance of about one kilometre and then landed in the target area.[9]

This achievement could not be compared with the results of the rockets, but the airmen were flushed with success. Urgent discussions took place between Field Marshal Milch and the air force Chief of Staff, General Hans Jeschonnek. They could already see England covered in a cloud of flying bombs launched from France and turning London into a heap of ruins. It was time to get Marshal Göring's decision as to what type of launching-pad would be the most suitable.

Further trials with the V-1 and V-2 were less successful; most of them failed and the designers had some difficult moments. And the overall war situation looked bad: British and American bombing-raids were increasing and new weapons were becoming more and more necessary. The air force held several conferences and even ordered the mass production of their flying bomb, although technical defects continued to preclude its use in combat. But Hitler had not yet made up his mind as to which of these two weapons, the V-1 or the V-2, should be given priority. It was decided that a special commission of the Long-Range Bombardments Development Committee would visit Peenemünde, acquaint itself with the installations there, watch demonstrations of each weapon and only then decide what should be done.[10]

On 26 May 1943 several eminent representatives of the government arrived at the island of Usedom: Minister of Armaments Albert Speer, Grand Admiral Karl Dönitz, Field Marshal Erhard Milch, General Friedrich Fromm, as well as the members of the Committee. The day was warm, even stuffy and, although there was no rain, the sky was covered in cloud.

Before the group of guests and experts was invited to the displays, everyone gathered in the mess in order to discuss both weapons. For the time being it was easiest to compare them theoretically. Both could carry 1,000kg of explosives and so in this respect there was nothing to choose between them. But the flying bomb, V-1, had a number of advantages over the rocket. It was cheap, since its cost, when mass-produced, was about £125. It was easy to control, easy to transport, and used little fuel, which in any case was ordinary 80-octane petrol. The rocket team, however, was well aware of the flying bomb's drawbacks. It had a relatively slow speed, 500 kph, and its low ceiling of about 2,000 metres allowed anti-aircraft guns and fighters to shoot it down in flight. It was also noisy and could be picked up on a radar screen; at night, because of its tail of fire, it could be seen at a distance and thus could not be used as a surprise weapon. Furthermore, the fixed launching-pad, with its characteristic outline, could be easily spotted from the air and made a good target.[11]

The rocket, V-2, was a completely different proposition. Because of its high ceiling of nearly 150 kilometres, right up in the stratosphere, and because of its speed of 1,500kph, it could not be attacked in flight and there was no defence against it. It was an ideal surprise weapon. The ease with which its launching-pad could be moved was another advantage: even the back of a lorry could be used. These advantages far outweighed the V-1's attractions, but the rocket's drawbacks were equally evident. First of all the cost of a mass-produced rocket was about £12,000, that is a hundred times more than that of a flying bomb; and its extremely delicate equipment made it a sensitive weapon and difficult to use. It required for fuel large amounts of alcohol and liquid oxygen, which was being produced in insufficient quantities. Each complicated part needed a great deal of production time.

After a lengthy discussion, and even before the demonstration, the commission reached the opinion that both weapons should be recommended for the priority rating.[12] Such a decision having been taken there was really no need to go on and see the missiles in flight, but the visiting dignitaries insisted and, anyway, the engineers would probably have felt hurt.

It was decided that the rockets should go first. It was midday when the magnificent cone rose into the sky and disappeared into the low clouds. After 5 minutes and 48 seconds the rocket fell into the sea after a flight of 280 kilometres, barely 5,000 metres from its target. Five hours later another V-2 firing was carried out and again the rocket fulfilled its designers' dreams, covering almost the same distance with equal accuracy.[13]

The flying bombs behaved differently. The first one flew only a short distance and crashed with a great noise, while the second one even failed to start. Field Marshal Milch did what he could to save the situation with optimistic remarks, and the engineers gave assurances that earlier tests had been successful, but the impression created was very poor. All this, however, was unimportant, since the commission had already decided that it would recommend both weapons. This decision was supplemented by the opinion that, despite technical deficiencies, they should both be mass-produced and used simultaneously.

Despite the undoubtedly great success of the V-2, the competition appeared, then, to result in a draw. But two days later Colonel Dornberger, director of the rocket programme, was promoted to general.[14]

3

On 29 June 1943 a further test with the V-2 (the 38th) was carried out at Peenemünde in the presence of the head of the SS, Heinrich Himmler. The rocket took off vertically but after a few seconds it began slowly to rotate, levelled horizontally and flew low over the island, exploding with a deafening roar on the runway of the airfield in the western part occupied by the air force. Eight tons of liquid oxygen and liquid alcohol blew a hole in the tarmac 30 metres in diameter.

Himmler's face contorted into a grimacing smile and he said: 'Now I can return to Berlin and order the production of close-combat weapons with an easy conscience.'[15]

It would have been a mistake to take his remark at face value. The head of the SS undoubtedly spoke with some sarcasm, but he attached great importance to the rocket experiments. This was his second visit to Peenemünde;* and in his own centre at

* The first had taken place on 16 April 1943.

Grossendorf, also on the Baltic, to the north of Gdańsk, some experiments with rockets were being carried out.[16] The ambition of the man who was sole ruler in his appointed kingdom was to take all these matters into his own hands.

Heinrich Himmler was not yet thirty when, in 1929, Hitler entrusted him with the organization of his personal bodyguard. At that time it amounted to barely 250 young men; but in 1933 this figure had reached 50,000, and during the war, together with the *Waffen SS* (the front-line divisions) it was several million. However, it was not only the number of soldiers which decided the strength of the *SS*, formed as it was from fanatical, superbly trained men geared to blind obedience and prepared for anything. In Himmler's hands the *SS* became in time a power not unlike a separate state, within the framework of the Third *Reich*. The *SS* possessed its own factories, its own experimental centres, its own farms and transport and, of course, its own slaves, who went in their hundreds of thousands to the numerous concentration camps. During the war in almost every camp there were armament factories belonging to various firms, which hired prisoners from the *SS* and paid well for them.* Yet all this did not satisfy Himmler: he was aiming at the creation of a personally-ruled state, and he secured from Hitler the right to his own territory. From this grew the plan to evict Poles from the area around Zamość and to introduce German colonists; after the war *SS* veterans with their families were to settle there.**

Himmler's sarcasm was in fact only a camouflage. This small, slight, grey and unexceptional man in thick glasses, the sort of man who, in civilian clothes, could easily be lost in a crowd, this man who hardly ever smiled and never betrayed the slightest emotion, who had no friends and sought none, had an iron will, unfettered by any moral scruples, relentlessly leading him to one goal: supreme power. He continued to recognize Hitler's authority, but only his. Was the *SS* chief's loyalty to the *Führer* sincere? Was he

---

* For a skilled worker the *SS* received 6 marks a day, and for an unskilled one 4 marks, while maintenance of a prisoner cost 87 pfennigs a day.
** See Appendix II, item 2.

not preparing for the right moment to seize that power for himself?*

Such was the man who became interested in the experiments on the eastern side of Peenemünde. He examined them several times. He had already had a three-hour conversation with Albert Speer about the whole rocket production programme, and after this discussion he had an even longer, four-hour one with Hitler himself.

On the same day that the rocket fell and exploded on the runway in Himmler's presence, the engineers hurriedly brought out another and prepared it for take-off. In the record time of 55 minutes the characteristic roar of the engine was heard, and this time the slender missile rose majestically, faultlessly reached its planned altitude and flew out over the Baltic at a speed of 1,700 metres a second. The rocket covered a distance of 232 kilometres and fell into the sea.[17]

Himmler was unmoved, not a single muscle twitched on his face and not one of the interested people observing his every reaction could say what he was thinking. It was only in the evening, in the mess, that a slight liveliness on the part of this silent man showed that the test-flight must have impressed him. He said not a word about it, but talked at length about German war aims and was very practical and precise. He was also extremely frank, which suggested that he considered those around him to be trustworthy. The main subject of his discussion was the war with Soviet Russia and the arguments justifying Hitler's decision to open this colossal front which absorbed nearly all of Germany's resources. The conquest of eastern Europe was, in his opinion, essential if the German *Reich* was to exist as a world power and to control the fortunes of the old Continent.[18]

That same evening Himmler went to Hitler's field head-quarters for a further discussion of the new weapons. Before, he had

---

* In April 1945, when Hitler was in encircled Berlin, Himmler tried to make contact with the Western Allies through a representative of the Swedish Red Cross, Prince Folke Bernadotte, and claimed to speak in the name of the whole of Germany. The Allies refused to talk to him at all and Hitler, when he heard of these attempts, threw Himmler out of the Party.

hesitated and weighed up various options; but now he was perfectly certain what was to be done. Previously he had had other designs, and during his first visit to Peenemünde he had tried to talk von Braun into handing over the work under his command,[19] which meant a move to Grossendorf. The engineer had politely refused and Himmler did not try to make him change his mind,* perhaps because he had not yet made up his own. However, Himmler had taken the precaution of arranging with General Fromm that the security net thrown around Peenemünde by the *Abwehr* would be reinforced by the *SS*, and the chief of police in Szczecin, *SS* General Mazuw, had received the necessary orders.[20]

By doing this Himmler, although still only a guest at the secret experimental station, left his mark there. He still possessed his own rocket testing-ground and could still decide one way or the other, but these achievements of Walter Dornberger's team, and the rocket's impressive flight, made up his mind. He was no longer in any doubt that both secret weapons, above all the V-2, required close further observation and that he would have to stretch out a hand for them as soon as the right moment arrived.

4

Early in the morning of 7 July 1943, Dornberger, von Braun and Dr Ernst Steinhoff boarded a Heinkel III and took off. It was foggy and they had been advised not to fly, but they ignored these warnings, for Hitler had finally summoned them to 'Wolf's Lair' (his field headquarters in East Prussia, from where he commanded the Russian front). The leader of the Third *Reich* had no time to come to Peenemünde himself, but he had agreed that they might come and demonstrate and explain everything about the rocket. They took with them a colour film of a perfect take-off on 3 October 1942, a large plaster model of a V-2 launching-bunker,

---

* J. Mader (op. cit., p. 167) contends that von Braun was an officer in the *SS* with the rank of *Sturmbannführer* (Major), but produces no evidence and does not give his *SS* number. Mader's book is so hostile towards the young engineer that it is difficult to consider it an objective source of information.

small wooden models of the vehicles, multi-coloured graphs and detailed plans.

Steinhoff was an excellent pilot and they reached Rastenburg without incident and landed successfully. The demonstration was to take place the same day, but Hitler was busy and made them wait for several hours, so they settled themselves in at the military hotel. The following day Albert Speer arrived and they all went to the cinema at the field headquarters. As well as the host and the team from Peenemünde there were several other people present: Head of Supreme Head-Quarters, Field Marshal Wilhelm Keitel, the Army Chief of Staff, General Alfred Jodl, Speer and General Walter Buhle.

Hitler's dreadful appearance shocked the guests, although his staff were no longer bothered by it. In a grey-green coat with no insignia, with pale face and trembling hands, he gave the impression of a seriously ill man. Only his eyes continued to sparkle.[21]

The film showed the whole operation, from the rocket being taken out of the hangar, brought to the launching-site and placed in a vertical position, to the dramatic picture of the surging flames and the slow, magnificent ascent of the shining missile higher and higher into the distant white clouds. Von Braun provided a concise commentary.

The film ended and for a moment there was silence. It was clear that the magnificent display of the rocket's flight had made an impression. Dornberger began to give some further information. Hitler hung on his every word and then leapt to his feet and began to examine the models. He was unusually moved and, when Dornberger had finished, he grasped his hand and squeezed it.

'I thank you. Why was it I could not believe in the success of your work? If we had had these rockets in 1939, we should never have had this war . . . Europe and the world will be too small from now on to contain a war. With such weapons humanity will be unable to endure it . . . '[22]

Speer had already shown Hitler the model of the rocket-launching bunker a few months previously and had obtained his permission to build it. Now the same model again became the subject of examination and discussion. Dornberger, like the other soldiers, felt that the bunker, which would become an easy target for enemy bombs, was impractical, and that it would be better to use a number of mobile, self-propelled launching stands. But Hitler's view prevailed. His staff had not seen him so lively and enthusiastic for a long time. He asked a great many questions and was interested in the smallest detail. He demanded that Dornberger and von Braun build, without fail, a rocket which could carry ten tons of high explosive and which could be mass-produced at the rate of 2,000 a month. With difficulty he was convinced that the construction of such a prototype would take five years' work and that there would not be enough fuel for such a powerful rocket.

Hitler's farewell to the Peenemünde team was very sincere. He shook hands warmly with everyone and told Dornberger that he had apologized to only two people in his life. The first had been Field Marshal von Brauchitsch and this was the second time. 'I never believed that your work would be successful.'[23] At the last moment, at Speer's instigation, he decided to make von Braun a titular professor and to sign the nomination himself.

When they were alone Hitler, still excited, took Speer to his underground bunker where they had a long conversation. He was very intrigued by von Braun; he could not believe that von Braun was only 31 years old and had already achieved technical miracles at Peenemünde which could alter the future course of events. This was in the pattern of Alexander the Great and Napoleon. He had been just about to sign a decree for a new tank construction plan, but had held back, and he now told Speer to change the document and put the V-2 on the same level as the tank programme, which enjoyed the highest priority. The rocket project was to receive immediately every assistance with labour, new materials and any other needs.

Later, having calmed down, Hitler returned to his earlier theme that this new weapon could alter everything: 'This is the decisive weapon of the war, and what is more it can be produced with relatively small resources. And what encouragement to the home front when we attack the English with it!'[24]

For the first time in a long while, Hitler went to bed on the early side for him (it was still only a little before dawn); and, just as he used to years before, he fell asleep easily. This sleep would not have been so untroubled had the dictator known that, even now, an ominous black cloud hung above these rockets for which he had suddenly developed such an enthusiasm. In London, barely nine days previously, the decision had been taken to attack Peenemünde from the air and destroy it as soon as possible.

# CHAPTER FIVE
## The Bombing of Peenemünde

1

Although the Long-Range Bombardments Development Committee in Germany had proposed that the secret weapons should be accorded equal status, and that both the V-1 and the V-2 should be put into mass-production, in practice the flying bombs remained the poor relation of the majestic rockets. The V-1 was a relatively cheap, pilotless aircraft, capable of carrying one ton of explosives into enemy territory, but it was easy to destroy and far less accurate than the ordinary bomber. It was not a dramatic new invention, nor did it capture the imagination. Hermann Göring's great influence had managed to obtain top priority for it, but no one seriously thought that this was a weapon which could tilt the scales of a war which was as good as lost. Thus whoever presented the secret weapon programme to Hitler, or tried to interest him in it, always mentioned the rockets. They were something completely new, they could inspire and excite the most tired mind.

The other side saw things the same way. When Duncan Sandys took over his new job he was instructed to collect information solely on the V-2. The British did not yet know all the details of both weapons, but what they did know was enough to make them concentrate on the rockets. There was also another very important reason for this. The Americans were showing interest, for they had heard that the Germans were experimenting with multi-stage rockets which would be capable of reaching the United States. This was in fact true. The A-4 (an early name for the V-2) was to be followed by further improved prototypes. It was planned that the A-9 would be lifted off the ground and carried a great distance by the A-10, which would weigh 85 tons at take-off. The Germans were of course unable to reach this level of rocket technology during the war and their ideas remained at the planning-stage,[1] but this was not appreciated at the time; there remained a threat, and American intelligence wanted to find out as much as possible about it.

Sandys paid particular attention to the experimental testing-site, and gathered much information about Peenemünde and the island of Usedom. The area of northern France was also being kept under constant observation, for it was known that the Germans were planning to build several large bunkers there, from which rockets were to be fired at London. There were three basic sources of information: the reports of secret agents, evidence from prisoners-of-war and aerial reconnaissance. The last two sources were exclusively in the hands of the Western Allies, in particular the British; the first one, however, appeared far more fruitful than the short phrase 'our agents' suggested. It embraced the results of the work of resistance movements in occupied European countries. Sandys collected information from every source, gave it to the experts for specialist analysis, selected the most important, the most convincing and thoroughly-checked facts and composed a short but comprehensive description of the new German threat. Within a few months the report was ready and Sandys signed it on 27 June 1943.

The report consisted of 17 typewritten pages, containing 16 intelligence reports, a great deal of information from three prisoners-of-war, statements from two political refugees from Germany and the results of seven flights over Peenemünde, which had produced a great many extremely valuable photographs.[2] The report contained no conclusions, since it was meant only as a discussion paper for a conference which was to take place a few days later. A small number of copies of the report, which was top secret, were sent to the members of the Defence Committee of the War Cabinet.

On 29 June, the very same day that Himmler visited Peenemünde and watched a successful rocket flight, the Defence Committee gathered in London in the underground office at Whitehall, the brain-centre of the Empire's war effort. The problem was so important that Churchill himself attended, together with the Deputy Prime Minister, Clement Attlee, the Foreign Secretary, Anthony Eden, the Home Secretary, Herbert Morrison, the

Minister for War Production, Lord Beaverbrook, the Minister of Information, Brendan Bracken, and Lord Cherwell and Stafford Cripps. The Chief of the Imperial General Staff, General Hastings Ismay, was also there as well as numerous scientists and experts, headed by Dr R.V. Jones.[3]

A decisive moment had arrived: the conference had assembled all those who were worried about the German rocket danger and all those sceptics who made light of it. That day one of the two sides had to win.

Duncan Sandys took the floor and set the proceedings in motion by showing photographs of Peenemünde. The slender, white rockets could be quite clearly seen. He followed this with a concise and realistic exposition presenting the overall intelligence picture. He concluded by urging the need for an aerial attack on Peenemünde as soon as possible.

Everyone was clearly impressed, but they did not all share the same feeling of drama. Morrison remarked that the high number of intelligence reports was suspicious, as was the ease with which the German positions had been photographed. This was after all one of the most closely-guarded war secrets. Lord Cherwell then raised other objections.

In his opinion the assembled material proved that the Germans had very cleverly planted it themselves. Was it possible, he asked, that they had outstripped British rocket technology by more than five years? Why were the rockets painted white? Surely so that they could be spotted so easily! Nor was he convinced that the Germans had started building great launching-bunkers in northern France, since they could so easily be photographed from the air. The testimony of prisoners-of-war was clearly at variance with the truth, particularly when they talked of extraordinary German fuels. It was essential to avoid falling into a German trap; Britain should be watching out for the other, really dangerous, secret weapons. Perhaps the Germans had already developed a pilotless jet-propelled radio-controlled aircraft?[4]

These were all serious reservations and Churchill did not ignore them, but his intuition made him take the opposite view. He therefore turned to Dr Jones for his opinion.

Cherwell listened in gloomy silence while his former pupil destroyed his arguments point by point. It seemed likely that

Peenemünde was one of the most important German research centres, while all the information received left no doubt that the enemy already possessed rockets of great destructive power and long range. The last report, which was very reliable, said that Hitler was already even planning a date on which the bombardment of London would begin, and that it was only technical difficulties that had postponed it.

Churchill, who was of a combative temperament, preferred this interpretation and seemed to be enjoying himself. He kept looking at Lord Cherwell and expressed his approval with gestures. It was clear that all the others shared this view.

Sandys was successful, and the Committee fairly quickly came to an unusually important decision:

'. . . that the attack on the experimental station at Peenemünde should take the form of the heaviest possible night attack by Bomber Command on the first occasion when conditions were suitable, and that in the meanwhile undue aerial reconnaissance of the place should be avoided, and attacks by Mosquitoes should be ruled out . . . '[5]

2

After a long spell of bad weather over the Baltic, the first sunny summer's day finally arrived. It was in the evening of 17 August 1943 when, after a 12-hour working day the great crowd of workmen returned to their barracks near the village of Trassenheide, close to Karlshagen on the island of Usedom. The camp lay not far from the sea on the north-eastern side, between the coast and the road and railway line, while the distance to the north-western promontory of the island, where Peenemünde was situated, was barely a few kilometres. Amongst the ten thousand men were Belgians, Frenchmen, Luxembourgers, Poles, Ukrainians: almost all of them had found themselves in Germany as a result of police raids which had sent them deep into the *Reich* to the hardest of labour. Sometimes deportees in Germany received a certain amount of relative freedom, but there was no question of that on the island of Usedom. Right next door lay the secret testing-grounds; everything was surrounded by great secrecy, the whole area was divided into closely-guarded sectors, everywhere there were sentry-posts and SS-men checking discipline, the diligence of the workers and security.

It was a beautiful evening and, although it was late and the sun had set, the workers were still walking around the barracks, forming small groups, chatting in low voices and humming songs from their own countries. For the most part they were working people, who had been torn from their work on the land, from small cottage industries or from industrial machinery which had not been engaged in war production; but there were also a number of intellectuals, some of whom even had high technical qualifications. Without exception they had been sent to the heaviest and dirtiest work—none of them worked in the actual factories producing weapons. Nevertheless, these factories and the testing ranges were so close that all the inhabitants of the international camp knew roughly what was going on there. Every day they could hear the roar of engines and in the evening they could watch strangely shaped objects flying out to sea. They could not fail to know that the nearby railway line and road constantly carried great loads going north.

These workers, herded into Germany, came from countries which had been under Nazi occupation for several years, and had been deeply and painfully humiliated. Each of them had also been ordered to work excessively for miserable food and pitiful wages. Furthermore, each hour spent at work helped German industry, and every completed day's work increased the enemy's military strength. It was thus not surprising that amongst these people there developed and hardened a feeling of hatred, whose only release could be the sight of the emblem of Nazi Germany being destroyed. Every night they heard the distant, powerful thunder of high-flying Allied planes, which they knew were heading for Szczecin, for Frankfurt and for Berlin. With satisfaction they imagined a hail of bombs falling on German cities. Sometimes the same rumble of aircraft could be heard over Peenemünde itself, but so far no bombs had fallen there. If they did, not only the German installations, but also the low barracks, filled with the two-tiered bunks of the foreign workers, might be destroyed. But anger and desire for revenge were so strong in these men that they seemed careless of their own danger.

Night fell. The large moon floated out into the sky and a wind rose from the sea, but the air was still warm and in the silent barracks the blackout blinds were raised. All that could be heard was the heavy breathing of the sleeping men and the slow footsteps of the guards. From somewhere in the distance to the north came the rumble of engines, but this happened so often that none of those who were still awake paid much attention. The rumble grew louder, but still it attracted no interest. Night after night there were raids on German cities, and Peenemünde lay in the path of those missions, so it was reasonable to suppose that the aerial armada would fly straight over the camouflaged area.

It was just a few minutes past midnight. The roar of aircraft was suddenly so great that sentries looked up and saw the sky above the island covered in hundreds of red points of light, which were slowly floating down to earth. There could be no doubt—the red lights were marking the target for approaching bombers. A few moments later the ground shook, great tongues of flame flickered and the deafening roar of exploding bombs was heard.

Every barrack was filled with the sound of bare feet. Men leaped from their bunks and filled all the windows. Their moonlit faces showed little fear, only interest, hatred and joy. An excited babble of voices merged with the detonations of the bombs and the howl of the engines. Suddenly the walls of the barracks creaked, flames appeared, boards and beams shook and a powerful rush of air threw people in all directions. Shouts, groans, screams for help and the guards' hoarse cries rang out. The camp seemed covered with falling timber, burning beams, great craters and rubble from which screaming men were running blindly. New explosions sucked them back into the vortex of death, they fell over, started crawling, tried to stand up and again went down, carpeting the vast area with their bodies. Out of the French barracks by the seashore, men in burning underwear were running into the water, but the explosions and splinters reached them even there.[6]

The planes flew over three times giving the dying men no chance of survival. Everyone now thought only of himself, looking for a safe place in vain, since the labour camp had no shelters. It was still dark when German thoroughness and efficiency took control over the panic and fear. Trucks drove up and began to collect the wounded.[7] They were rescued from burning ruins, pulled out of deep craters into which they had rolled after being struck by flying fragments; groans and cries guided the rescuers to those buried under piles of rubble. Hundreds of corpses lay silently amid the smouldering ruins, but no-one started to collect them. Amongst them lay also those unknown and nameless men who had been deported from Luxembourg[8] and from Poland. It was their secret messages, sent out at great personal risk, which had reached London and been the reason for the night attack. They had paid for this with their lives, but German hopes for turning the tide of war seemed to have been shattered.


3


At the beginning of the war Hermann Göring had said that not a single enemy aircraft would appear in the skies over Germany; but several years passed, and night after night British Halifaxes, Stirlings, Lancasters and Wellingtons set off for the German cities, increasing the destruction which was already sapping the strength of the civilian population to resist. Soon afterwards these British bombers were joined by the powerful squadrons of American Liberators and Flying Fortresses, which made only daylight sorties and dropped their bombs from a great height. The Germans defended fiercely; they increased their anti-aircraft artillery, imposed a thorough blackout and introduced improved night-fighters. Their resistance stiffened and the Allied air force suffered heavy losses.

After that conference on 29 June, when the Defence Committee together with Churchill decided that Peenemünde should be bombed as quickly as possible, Air Chief Marshal Sir Arthur Harris received the order to carry this out within the shortest possible time, making allowances for the weather.[9] The first precondition was a full moon which would fall in the middle of August, so this had to be taken into account and plans made for the nights on either side of this date. The actual preparations were the airmen's responsibilities, but the targets had to be designated by those who were clamouring for the attack. The key figure was Duncan Sandys in whose hands lay all the complicated threads of intelligence; he knew how the German experiments could most effectively be sabotaged. As we have seen, the flying bombs were thought to be the less dangerous, so the attack was directed exclusively on the eastern side of the promontory where work on the rockets was centred.

This area was divided into sectors, so it had to be decided in which sequence they were to be attacked. Harris, who for some time now had been directing the air offensive against German factories and cities was of the opinion that the technical installations should be destroyed first; but Sandys convinced him that it was the German scientists who were the greatest threat, and that the main attack should be directed at their living-quarters. This target was given the letter 'F', and the first wave of bombers was to aim for it. The second target, designated 'B', comprised the great pilot rocket factory, while the third target, designated 'E', comprised the main development works and also the administrative office. The planning completely ignored the rocket launching-stands on the north-eastern tip of the promontory: little importance was attached to them.[10]

The Peenemünde mission was critical and was given one of the highest priorities of the war. Sir Arthur Harris had to plan it so that the risk of failure was virtually nil. Everything indicated that Peenemünde, so vital for the German war effort, would be heavily defended: the plan therefore had to be devised so that the Germans would not guess that this was in fact the main British target. It was not just a dangerous mission, it was a tricky one; the Germans must be taken completely by surprise so that the scientists and technicians could not shelter themselves or hide the valuable plans and documents underground.

The great raid on Hamburg, which began on 24 July and continued for nine nights, causing the death of more than 40,000 people and the evacuation of a million, was followed by smaller attacks directed at other cities, particularly Berlin. British planes flew there almost nightly and each time they went over Peenemünde, causing alarm amongst the Germans, but nothing more. This created the impression that the British knew little about the experimental station and that their main target was the capital of the *Reich*. The attention of the German defences, in particular the night-fighters, was therefore directed at Berlin: and the British encouraged this conviction.

Night raids, even with a full moon and radar direction-finding, required a very precise indication of the target area. It was the task of special Pathfinder squadrons to find the target and cover it with parachute flares which fell slowly to the ground like burning Christmas trees. With such illumination and target indication the bombers no longer had any difficulty in finding their way. The Pathfinder squadrons were commanded by Air Vice-Marshal D.C.T. Bennett, stationed at Huntingdon. He received from Marshal Harris orders to plan a mission for his aircraft. Eight of his Mosquitoes were to prepare themselves for an attack on Berlin. Their task was to decoy the German night-fighters and create the impression that the capital was the main target for the night. This was important, for the Germans were picking up British radio signals and from their intensity knew that something large was brewing.* The whole operation could fail if it was discovered that Peenemünde was to be the target.

By mid-1943 British Bomber Command had expanded and had acquired a great deal of experience in night raids, but with every night the Germans were also improving the standard of their defences. Some new surprise element had to be introduced into the plan of the raid. In the night attack on Turin the technique of using a Master Bomber was employed for the first time. This idea was to be repeated over Peenemünde. It consisted of the commander of the attacking force circling the target area throughout the whole raid to direct operations on the spot. His aircraft was equipped with all the most modern aids including radar, while an air-to-air radio link-up gave him continuous contact with the commanders of the individual squadrons. To this difficult and dangerous task was appointed Group Captain John Searby who, despite his youth, had already led a number of sorties over German cities.[11]

Early in the morning of 17 August, after first acquainting himself with the weather report and then weighing up several important factors, Sir Arthur Harris informed all the previously

---

* The British did not at that time know that the Germans were able to break the code of the lower echelons of Bomber Command, and it was only a very pedantic avoidance of the name Peenemünde over the air which kept the plan a secret (D. Irving, op. cit., p. 100).

alerted squadrons that they should be ready for a night attack. It had already been decided that 433 bombers were to take part (Halifaxes, Stirlings and Lancasters) as well as 65 Pathfinders, with a total crew strength of about 4,000. Their H.Q. was at that time in Wyton, so both Air Vice-Marshal Bennett and Duncan Sandys went there. This was the home base of 83 Squadron, and in the afternoon, after confirmation of the weather, the squadron's crews were assembled and Group Captain Searby held a short briefing. Listening thoughtfully the young veterans of night raids heard that they were to attack and destroy a German research centre and a large factory producing new equipment for night air defence. The raid would be carried out in three waves, with the flight over the sea low-level to avoid detection by the German 'Frey' radar net. On reaching Denmark the aircraft were to climb to an altitude of 2,300 metres from which the attack would be carried out. It had to be successful, otherwise it would have to be repeated. They had to reach the target area just after midnight and the attack was to last about 45 minutes. The name Peenemünde had still not been used as it was feared that unauthorized ears might hear it, or that someone might be indiscreet, since several hours still remained before the raid. The operation was code-named *Hydra*.

Sometime earlier Vice-Marshal Bennett had ordered 139 Mosquito Squadron to send eight aircraft over Berlin and attack the city at 23.00 hours.

4

In occupied Holland, Air Force General Jozef Kammhuber, commander of the Twelfth Air Corps, was, as usual in the evening, in his office in the town of Zeist. Every night British bombers flew over Germany and the night-fighters had continually to be manoeuvred so that they would appear where they were most needed.

The evening was fine and there was a full moon, so an attack might well be expected. The General therefore, following routine, called all his subordinate units to check their state of readiness. During the afternoon the radio monitoring station in Paris, code-named *Seeräuber* (Corsair), had sent the information that the volume of British air force radio signals was increasing considerably. This could mean some large operation. Several minutes later he was handed a report that something must have happened, since his communications centre at Arnhem-Deelen had stopped operating.

Technicians hurriedly searched for the cause of this breakdown,* while the General, cut off from the outside world, impatiently paced his room. Meanwhile the Staff of the *Luftwaffe* received news from the Admiralty that sea-going observations points in northern Denmark had informed them of a large aerial armada approaching from England. This information was immediately transmitted to General Hubert Weise, Commander of the *Reich's* internal defence, stationed in Berlin.

The approach of a large number of bombers alarmed the German night-fighter units and everywhere there was much speculation as to their target. The German units started contacting each other, exchanging opinions, and reached the conclusion that this time the target was Berlin. Weise was of the same opinion and he ordered Major Hajo Herrmann, the commander of a special pursuit unit, *Wild Boar*, to scramble his three squadrons, stationed at Bonn, Jüterborg and Rheine. This was a new formation, as yet untried in combat, composed of first-class pilots and with aircraft partially adapted to night-fighting. It had been formed on Göring's special orders, because of the Marshal's dissatisfaction with his fighters' results so far.[12]

The centre at Arnhem-Deelen remained out of action and General Kammhuber was still cut off from his units and his superiors; the alarm caused by the approaching British bombers spread. The first Mosquitoes were already over Berlin and the howl of air-raid sirens in many places highlighted the danger; local commanders, cut off from Twelfth Corps headquarters, had to take their own decisions. General Junck, in command of the Fourth Fighter Division in Metz, ordered his aircraft into the air and soon afterwards a similar order was given in Belgium and Schleswig-Holstein. Within a few minutes 158 Messerschmitts and Torniers

---

* D. Irving (op. cit., p. 114) states that in this communication centre there were two Germans who were British agents. It is not clear, however, whether it was they who caused the breakdown.

were in the air. All this took place around ten o'clock in the evening.

It was still not clear where the British aircraft were heading and the German night-fighters were picking up signals that the target was to be Bremen, then Wilhelmshaven, finally Kiel. It was only at about eleven o'clock, when the eight Mosquitoes over Berlin began to drop flares and bombs to create the impression of a larger raid, that from Metz, the HQ of the Fourth Division, came the order to the pilots of the Twelfth Air Corps: 'All night-fighters to Berlin!' Major Herrmann, finally convinced that the attack was aimed at the capital and that the enemy's objective had been understood, ordered 55 of his daylight fighters into the air.[13]

The inhabitants of Berlin leapt from their beds and sought safety in the shelters; the sky was pierced by the beams of the searchlights; and the anti-aircraft artillery thumped, while over 200 fighters chased around high over the city, eagerly seeking a target for their cannon and machine guns. Chaos ensued and no-one really knew what was happening. The German airmen were ceaselessly flashing their little identification lights, trying to stop their own artillery from firing on them, while the soldiers on the ground, confused by the roar of the engines, took every plane to be an enemy, and Major Herrmann's daylight fighters, unused to fighting in the dark, only added to the confusion.

Field-Marshal Milch, who was at the time in Berlin, left his shelter to see what was happening. He noticed the signals of his own aircraft and realized the danger. The anti-aircraft guns had twice already reduced their range, to 7,000 and then to 6,000 metres, so as not to hit their own airmen. Milch saw that they would have to cease firing completely, but he couldn't give the order since the defence of the capital was so important. He telephoned both Göring and Hitler's field HQ. Göring agreed, but Hitler did not. This decision was confirmed by the Air Force Chief of Staff, General Jeschonnek. For two hours 89 heavy batteries fired into a sky which held only eight enemy and more than 200 German aircraft.[14]

Major Herrmann flew over Berlin in his fast Focke-Wulf 190 and immediately joined the battle. He was, however, too experienced a pilot and had taken part in too many night fights not to discover fairly quickly that there was some misunderstanding. He had already used a great deal of fuel and still couldn't find the enemy, constantly coming across German fighters. He climbed high over the battlefield and looked all around. Too few bombs could be heard and too few fires could be seen to accept that the capital was really under a great aerial attack. His gaze, covering the whole area, turned also northwards and for a moment the Major caught his breath. At a distance of some one hundred, or perhaps one hundred and fifty kilometres cascades of lights could quite clearly be seen and there were sudden flashes, which could only be caused by exploding bombs. Major Herrmann realized that all the German fighters over Berlin had been deceived and that the British target was not the capital. His first reaction was to order his men to turn north immediately, but he realized that their fuel tanks, like his own, could now supply only a few minutes' flight. They had, almost immediately, to find airfields.

5

At precisely the time when Churchill was preparing himself for a night-time conference in Quebec with President Roosevelt, during which they were to divide Europe into spheres of influence,* Group Captain Searby was approaching the Baltic coastline north of Szczecin at the head of his armada. The shortest route to the heart of Germany was over Holland, but the British always used the northern route over Denmark so as to fly as little as possible over German-occupied territory and thus lessen the effectiveness of German defences. The long distance meant that fighter-cover was impossible. The armada headed for the small island of Ruden, a few kilometres to the north of Peenemünde, which was to be a landmark. The weather was holding and the moon still shone, although the sky was now covered in light cloud which hindered visual navigation.

Group Captain Searby's first impression on reaching the target was one of a great silence which lay over the factory buildings,

*    It was then that the dividing line, more or less similar to to-day's, was settled. Countries to the east of this line were to be within the Soviet sphere of influence.

construction halls and houses far away below. Not a single shot rang out, not a single searchlight stabbed the night; only some smoke curled up from a few chimneys obscuring visibility. However, there was no time for thought, for midnight had already passed and the first Pathfinders had begun to drop their red parachute-flares. The designated target area stretched from the north-west to the south-east and the red markers drifted over it; but Group Captain Searby, making great circles over Peenemünde, realized that they were too far to the south. Fortunately some of the pilots also noticed this mistake and dropped yellow flares on the very centre of the target area. Further aircraft arrived and poured out bundles of green lights on the same spot. It was 00.17 hours when the Master Bomber gave the order for the bombers to concentrate only on these. The first wave of 227 aircraft roared over the designated target and thousands of kilograms of bombs hurtled down on the housing complex of the German engineers and scientists. Unfortunately one third of the attackers, navigating by the thick cluster of red markers, dropped their bombs two miles further south on the workers' barracks and on a concentration camp, killing hundreds of their faithful allies.[15]

Group Captain Searby, having made a wide circle, again found himself over Peenemünde and could not control his surprise. Contrary to expectations that they would encounter furious resistance and suffer heavy losses, the target, already covered with fires and smoke, was barely replying at all. A few searchlights appeared, some anti-aircraft guns opened up, but rather desultorily and mainly from a ship lying about one-and-a-half kilometres off-shore; and still there were no fighters.

The target for the second wave was the large pilot rocket factory, given the letter 'B' during the planning. Again a mistake was made, caused by the original incorrect placing of the red flares, and once again the green lights were dropped too far to the south. But above Peenemünde circled the Lancaster of the attack commander, who could see everything, and he issued the order to ignore the green flares grouped towards the south, and concentrate the attack on the northern cluster. Within 8 minutes 113 Lancasters had carried out their mission. The third and final phase of the night attack remained.

Group Captain Searby saw great clouds of smoke rising below

and realized that, in addition to the fires caused by the bombing, the Germans must have their own smoke-screen. Therefore he gave the order for the 126 Lancasters and 54 Halifaxes, moving in for the kill, to circle over Ruden and then to fly over the target by their watches. This increased the chances of success, since the green lights could disappear in the clouds of smoke. Some of the crews followed these instructions, others looked for the lights, and again the spread was large, although a few aircraft aimed well and caused great destruction of laboratory and administrative installations.

During the first wave of the attack a few individual German fighters had appeared over Peenemünde. They had seen the distant glare, and, realizing what was happening, had ignored the command to converge on Berlin; there were already thirty of them. Some of them came from the *Wild Boar* formation, while the rest, belonging to the Third Night-Fighter Group, had flown over from the region of Copenhagen. They had been ordered into the air just before midnight and had been instructed to lie in wait for British bombers returning from the capital; but the great fire and streams of lights over the island of Usedom drew them in that direction. They flew in at the high altitude at which the British usually carried out their raids, and thus did not engage them immediately; but they soon dropped, and the slow, heavy bombers found themselves in a difficult situation. One o'clock was approaching, the raid was dragging out and still thirty-five aircraft were waiting for their turn to make their final run, while the German fighters were spiralling down and picking them off with ease, lit up as they were by the fires and the moon.

Searby flew over Peenemünde seven times and up to the last moment was in control of the operation. Finally, when the last bombs had been dropped, he was able to issue the command to return home. The aircraft, stretched over a wide area and under attack by the Germans, set off towards the north-west over Denmark, and the commander could now think of his own safety. It was a miracle that his Lancaster had not been hit by the British bombs, since he had been circling at low altitude, observing the effects of the attack; and now, after the turn towards the north, he barely succeeded in escaping from a Focke-Wulf, which he managed to shoot down.

The roar of the engines died down and slowly disappeared, while behind, down below, there remained fires, smoke and ruins; 1,593 tons of explosive had fallen on Peenemünde, as well as 281 tons of incendiary bombs.[16]

## 6

The peaceful calm of the summer evening in Peenemünde had relaxed General Dornberger; he had sat late into the night in the mess, together with von Braun, talking to Hanna Reitsch, the famous test-pilot, who had come to Peenemünde to help with the V-1 tests.* She was able to go where she wanted, since Hitler knew her and had a very high opinion of her. Her personality and attractiveness drew men, and the mess had filled with engineers and officers of various ranks, enjoying a few hours' relaxation.

The wail of the air-raid sirens alarmed no-one, for they were heard almost every night just like the distant rumble of aircraft, to which people had already grown accustomed. The carefree atmosphere continued even when the rumble became a howl; the glasses began to dance on the table and the lights flickered several times. Suddenly the whole building shook and the deafening roar of several explosions, followed by several more, was heard nearby. The laughter died away; everybody sprang from the tables and quickly, but without panic, moved towards the shelter, which was situated next to building number 4. About 300 people gathered underground, many of them those who had that night stayed longer in the mess than usual. This had saved their lives.

For a whole hour the shelter was shaken by explosions. Several bombs fell right next to it, but the massive thickness of concrete resisted. The lights went out, nobody spoke while they waited in gloomy silence for the inferno raging outside to die down. Finally the monotonous long-drawn out wail of the siren was heard, and someone gave an order: 'Everyone outside to help!'

Dornberger went up to the surface and looked around. A full moon was shining, buildings, construction halls and barracks were burning, and smoke covered the ruins. The first impression was terrible; it appeared that everything had been destroyed, that not a

---

* See Chapter One, section 5.

single wall remained intact, not a single beam untouched by fire. Together with von Braun and several girls from the office staff, who had also been in the shelter, they started to salvage the most valuable documents. Building number 4 had been hit several times and seriously damaged; the roof had collapsed, the door and window-frames were burning, but the staircase was still standing. Covered with dust, eyes smarting, they squeezed up close to the wall to reduce the weight on the crumbling stairs, and reached the second floor where they rescued secret drawings, diagrams and papers from a fireproof safe. A sentry was found and then posted, with bayonet fixed, over the precious documents.

Dawn broke and Dornberger and von Braun got into a Storch in order to assess the damage from the air. The whole area looked like a photograph of the moon: everywhere there were craters, holes and heaps of concrete, resembling, in the grey light of early morning, fantastically broken rocks. It immediately struck them that the western side of Peenemünde, the V-1 area, was completely untouched. They were too upset with what had happened to feel any satisfaction that even the enemy had seemed to appreciate their importance and had struck only at them.

They had as yet no information about the attackers' intentions,* but this first quick survey produced the impression both that the enemy knew exactly what he was doing, and that an error had crept into the raid. On the one hand, although the bombing had concentrated exclusively on the eastern side of the promontory, that is on the rockets, several bombs had been dropped on the liquid oxygen plant and the power-station, which were both on the western side. This proved that British intelligence knew the exact location of the important buildings. On the other hand a great many bombs had fallen on the foreign workers' camp, and surely that could not have been the target for the Allied raid. It appeared that, as a result of an error, the whole attack had been concentrated too far to the south. Because of this a number of buildings in the northern part of the area, where the development works were situated, had survived. The wind tunnel and the measurement house were completely untouched. The engineers' and inventors'

---

* W. Dornberger (op. cit., p.119) states that in shot-down British planes they found plans of the raid with the designated targets.

living-quarters had been the hardest hit.[17] There could be no doubt that this had been one of the raid's main targets. Dornberger knew that in the complex there were no shelters and that the families living there, by now used to alarms which had always turned out to be false, never left their beds. He was afraid to think what had happened to these people that night.

It was approaching nine o'clock in the morning when they both got out of the aircraft and with heavy hearts turned in the direction of the ruined offices. A few hours earlier they had already telephoned the news of the British raid to Berlin and to Hitler's field H.Q., and now they had to get down to a thorough assessment of the damage so that an accurate report could be prepared.

The first dreadful impression was softened somewhat when detailed information began to flow in from various sectors of the widespread area. The north-eastern part of the promontory, where the test-firings took place, was completely untouched. The area lying several hundred metres further south, and comprising eighty buildings for development and tests, had suffered heavily. Fifty of these buildings had collapsed, burned down or had been heavily damaged; amongst them was von Braun's laboratory in building No. 4. Even further south, where the rockets were actually made, the damage was very much lighter and the two great assembly halls had not been hit at all. However, the effects of the raid on the living-complex for the 3,000 scientific workers were dreadful to behold. Of the hundred buildings concealed in the trees not one still stood intact. Furthermore, all that remained of the foreign workers' settlement was a great heap of rubble. There had been thirty large barracks, of which eighteen had burned down and most of the rest had been damaged.[18] The concentration camp had suffered severely. From the human point of view the most tragic fate was perhaps that of several hundred German girls from the women's auxiliary service, who had been working for the anti-aircraft defence. The building in which they had been living was situated not far from the foreign workers' settlement, right by the sea. A number of bombs had fallen there and completely destroyed it. Tight-lipped, Dornberger listened to a report from which it transpired that the girls' supervisor had, as always, locked the building in the evening to protect her girls from prowlers. She had died almost at once, since she slept on the top floor, but with her had gone any chance of opening the doors quickly.[19] The girls had tried to escape by jumping from the windows and running towards the sea, but many had been burnt to death.

In many places the sewers and the power lines had been destroyed, the water mains had been ruptured, the railway tracks presented a fantastic tangle of bent rails and the road, running down the middle of the island, was quite useless.

It was difficult to assess at once the extent of the damage and how much time would be needed to get the rocket programme on its feet again. The destruction of the buildings in the northern area was great and it would take weeks to rebuild them. The rocket production sector looked more promising, but even there there was a great deal of work to be done. Dornberger reckoned that temporary repairs could be effected within six weeks, while nine months would be needed for a complete recovery,[20] but this opinion was based on a very cursory examination.

It was easier, but more painful, to calculate loss of life. The living-complex had been completely destroyed and, according to Dornberger, 178 people had perished there. This seems to be a low figure, perhaps intentionally reduced, but it may be correct, since many of the leading scientists had stayed longer in the mess that night in the company of Hanna Reitsch. Nevertheless von Braun had lost a number of his close collaborators, among them Dr Walter Thiel, a man with a first-class analytical mind who had been closely connected with the rocket programme and the use of liquid fuel. Another great loss was that of the senior engineer, Helmut Walther. Dornberger reported that the total loss of life had been 735 people, but that most of these were from the foreign workers' camp.[21] There is no other trustworthy source with which to compare this figure, but the ratio between the German personnel and the foreign workers does not appear to be accurate.* Dornberger's report also omits all mention of the death of the German girls of the women's auxiliary service.

---

*   After the war, in the cemetery of Karlshagen, a stone cross was erected and on it was the inscription: 'In this grave lie 91 Poles, 23 Ukrainians, 17 Frenchmen, 16 concentration camp prisoners and 66 whose nationality is unknown, altogether 213 people deported to hard labour. God says "I know their names".'

Albert Speer arrived in Peenemünde the same morning in his private plane. Before landing on the airfield on the western part of the promontory he examined the whole bomb-cratered area from the air. Later, in conversation with Dornberger, he acquainted himself with the details of the damage. He had still to fly to Schweinfurt, which had suffered from an American raid the previous day, and then to go direct, to Hitler's field HQ with an accurate report.[22]

When the first shock had worn off, the most immediate tasks been accomplished, and when, finally, the fires had been put out and the wounded collected, Dornberger permitted himself a few hours' sleep. He awoke with a heavy head and again went to see the ruined and damaged buildings. Thinking over the precision of the night raid, he could not help asking himself several questions: how had the enemy managed to obtain such accurate information? How had they known which targets should be bombed, and who had provided them with all these details? He was afraid of this thought and tried to put it from his mind, but it would not go: someone on the inside, someone from Peenemünde itself, was an informer.*

7

The British lost 40 bombers over Peenemünde and one Mosquito was shot down over Berlin; but this low figure could easily have been 200 had the Germans not made a great many surprising mistakes that night.

Above all they had been deceived by Air Chief Marshal Harris' strategy of decoying them over Berlin and drawing most of the German fighters to the capital. This diversion succeeded brilliantly, but it alone was not responsible for the success of the whole operation. For some unknown reason the Germans that night abandoned all their normal precision and patience and ordered

---

* In his memoirs Dornberger states that one of the Germans in Peenemünde said that in some German illustrated magazine he had seen a crossword giving full details of the exact location of the research station together with information as to what was happening there.

their night-fighters into the air immediately after the first reports
that an enemy fleet was approaching. Certainly the breakdown of
the station at Arnhem-Deelen and General Kammhuber's isolation
were also contributory factors, but even this did not justify the
hasty use of almost every night-fighter a good hour before they
could engage the enemy. They simply wasted fuel flying around an
empty sky. Ordering them to Berlin was just another in a series of
mistakes, and in pursuit of an enemy who wasn't there they used up
the rest of their fuel. By the time the mistake was discovered and
the planes had been ordered to Peenemünde, the distraught airmen,
who were only too eager for a fight, had to look for a place to land.

Indescribable scenes took place on the airfield at Brandenburg-
Briest where most of the fighters went. The ground staff
continually fired off red flags warning that there was no more
landing space, but the pilots, flying on their last drops of fuel,
completely ignored them. More than thirty aircraft crashed on the
tarmac, colliding with other planes, breaking up and starting fires.
This was a terrifying total when compared with the nine German
machines lost in combat.

Duncan Sandys waited all night on the airfield at Wyton, and as
soon as the first Pathfinders returned he received preliminary
information about the raid's success. The bombers then began to
come home. Group Captain Searby flew in, and although he
restrained himself from any premature comments until some of the
457 photographs taken during the attack had been developed,*
there was no doubt that a great victory had been achieved. It was
daybreak when Sandys called Churchill in Quebec with the good
news.[23]

The German defeat brought yet another death. During the decoy
raid over Berlin the *Luftwaffe* Chief of Staff, General Hans
Jeschonnek, received two telephone calls in Goldap: the first one
from Milch, the second from Göring. Neither of them could
control their fury and both put full responsibility on him for the
chaos over Berlin and the lack of co-ordination between the
fighters and the anti-aircraft artillery. Göring furthermore accused

---

* An examination of these photographs showed that the bombing had
  covered an area no more than five kilometres from the designated
  targets.

him of always obeying Hitler's orders, whatever the situation, like a recruit.

Jeschonnek was already depressed by the reports from Schweinfurt; now, at seven in the morning, came the tragic news of the disgrace over Berlin and the destruction of Peenemünde. At nine o'clock his secretary entered his office and found the General dead on the floor. In his cold hand was a pistol, and nearby lay a card: 'I cannot work with Göring any more. Long live the *Führer!*'[24]

# CHAPTER SIX
## V-1 in France and Denmark; the *SS* and the secret weapons; 'Dora'; experiments in Poland; 'Enigma'

1

On a scorching summer day in 1943, Colonel Max Wachtel, a tall, well-built man of about 45, briskly entered the Palais de Luxembourg in Paris wearing artillery uniform. He showed the sentry his papers and went up to the first floor where General Karl Koller, Chief of Staff of the Third Air Fleet, had his office. Colonel Wachtel, commander of the special anti-aircraft regiment, code-named 155(W), had been brought to Paris very urgently,[1] and once in the Palais he reported straight to the General.

Wachtel had taken part in the French campaign and later been at the front outside Leningrad. From there he returned to Germany at the beginning of 1943, to be summoned by his former superior officer, now commander of the anti-aircraft artillery for the whole country, General Walter von Axthelm. On 3 January he had been in Peenemünde as an observer at the successful launching of the V-1 flying bomb and had been very impressed by it. He had put in an optimistic report to the Chief of Staff of the Luftwaffe, General Jeschonnek, and subsequently had a long conversation with Field-Marshal Milch about the launching-pads from which the V-1 was to be fired on London. Milch, like Speer, was of the opinion that several big bunkers should be built, which could withstand *any* bombing, and in which the necessary equipment and a stock-pile of several thousand bombs could be accommodated. Von Axthelm considered that it would be better to construct about a hundred small but effective launching-pads. For even if the concrete bunkers could withstand the bombing, the supply lines could still be destroyed and the bunkers would be useless, whereas no attack could put all the small launching-pads out of action. Finally Göring came down on the side of the General and the decision was taken for the building of the launching-pads to begin at once.[2] At this time the flying bombs were still in the experimental phase and were far from being militarily effective. Moreover the decision to mass-produce them had not yet been taken. Perhaps it was premature to construct the launching-pads, but the war was going badly and more urgent measures had to be taken.

General von Axthelm had summoned Colonel Wachtel to take charge of this matter. He ordered him to prepare for widespread use of the flying bombs. In great secrecy he was to organize a special anti-aircraft unit which was at once to start finding suitable sites for the launching-pads, building them, and learning to fire the V-1s. Wachtel was to assure himself that there was adequate liaison and the necessary supply-lines. He had to start from nothing, for so far no-one had done anything of this kind and no-one had the necessary experience.

During the middle of May Wachtel went to Peenemünde to acquaint himself with the operation of the flying bombs and establish along what lines he ought to carry out the preliminary work. His task was made easy for the western side of the testing-grounds, where the experiments with the V-1 were carried out, was commanded by Major Stahms, the brother of General von Axthelm's chief of staff.[3]

Within a few days a command group had been formed to undertake the special tasks and sworn to complete secrecy. After theoretical consideration and trials it was decided that each launching-pad would be manned by 15 soldiers plus expert technical personnel. In Brüsteort, four anti-aircraft batteries were organized, of which each was to take over four launching-pads. One officer went to France to examine the terrain and choose appropriate sites for them to be erected: the most suitable were narrow valleys, meadows and gorges, running from south to north towards London. Another officer, also in France, took over the organizing of the radio and telephone network and aerial liaison. Colonel Wachtel himself was in constant touch with Organization Todt, which set about building some hundred launching-pads using 40,000 Frenchmen and workers of other nationalities deported from the occupied countries.

The command of the special unit was in Zempin, 13 kilometres south of Peenemünde. When it was finally formed the unit was renamed as a regiment with the code-name 155(W). Militarily, as anti-aircraft artillery, it was under the command of General von Axthelm, but operationally it was under the commander of the LXV Army Corps, General Erich Heinemann. Although the construction of the launching-pads was carried out by Organization Todt, the air command for the region Belgium-Northern France, under General Wimmer, was formally responsible for it; supplies on the other hand were the responsibility of the Third Air Fleet commanded by Field-Marshal Hugo Sperle. It was necessary to keep in constant touch with the commanders and staffs of all these units. Difficulties and problems of competence were constantly arising and this caused Colonel Wachtel considerable trouble.[4]

Some months later all the preparations were well forward and the first launching-pads ready. If the flying bombs had now reached the stage of readiness for mass production and if this production had been operative, the bombing of London could have commenced very shortly afterwards. Yet in spite of feverish work things were still delayed and the delivery of the first 'cherry stone'* had to be waited for. The whole operation was given the code-name *Rumpelkammer* (Junk-room),** and was surrounded by the most stringent secrecy.

Colonel Wachtel sat opposite General Koller and listened to him carefully. The urgent summoning of the colonel to Paris was caused by the information that British Intelligence knew his name and appearance and what he was doing, and that they would try to put him out of action. He was to remain in Paris for some days and in the meantime counter-intelligence would prepare papers for him in another name. There would no longer be a Colonel Max Wachtel in the army list; in his place would be Colonel Martin Wolf. Wachtel would also have to grow his small beard and side whiskers.

Later Colonel Wolf also disappeared and his place was taken by Lieutenant-Colonel Michael Wagner in an air force uniform. Sometimes this person appeared in civilian clothes, sometimes as an engineer in the uniform of the Organization Todt. His subordinates also took off their uniform tunics at times and put on civilian jackets.[5] This did not help much to camouflage their origins, for

---

*    So the Germans jokingly called the V-1 (*Kirschkern*).
**   This name was first used in May 1944.

they still wore army breeches and top boots, which must have been noticed by the trained eyes of British agents. In a short time they were also observed by the French underground movement, which carefully noted everything that was happening on its territory and sent urgent reports to London.*

2

During the conference in the underground war room in Whitehall, where the decision to bomb Peenemünde was taken, Lord Cherwell, rejecting the possibility of the Germans having rockets, had tried to draw the attention of those present to a pilotless jet aircraft. At that time the British efforts concentrated exclusively on rockets and the night attack was directed solely against them. But the flying bombs were not forgotten.

Generally they were regarded as less menacing than the rockets, but minute attention was still paid to all available information on them, from photographs and reports arriving from the continent. British intelligence wanted to know more, and made attempts to obtain drawings or parts of the bomb. In this they were lucky, but only by sheer chance. On 22 August (that is, only a few days after the great air-raid on the eastern part of Peenemünde) one of the bombs taken up by a Heinkel 111 and released from it to fly alone, carried on farther than planned and fell on the island of Bornholm, in a field of tulips near Bodilsker. It failed to explode.[6]

As in Poland under the German occupation, the Danish police were still in operation, working with the German authorities on criminal cases. But they were also in contact with the Danish resistance movement. A police inspector, John Hansen, happened to be nearby and he reached the place where the bomb had fallen almost at once; together with a friend, a Danish sea-captain, Hasager Christiansen, he took a number of photographs and hid

---

* It looks as if Wachtel is exaggerating when he writes about the threat to his person. In his memoirs, on the last page there is a photo-copy of a letter written to him by Duncan Sandys on 11 January 1960 and beneath it the words: 'We wanted to kidnap you'. But in the letter, written in English, there is not a word of this; it is purely a courtesy letter.

some of the parts of the bomb. Within half an hour the Germans turned up, but Hansen was able to add, later, a sketch of the whole weapon.* A report was drawn up and eight copies, via eight routes, were sent to London.[7] One of the couriers was arrested and all the material together with the photographs fell into the hands of the German security forces, but another copy reached England within a few days. It was brought by a Major of the Danish Intelligence, V.L.U. Glyth who, pursued by the *Gestapo,* escaped to Sweden at the very last moment.[8] This was the first flying bomb, V-1, to have fallen outside German territory and the Danish report was a revelation to the scientists in Great Britain. They were able to compare it with what had come from Poland** and were in a position to attempt the reconstruction of a prototype.

The details received, including the definite statement that the flying bomb was propelled by a jet engine, made a great impression in London and Air Chief Marshal Sir Charles Portal was of the opinion that this weapon might be even more of a threat than a rocket. Unexpectedly Lord Cherwell, who had warned against it, estimated it quite differently. In his opinion the details collected proved that the warhead of the bomb could be little heavier than 500 kilograms so that the whole object was implausible and could not be dangerous.

In spite of the difference of opinion the flying bomb was treated very seriously and various preparations were put in hand. Duncan Sandys received instructions to examine the question of flying bombs as closely as that of rockets; even the carrying out of the *Black Plan* was considered, namely the programmed evacuation from London of the Cabinet, Parliament and 16,000 essential officials; and the Ministry of Production was asked whether it could supply the capital with 100,000 Morrison shelters. It was expected that attacks by flying bombs, the V-1, might commence as early as September 1943.[9]

3

The attack on Peenumünde must have saddened every German in

* See illustrations.
** See Chapter Three.

the small, ruling elite, which knew the truth. So it can be assumed that Himmler must have felt it to be a particularly painful and well-aimed blow by the enemy; but not one muscle moved in his face when the news was brought to him. Cold and stiff, he made no comment at all to those around him on this event, but he ordered that *SS* General Dr Hans Kammler should report to him at once.

Kammler was a dark-haired man of forty, talkative but unwilling to listen, energetic and decisive. No moral consideration ever restrained his actions.[10] A civil engineer in charge of the Building Department of the *SS* Chief Economic and Administrative Office (WVHA),* he was among other things also responsible for the planning of concentration camps. He supervised and confirmed the plans for the huge sub-camp of Birkenau, part of Auschwitz, where four great gas chambers and crematoria operated, in which over 3,000,000 people were killed.[11]

Himmler had a long conversation with him and then made a telephone call to Hitler's field H.Q. and asked to be received as soon as possible. He arrived there on the morning of 22 August and, together with Albert Speer, discussed the situation with the leader of the Third *Reich*.

Himmler's plan was simple and in accordance with his usual methods: the *SS* existed only to serve their country; the rockets were threatened because someone had betrayed Peenemünde; everything connected with the rockets should be put in the care of the *SS*.

The conference lasted until evening and resulted in Hitler deciding that the V-2 should be handed over to the *SS* and that further experiments and the mass-production should be moved to safe places, which enemy aircraft could not reach. The experiments involving firing the rockets would be moved to central Poland; the development works to caves in the steep mountains near the Traunsee, in Austria; and mass-production to an underground factory in the Harz mountains, not far from Nordhausen.[12] The eastern side of Peenemünde was, however, to be rebuilt, but so camouflaged that from the air it would give the impression of a deserted battlefield.

The chief argument used by Himmler, and the one that finally

* *Wirtschafts-und Verwaltungshauptamt.*

convinced Hitler, was the security aspect and the work-force. The transfer alone of the experiments and mass-production of the rockets beyond the reach of enemy aircraft was not enough: they also had to be completely isolated to ensure their safety from any other form of attack and destruction. This isolation could be obtained by putting concentration-camp prisoners to work on the rockets. Himmler had more than enough of them and he added the promise that he would accommodate them on the spot and even deprive them of the right to correspond with their families,* cutting them off completely from the rest of the world.[13]

Immediately after Hitler made his decision, Dr Hans Kammler was entrusted with this task by Himmler. This took place on 1 September, and the young engineer, within the space of a few days, became an important and influential person. Soon all those who came into contact with him officially found that he was ruthless, unfeeling, fanatical, never resting for a moment and demanding the same qualities from others, and that he had no scruples whatsoever. Himmler backed him up to the hilt on every occasion, for Kammler was a devoted henchman similar in personality to himself. Whenever possible, he took him to conferences with Hitler. The head of the *SS* had his eye on the whole of military production and meant to take it all into his own hands. In these plans Hans Kammler played a very important role, for it was he who was to take Albert Speer's place.[14]

4

In March 1937, in the vicinity of Weimar, not far from the oak under which Goethe used to sit, near the town of Buchenwald, a concentration camp had been set up. At first life in it was very hard, for criminal prisoners were the ruling class and rivalled the *SS*-men in brutality; after some years, however, political prisoners began to come to the top. Before the war these were exclusively Germans and Jews; later, after the *Reich* had conquered a large part of Europe, there were also Czechs, Poles, Belgians, French,

---

* Normally prisoners were allowed to send one letter a month from a concentration camp, and to receive one.

Dutch, Russians and others. The majority of privileged positions in the camp passed into the hands of the red triangles* and, although they formed new cliques and employed a new form of discrimination, life became more bearable. The barbaric stealing of the prisoner's starvation rations ceased, labour was distributed more fairly, and a camp hospital functioned.

Every German concentration camp had numerous sub-camps and Buchenwald was no exception. They were generally set up near factories, road intersections, bridges and buildings in process of erection—anywhere that human labour was required. Sometimes in these small camps life was more bearable than in the central camp. Some factories looked after their prisoners, since they needed them, and gave them extra rations; but generally it was considered that the sub-camps were bad and that it was better to stay in the central camp. Every enterprising prisoner if he managed to survive a few months, somehow made a place for himself; he found easier work, got into relatively better barrack, obtained some small position of responsibility or worked under a humane *Capo.*** Everyone feared a departure into the unknown.

During the second half of August 1943 the news went around the camp that a small transport would be going to set up a new sub-camp in the Harz mountains. Such transports were the most feared, and the prisoners hid in their barracks and places of work to avoid getting onto the list; but finally 107 Poles, Russians and Germans were chosen and with an escort of 40 *SS*-men loaded into trucks. The transport left on 27 August and ended up in mountainous territory not far from Nordhausen. A few days later, on 2 September, a second much larger transport arrived, consisting of 1,223 prisoners, mostly French, Polish and Russian. In September still further groups arrived and the number of deportees rose to 3,300. They were accommodated in tents, for first of all they had to build barracks for the *SS*-men. The sub-camp was given the name Mittelbau, but has come down in the history under the code-name

---

* In the German concentration camps every political prisoner wore a red triangle on his shirt and trousers and every criminal a green triangle. A letter on these triangles showed his nationality; only Germans did not have a letter. See *Fighting Auschwitz,* op.cit.
** The prisoner in charge of a larger group of fellow prisoners.

*Dora,* which the German authorities used purposely to make it more difficult to find. The first commandant of *Dora* was *SS* Major Förster, but after a month his position was taken over by *SS* Lieutenant-Colonel Otto Förschner from Buchenwald, who, in January 1945, as a result of evacuation of Auschwitz, handed over to the last commandant, *SS* Major Richard Baer. The number of prisoners in *Dora* constantly increased and in November 1944 was over 13,000.[15]

As well as the numerous Poles, Russians, French, Germans, Czechs and prisoners of other nationalities, brought from Buchenwald, the *Dora* also took in two other categories of German slaves. The first of these were Italian soldiers from Marshal Badoglio's army, whom the Germans had picked up after the coup in Italy and the severing of the alliance with the Third *Reich*.[16] They were allowed to wear their uniforms and were allotted a separate barrack under the command of their own officers, but nevertheless they had been put in a concentration camp and ordered to work on military production. When they tried to protest and six of them refused to assemble the V-2, they were shot.[17]

The second group was composed of foreign civilian workers from the firm 'Wifo'. In the late autumn of 1943 several hundred of them were added to the prisoners and shut up in the tunnels. This was because of the special security regulations concerning the production in the underground factory.

The fears of the prisoners from Buchenwald before their departure into the Harz mountains proved to be well-founded. They had been brought to work in a factory below ground, hollowed out of the rock of the Kohnstein mountain, and to exceptionally hard and exhausting work.

Drilling into the rock had first started in that area in 1933, when the I.G. Farben factory installed fuel tanks there. Eventually, besides two tunnels A and B, each 800 metres long, 200 metres away from each other, and wide enough for two railway-lines in each, 18 side-chambers had been hollowed out. The whole complex was 5,000 metres long, with a floor-space of 50,000 square metres and a cubic space of 350,000 metres. Twelve ventilation shafts were installed, which changed the air every day; special heating kept a constant temperature of 17° C, with 7% humidity; all the corridors and chambers were electrically lit.

1. Walter Dornberger and Wernher von Braun

2. Reginald V. Jones

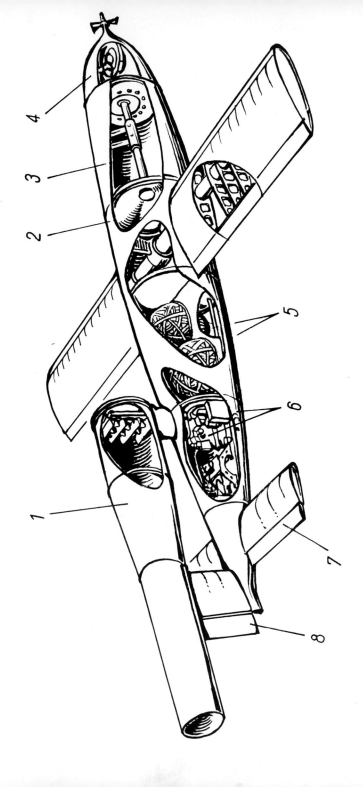

3. The V-1

*1.* pulse-jet engine *2.* fuel tank *3.* warhead *4.* magnetic compass *5.* compressed air tanks *6.* batteries *7.* altitude vanes *8.* direction vanes

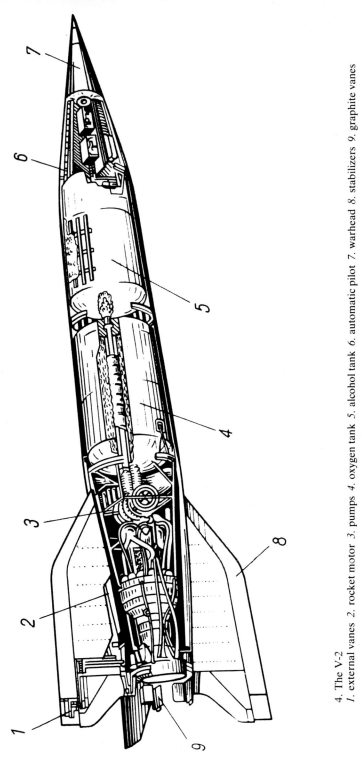

4. The V-2

1. external vanes  2. rocket motor  3. pumps  4. oxygen tank  5. alcohol tank  6. automatic pilot  7. warhead  8. stabilizers  9. graphite vanes

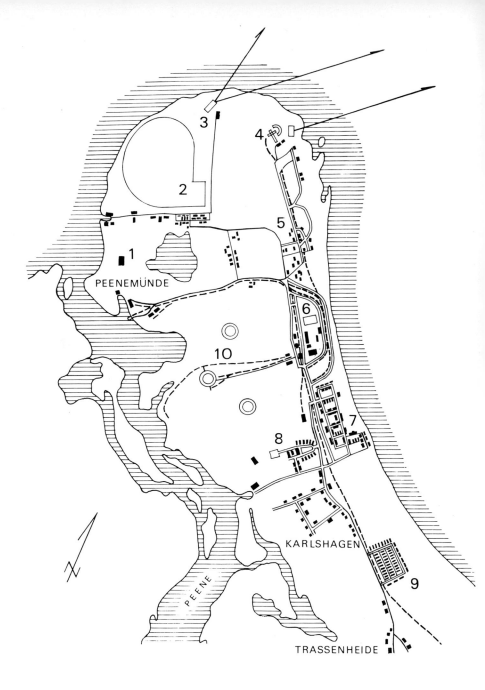

3

4

2

5

1

PEENEMÜNDE

6

10

7

8

KARLSHAGEN

9

PEENE

TRASSENHEIDE

5. Peenemünde
*1*. power plant *2*. airport *3*. V-1 launching-pads *4*. V-2 test stands *5*. development site
*6*. pre-production site *7*. settlement *8*. army camp *9*. workmen's barracks *10*. test stands

6. Relative sizes of the V-2, the V-1, a 2,5-ton bomb and a human figure

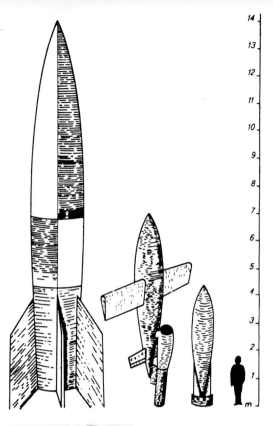

7. Hitler watching a rocket-demonstration at Kummersdorf West

8. Albert Speer

9. Lord Cherwell

10. Duncan Sandys

11. V-1 with cockpit

12. Hanna Reitsch

13. Constance Babington-Smith

14. Max Wachtel

15. Antoni Kojan

16. Jerzy Chmielewski

17. Roman Träger

18. Heinrich Himmler

19. John Searby

20. Sketch of V-1 made by a resistance worker at Bornholm

21. Part of V-1 which fell on Bornholm

22. V-2 launched at Peenemünde in 1943 (*original German photograph*)

23. Von Braun (with hat) and German ace-pilot Adolf Galland (on his right) at Peenemünde

24. Himmler (with white scarf) and Dornberger (on his left) at Peenemünde

25. Aerial view of Peenemünde (*photograph taken by the RAF in June 1943*)

26. Peenemünde before and after the bombing

27. Housing-estate at Peenemünde after the bombing

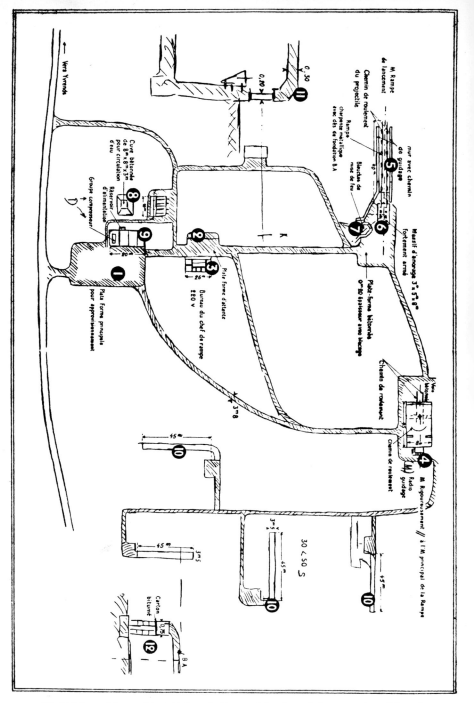

28. V-1 launching-pad installations in France (*sketch made by a member of French underground intelligence*)

29. British fighter tipping V-1's wing

30. Władysław Ważny mortally wounded by Germans and supported by French gendarmes

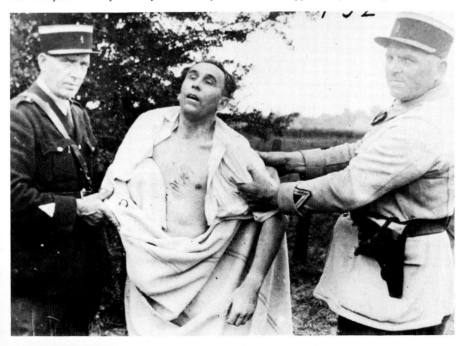

31. Stalin

32. Eisenhower and Churchill

33. Aerial view of Blizna (*photograph taken by the RAF in May 1944*)

34. German signpost in Polish and Ukrainian at Blizna

35. German signpost at Blizna

36. Janusz
Groszkowski

37. Marceli
Struszyński

38. German leaflet in German and
Polish distributed amongst local
population where V-2s were falling

39. Part of V-2 which fell in Sweden

40. German cipher machine *Enigma*

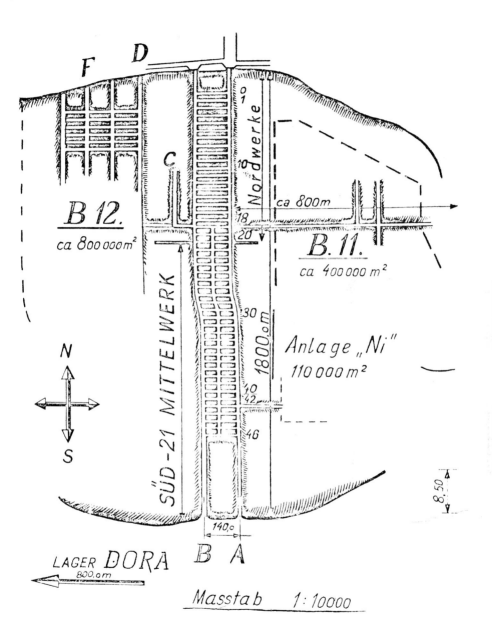

41. Underground factory in Kohnstein mountain

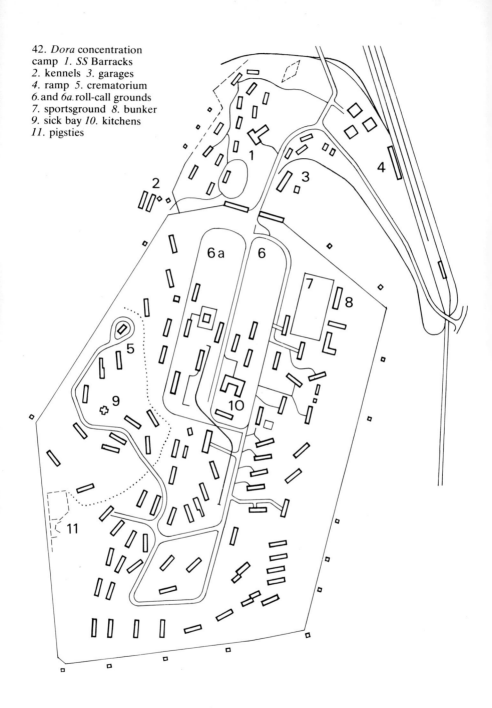

42. *Dora* concentration
camp  *1. SS* Barracks
*2.* kennels *3.* garages
*4.* ramp *5.* crematorium
*6.* and *6a.* roll-call grounds
*7.* sportsground *8.* bunker
*9.* sick bay *10.* kitchens
*11.* pigsties

43. Entry to the tunnel in Kohnstein mountain

44. *Dora* concentration camp

45. V-2 assembly in Nordhausen

46. American soldier standing by V-2 after the capture of Nordhausen

47. The *Meillerwagen* V-2 trailer, and 48. with load

49. V-1 assembly in Nordhausen

50. Political prisoners of Boelke-Kaserne concentration camp (sub-camp of *Dora*) killed by Allied bombs

51. Antwerp after V-2 attack

52. V-2 fuel tanks at underground factory in Nordhausen being surveyed by two former political prisoners (with rifles) and an American soldier

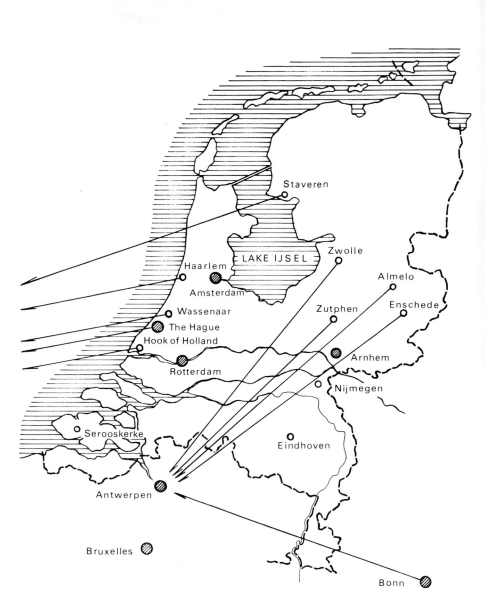

53. Holland: V-2 attacks on London and Norwich from Staveren, Haarlem, Wassenaar, The Hague and Hook of Holland; V-1 attacks on Antwerp from Zwolle, Almelo, Zutphen, Enschede and Bonn

54. British and Soviet officers at Blizna in September 1944

55. British and Soviet officers examining part of a V-2 at the River Bug

56. British officer photographing part of a V-2 at the River Bug

57. Part of a V-2 launching-pad

58. Post-war picture of the road leading to Blizna

59. Blizna at the present time

60. The ruins of Peenemünde

The drilling went on, and during the years 1936-38 both tunnels were lengthened by a further 1,800 metres and 28 new side chambers hollowed out bringing the total to 46. A new tunnel C was also added, to the west of tunnel B, starting at the level of the eighteenth chamber. The whole area of the tunnels now amounted to 125,000 square metres, and the cubic space to 875,000. These newly-drilled chambers were still unfinished and required a lot of work before they could be used.*

After two months of living in tents, towards the end of October the whole sub-camp *Dora* was transferred underground. The prisoners were shoved into chambers 44-46, which were still in a raw state, dark, damp and full of an irritating dust. Normally in the German camps the bunks were three-tiered; here four tiers were set up. They worked and slept in two shifts: when one went to work the other lay down on the same filthy litters and covered themselves with the same damp blankets. There were no latrines at all; empty carbide barrels, cut in half, were used; it was necessary to walk about a kilometre to the water-taps. In the beginning 70-80% of the prisoners were employed in unloading, transporting and setting up the machines, about fifteen hundred worked at building the camp, only a very small percentage got into the group of specialists and the rest drilled the rock. From the end of November, when the machines had been installed, all the prisoners, except for those building the camp, were employed at assembling rockets. Since after 12 hours of hard labour a further six and a half hours had to be spent on roll-calls, getting to work and standing in a queue for food, as well as finding a place to sleep, barely five and a half hours were left for rest. There was very poor and insufficient food, brutal treatment and constant very hard work, so the mortality rate was high.[18]

The underground factory in which the prisoners of *Dora* were set to work belonged to the company *Mittelwerk,* which had been set up especially for the purpose of mass production of the secret weapons. Its head office was in Berlin, and it had at its disposal two factories: the one in the Kohnstein mountain with the prisoners of *Dora* as a work force and Albin Sawatzki as director, where the V-2 was to be produced, and the Volkswagen factory in Fallersleben,

---

*   See illustrations.

where production of the V-1 was begun.*

The military position of Germany was worsening, so everything had to be done in great haste. Even before the arrival of the engineers, technicians and civilian workers (amounting to thousands), before the prisoners had been given any sort of accommodation, and before the machines had been set up, the first huge order arrived. It came from General Emil Leeb, head of the Army Weapons Office, bore the date 19 October 1943, and concerned the production of 12,000 rockets, 900 a month. Each of them was to cost 40,000 marks.[19]

This order increased the pressure even more, and the effects fell above all on the prisoners. They were driven to work with sticks, they were not allowed to rest for a single moment, any negligence was regarded as sabotage. It is not surprising that their output fell off and the mortality rate rose. *Dora* did not yet have its own crematorium, so trucks carried hundreds of corpses to Buchenwald more and more frequently.

This state of affairs became so disturbing that Albert Speer, who took a great interest in the progress of the work and received constant reports, decided to make a personal inspection. He arrived on the spot on 10 December and, surrounded by a numerous suite, walked through the tunnels and corridors, observing the prisoners closely. They looked straight through him, as if he were transparent, their hands raised automatically, their striped caps taken off and put on again when the group of dignitaries moved away. It could be seen that they were at the end of their strength and a further inspection revealed that they were living and working in barbarous conditions. Speer realized that with such a work force the planned rocket production would never be attained; there must be immediate changes in their living and working conditions. He held a long conference with the management of the factory and the camp command and gave a number of orders which were to be carried out in the shortest possible time.[20]

First of all it was decided that the camp under construction must be finished as soon as possible so that the prisoners could be taken out of their underground lodgings, particularly since the space was

* American bombers caused part of the production of the V-1 also to be transferred to the underground factory in the Kohnstein mountain.

needed by 'the expanding factory. Naturally the *SS* barracks had priority, but as soon as they were finished all efforts were directed to building barracks for the prisoners. It was already the end of 1943, and the Germans had for some months been applying the principle that the several million political prisoners must be regarded primarily as hands to work and not as human material destined to march away into another world. Even in Auschwitz, which was a death camp and in which people were murdered *en masse* in gas chambers and by phenol injections, from the middle of 1942 selections were made from the transports destined for slaughter, and people capable of manual labour were taken into the camp. This involved Jewish transports as well.[21] *Dora* also received prisoners who at this stage were not under sentence of death at all, but were there to speed up the production of the secret weapon. So in December 1943 barracks for these prisoners started going up; the work went quickly, for by 31 December, of a total number of 11,000 prisoners, 5,500 found themselves in a normal camp.[22]

The camp was set up in a mountain valley less than a kilometre from the entrance to tunnel B, to the south. All the living quarters were wooden, but well supplied with sanitary and heating appliances. Each barrack was divided into a sleeping compartment with two-tier bunks occupied by two prisoners and an eating compartment with tables and stools. There was always running water in the barracks and the prisoners could also take showers. The domestic buildings were of brick, with modern equipment for the kitchen and laundry. A hospital was also built, consisting of eight barracks with equally modern equipment; there were also a cinema, a canteen and a sports-ground with a swimming pool. The ground for the roll-calls and all the roads in the camp were cemented. In the middle of 1944 a brothel was also set up in the camp, in accordance with the general *SS* regulation concerning all concentration camps. There also existed a special psychological and vocational selection unit, with modern equipment, which was to determine the professional qualifications of the individual prisoners. Naturally there had to be a crematorium and a camp prison, called the bunker, and the whole camp was surrounded by high-tension wires and guard towers.

Speer's intervention also brought about an improvement in the food in a way quite exceptional for German camps. Within the camp there were pigsties and the prisoners began to get soup with macaroni and pieces of pork.[23]

Many former prisoners of *Dora* in their accounts, especially in the early period after the war, have described the camp in the darkest colours, and some historians have even called it an extermination camp; but in fact this was not so, for the production of the underground factory was very important to the Germans. This opinion could refer only to the preliminary stage and to the end of the war and the evacuation. Mortality in *Dora* was high; in the worst period it reached 15%; but it could not be compared with the mortality in Auschwitz, where, apart from the 3,000,000 people in transports taken straight to the gas chambers, of 404,000 prisoners who entered the camp, 340,000 died on the spot—i.e. 84%.[24]

However, before the improvements were made and before the greater part of the prisoners were transferred from the tunnels to the camp, which was only in April 1944, conditions were extreme and they were made still worse by the security regulations. The underground factory was one of the best-guarded places in the Third *Reich,* so the prisoners were ceaselessly spied upon and accused of sabotage at the least excuse. As well as the camp *Gestapo* and the huge network of informers, there were also in the factory military counter-intelligence agents in the roles of engineers, craftsmen and workers.

All the same, it was not only the low morale of the prisoners that held up the execution of the ambitious plans. Technical aspects were also decisive. Mass-production was attempted too soon, while the secret weapon still had many imperfections. Rockets often exploded immediately after take-off or during the flight, and further tests were necessary to iron out these faults. Moreover the target of 900 rockets a month was quite unrealistic and it was never reached. In spite of constant urging on and the great tempo of work, it was only on 1 January 1944 that the underground factory, called the Central Works,* sent out the first three rockets completely assembled on the spot.[25]

---

\* On 1 October 1944 the camp *Dora* became independent under the name *KL Mittelbau* (concentration camp *Mittelbau*), and all the local sub-camps came under its jurisdiction.

This disquieted the designers of the V-2, and on 25 January von Braun visited the tunnels in the Kohnstein mountain. Almost all the machines were already installed and about 10,000 prisoners were working on them, but the condition and appearance of the prisoners did not augur well. The young engineer walked round all the corridors in silence and left despondent, his mind full of unpleasant thoughts. He did not know that not far away, quite apart from his technical and labour problems, a danger was lying in wait, which would strike him suddenly and threaten his life.

5

During the second half of November 1943, in a private apartment in Warsaw, the clandestine monthly briefing of some staff officers of the Home Army HQ was taking place. Besides the commander, General Tadeusz Komorowski, only four others were present, among them the chief of intelligence, Lieutenant-Colonel Marian Drobik.[26]

The briefing had barely started when there was a violent knocking at the front door. At that time in Warsaw this almost certainly meant a raid by the German police; so the company froze into silence, for there was no way of escape from the fourth floor, and Drobik went into another room. After a moment it turned out that it was a false alarm and everyone sighed with relief, looking around for Drobik. He appeared in the doorway, muttered a few words and fell like a log to the floor. His nerves, stretched to the utmost for years, had given way, and expecting the Gestapo, he had taken poison.[27]

The colonel was revived but he was ill for a long time. He had been under a great deal of pressure, for the Gestapo had struck several times against the provincial intelligence network of the Home Army and left big gaps in it. He had to resign from his position, and at the end of November it was taken over by Colonel Kazimierz Iranek-Osmecki, a man at the height of his powers, who had undergone appropriate training in England and been dropped into Poland by parachute in March 1943. He was well prepared for the job entrusted to him: he knew the Western view of the war, and he was at home in Poland, since at the turn of the year 1940-41 he had been there for a while, after carrying out the mission of an emissary.[28]

The new chief of intelligence knew about the bombing of Peenemünde, for the Polish network in Germany had reported on this fairly quickly, but he did not know about Hitler's decision regarding further work on the rockets and he had no date concerning the transfer of the V-2 experiments onto Polish territory.

In the meantime the Germans, decisive and methodical, as usual, had been working feverishly for several weeks on the terrain around Blizna, a small village at the confluence of the rivers Vistula and San, in Southern Poland. The area was densely forested and sparsely inhabited, and the German authorities had been interested in it since 1940. The villagers had been evicted and an *SS* proving-ground set up in the shape of a square with sides of more or less 20 kilometres in length. It was called *Heidelager*. Towards the end of 1941 Soviet prisoners-of-war had been brought there and killed off almost to a man by very hard labour and starvation. After them had come political prisoners, for whom a small concentration camp was organized.[29] Now, after Hitler's decision and the taking over of the rockets by the *SS,* further building of the whole area went forward quickly. The railway siding, running from Kochanówka, was repaired and lengthened; the road surface was changed; a number of new barracks for soldiers were erected; a large part of the forest was wired off; and a large cement slab was laid down in an artificial clearing. On 28 September Heinrich Himmler paid a visit to the camouflaged and strictly-guarded area and inspected everything carefully.

After his departure the speed of the work was stepped up and everything began to be carefully camouflaged. On the place where the burnt-out village of Blizna had stood the prisoners set up a new mock village. The outlines of cottages and outbuildings, made of hardboard, were brought from Germany; fences were erected and linen hung on them; dummies of men, women and children stood around, and flowers were sown. From the air the illusion of an inhabited village must have been complete.[30] At the railway siding trains began to arrive composed of long flat trucks, covered with canvas, hiding long objects. Sometimes among the flat trucks, strangely-shaped cisterns were seen.

The Home Army intelligence received good information from this area, for the Germans had left there the Polish forestry commission, almost all the personnel of which belonged to the underground. For several years nothing significant had come from this source, but the area now suddenly became important and the reports sent from there, via the district of Cracow, acquired new consequence.

Two reports arrived at the end of November and the beginning of December 1943 which aroused Colonel Iranek-Osmecki's interest. They spoke of the build-up of Blizna and the proving-ground there, of mysterious transports, of an increase in the military garrison, and of great security measures. The colonel compared these reports with information from Germany, and his thoughts turned to the possibility of secret weapons and the experiments connected with them; but he lacked the links to prove anything. By coincidence proof came into his hands on the same day.

During the middle of December a new report arrived giving details of observed flights and explosions. Then the city intelligence network reported that in Warsaw a German car had crashed killing all passengers, and Home Army counter-intelligence was able to state a few days later that the passengers were experts working on the secret German weapons and that they had come from Mielec, situated not far from Blizna.[31]

The colonel was now almost sure that experiments were being carried out in Blizna on the same secret weapons whose installations had been destroyed in Peenemüde. He immediately requested additional information from the Cracow District and at the same time set in motion his own central network, in case the local cells were to fail for any reason.

In January 1944 the experiments became more intensive. Missiles were being fired off regularly, day and night. They usually flew in a northerly, north-easterly or westerly direction, but their dispersal and range were very varied. Sometimes they exploded quite near Blizna, sometimes they travelled far and fell near Częstochowa, Końskie, Rejowiec and to the north, as far as the river Bug. This was where most of the missiles fell, making huge craters in the ground (20 metres in diameter), destroying buildings, tearing up trees.

The Germans had a number of motorized patrols stationed in the countryside where the missiles were due to fall, and these patrols would rush to the scene of the explosion, seal it off and gather up all the fragments and parts of the mechanism. These were often in fairly good condition, for the warheads of the experimental missiles were filled with sand. Patrols of the Home Army did the same, and almost every day a race took place between the Germans, acting openly, with every technical facility at their disposal, and the underground army, which had to operate in secret but was on its own territory and received willing assistance from the local population. In the fight to get there first, shots were exchanged several times between the Germans and the underground patrols.[32]

6

However, it was not only reports from Poland which enabled British intelligence to build up a more precise picture of the German work connected with the retaliation weapons. Only now, thirty years after the war, are details being revealed of the top-priority secret effort, which successfully cracked the code of the enemy's most secret signals, which the Germans thought were impossible to break.

The German cipher was based on a machine called *Enigma,* which was built in Germany for this purpose in 1928, introduced into the forces and later modified and refined. It looked like an elaborate electric typewriter, but instead of printing on paper it was equipped with a display of twenty-six illuminated letters: when a key was pressed down, instead of a letter a light appeared. With the help of an electro-mechanical device and three revolving drums it was possible to produce over 100 milliard* combinations, and further technical improvements allowed this figure to be multiplied many times. To get any idea of these astronomic figures, we must resort to an example: if all the people now living on the earth (about 4 milliards) were to work on one *Enigma* combination ceaselessly, day and night, they would get the correct connection within 6 milliard years. In order to read the signals ciphered by *Enigma,* one had first to have an identical machine, then know the

* 1,000,000,000.

pattern to which it was set (which was changed periodically), and also have the individual key of the given radiogram.[33]

No wonder the Germans considered their invention to be one hundred per cent safe. But they were mistaken; their top secret radiograms, signalled during the war, were—amazingly—being read by Polish cryptologists. In the Second Bureau (Intelligence) of the Polish General Staff there was a Cipher Department with a section for German codes (B.S.4). The head of the section was Lieutenant-Colonel Gwido Langer and in it worked three eminent mathematicians and cryptologists: Marian Rejewski, Jerzy Różycki and Henryk Zygalski. To them, in 1932, was entrusted the task of breaking *Enigma*.

The Polish Intelligence network in Germany gathered details, monitoring stations picked up German ciphered radiograms and the Department maintained constant contact with French Intelligence, represented by Captain Gustave Bertrand. From 1932 the French had had a valuable informant in Germany with the code-name *Asché*,[34] who worked in the cipher section of the *Reichswehr*. Thanks to the jointly-gathered information and to the possession of an *Enigma* cipher machine used in industry (much less complicated, but still useful), it was possible to reconstruct in Warsaw an *Enigma* of the military type. This was largely the achievement of the three cryptologists who, at the end of 1937 and the beginning of 1938, working on the lines of a theory of group permutation, finally uncovered the secret of the German machine.[35]

This was of the greatest value from both the technical and the military point of view, and it could only be appraised by a specialist. It is therefore worth quoting the words of Gustave Bertrand on the breaking of the code:

'. . . This made it possible to give such information of the enemy, of such range and of such quality, as had never been put at the disposal of the General Staff by its Second Bureau . . .

Where the Polish cryptologists are concerned, to them alone belongs all the merit and all the praise . . . They have overcome difficulties which the Germans considered impossible to overcome.'[36]

As well as the work of the Polish and French intelligence

services, great efforts in this connection were also being made by British intelligence, which was in contact with the French. Political events brought it together with Polish intelligence and in January 1939 for the first time the cryptologists of all three countries met in Paris. Valuable information was exchanged there, but what was really decisive was a conference in Warsaw, which took place in July, just before the outbreak of the Second World War. From France came Major Gustave Bertrand; from Great Britain, Commander Alastair Denniston, head of the British Coding Service, and Dillwyn Knox, the leading Briton in this field. The Poles had decided that in the face of the inevitable war the achievements of their cryptologists should be made available to their western allies. They told how they had broken *Enigma*, gave technical details, and each of the heads of the Allied missions was given a duplicate machine, specially constructed in Poland.

The German attack came and Lieutenant-Colonel Langer with the cryptologists arrived in France, bringing two duplicates of *Enigma*. There he directed a group of 15 co-workers, which under the name of *Equipe Z* was incorporated into the Fench cryptological unit led by Major Bertrand and bearing the code-name *P.C. Bruno*. They worked in the castle of Vignolles, 35 kilometres south-east of Paris, and their chief task was to find out what modifications the Germans had made to *Enigma* in the meantime. It turned out that these were not great, and on 17 January 1940 the Polish cryptologists broke the German key of 22 November of the preceding year. From then on it was possible to read the secret coded German radiograms. Up to June 1940, 1,151 radiograms concerning the Norwegian campaign, 5,084 concerning the fighting in France and 2,100 on other matters were read.[37]

At the same time, in Great Britain, thanks to the duplicate of *Enigma* received from Poland by Commander Denniston, work could be done on its utilization. In Bletchley Park, 75 kilometres north of London, a well-equipped cipher centre, called the Government Code and Cipher School, was set up. In it were gathered several prominent mathematicians—Knox, Milner Barry, Gordon Welchman, Oliver Strachey, Allan Turing—led by J.H. Tiltmann. They carried the Polish discovery further and set up their own machines to decipher *Enigma*. A special network under the code-name *Ultra*, directed by Group Captain Frederick W.

Winterbotham,[38] was used to deliver the deciphered signals to the headquarters and men concerned.

The western front collapsed, Paris fell and the cryptologists in *Equipe Z* were evacuated to Algiers. Major Bertrand made contact with the Vichy Government and with its tacit agreement took his whole group to unoccupied France. The castle of Fouzes near Nimes was bought and there the work was taken up again with the aid of the Poles, still headed by Langer. His group was now given the code name *Outpost 300*. German modifications in the use of *Enigma* were still being followed and signals deciphered. Four more duplicates of *Enigma* were also assembled.

In November 1942 the Germans occupied the whole of France and again the group of cryptologists had to be evacuated. Some of them, including Langer, unfortunately fell into German hands, but some reached Great Britain through Spain, among them Rejewski and Zygalski. They joined the Signals Battalion at the Polish General Staff where they worked to the end of the war, in constant touch with the British cryptologists at Bletchley Park.[39]

The results of the cryptologists' achievement, developed so successfully by *Ultra*, were very significant. Top secret German signals were read during the course of the fighting in France, the Battle of Britain, the German offensive in North Africa, and in the heated days of the Allied landings on the continent of Europe; and finally, German communications on their secret weapons were deciphered.

After the bombing of Peenemünde and the transfer by the Germans of the ballistic tests to a place still at that time unknown, Dr Jones strengthened the ties with Bletchley Park, which he had maintained since 1940. It was to be expected that the Germans would start to send radiograms on this subject, which might be intercepted and deciphered. The first fragmentary information from this source was compared with despatches from Poland and confirmed that the tests had been moved to Blizna. Dr Jones refers to this in his report of August 1944,[40] but does not mention *Ultra*, for it was secret at that time. Later, in further German despatches, it was possible to pick up information that a very long-range missile was involved and that it could not be a flying bomb. Establishing this was important, for the reports from Poland in this phase were not sufficiently precise. At that time it was not yet known there that the Germans had two kinds of secret missiles: V-1 and V-2.[41]

Events in the Second World War were sometimes strangely connected. It is almost certain that none of those unknown, local underground soldiers in Poland, on the River Bug and at the confluence of the Vistula and San, who with the greatest difficulty collected information on the German rockets, could have imagined that their reports were checked and confirmed in London thanks to the discoveries of Polish cryptologists and mathematicians.

# CHAPTER SEVEN
## 'Bodyline' and 'Crossbow'; the resistance and the V-1 in France; the underground and sabotage in 'Dora'

1

On 27 August 1943, barely ten days after the bombing of Peenemünde, 185 Flying Fortresses of the US Eighth Air Force, stationed in Great Britain, carried out an air-raid on a bunker in Watten, built as a launching-pad for the rockets.\* The air-raid was planned to take place as soon as the building of the huge construction was completed, but before the cement had set. The 370 tons of bombs caused such destruction that the Germans decided not to rebuild.\*\* They started to prepare a new bunker in Wizernes; hidden underground, with wide branching corridors, it was never quite finished because of constant bombing. In July 1944 the RAF's six-ton bombs finally destroyed it.[1]

Such an accurately planned attack, which shattered the German construction work during those very days when the cement of the powerful vaults in Watten was hardening, proved that Allied intelligence, both on the ground and from the air, was operating excellently; yet the British War Cabinet considered that the efforts of the Intelligence Service had failed. It was of the opinion that there was still no certainty as to whether the Germans did have long-range rockets, and the quarrel among the scientists, which had been going on for several months, flared up again.

Lord Cherwell again rushed to the attack, and Dr Alwyn Crow seconded him; both demonstrated that the aerial photographs showed objects which, because of their ballistic and aerodynamic

---

\* See Chapter Six, section 1.

\*\* Albert Speer decided that under the ruins a factory for liquid oxygen should be installed. The Germans used this method several times, considering that the ruins left above would deceive aerial reconnaissance and avert another air-raid.

instability, could not be long-range rockets. They also did not wish to believe that the Germans had managed to produce a liquid fuel so far ahead of anything known at that time.

Duncan Sandys was under constant pressure from the opposing views and was forced in September to set up a Special Scientific Committee composed of nineteen experts. From the code-name given to the rocket at that time it was called the *Bodyline* Committee. It was assisted by a group of experts specially assigned to research into liquid fuel, and to this 'Fuel Panel' Isaac Lubbock (who was working with Shell on pioneer experiments in this field) was urgently recalled from the United States. The committee was interested not only in the way that the rocket was propelled, but also in the mechanism which drove the fuel into the combustion chamber.

Lubbock, during his stay in America, had familiarized himself with the great development of research, various types of fuel and the motors connected with them. He had watched many experiments and he believed that the Germans could have solved the problem of propelling rockets in such a way as to allow them to fly for a distance of 300 kilometres with a considerable explosive load. Sandys therefore asked him to prepare a blueprint of a rocket with all the important parts, the same size as the objects shown in the photographs from Peenemünde, and propelled by liquid fuel. The blueprint was completed in four days and resulted in a monster which weighed over 52 tons without the warhead, almost 43 tons of which consisted of fuel.[2] In spite of such a great error in proportions, Lubbock took account in his deductions of all the most important elements of the menacing weapon, and his sketch was used in the continuing search for a correct solution.

Towards the end of October the *Bodyline* Committee prepared a report for the War Cabinet, which was a compromise resulting from the differences of opinion among the scientists. It gave three hypotheses as to what the Germans might have in their possession:

(a) a multi-stage rocket using a technique known in this country (i.e. solid fuel), possibly having a warhead of one to ten tons in weight and a range of about 220 kms;

(b) a single-stage rocket using an existing American technique for liquid jet motors, with a warhead of five to fifteen tons and a range of about 220 kilometres;

(c) a single-stage rocket using the same technique as (b) but assuming a 15 per cent increase in specific thrust, as obtained in laboratory tests in America, with three different variants as to the weight of the warhead and range: a warhead from ten to twenty tons, range about 220 kilometres; a warhead from five to twelve tons and a range of about 320 kilometres; a warhead from one to five tons and a range of about 480 kilometres.

The report was signed by twelve members of the Committee. Among them was Dr Crow, who nevertheless stipulated that he did not consider that rockets (b) and (c) were possible. Lord Cherwell did not sign the report.[3]

From the Continent additional information on the German secret weapons was coming in; airmen were taking photographs in northern France, gathering proof that the Germans were erecting suspicious-looking buildings; and in London they were still quarrelling about rockets. Churchill sometimes took part in the meetings and was annoyed that the discussions came to nothing. Already in September Sandys's Committee had handed over the matter of the V-1 to the Air Ministry, in order to concentrate wholly on rockets. Now the representatives of the Intelligence Service began to argue that there was duplication and that it would be better if the whole matter were handed over to the Air Force. After all, it was a case of flying objects. Sandys therefore found himself under various pressures, at a time when he would have preferred to concentrate his energies on the matter of supplies for the invasion of the Continent—operation *Overlord*, which was already being prepared in the greatest secrecy. So, on 18 November, during a conversation with the Chiefs of Staff, he accepted a proposal to recommend to the Prime Minister that the Special Committee be disbanded and that he be released from his duties there. This recommendation was accepted.

With Sandys's resignation interest in the rockets waned. Everything connected with the V-1 and V-2 passed into the hands of Air Marshal Norman H. Bottomley, Deputy Chief of Air Staff, and became routine work. The name *Bodyline* disappeared, and at the turn of 1943/44 a new one was adopted: *Crossbow*.

This committee was briefed to look into the German flying bombs and rockets, but for several months it concentrated almost entirely on the V-1, for the immediate danger from them appeared to be more real. It was known, of course, that after the bombing of Peenemünde the Germans had transferred the experiments on the V-2 to Poland, for this had been reported by Home Army Intelligence and agents of the British Intelligence Service, watching the movements of German transports; but it was thought that the possibility of mass-production was still fairly distant. As a matter of routine several aerial photographs of Blizna were taken, but no interest was shown in them. Only two urgent despatches in May and June 1944 were a reminder that the rockets still existed and that they were probably the greatest danger threatening London.[4]

2

The situation in France after the collapse of the Western front in June 1940 assumed a quite exceptional form. At first the Germans occupied only the northern and western parts of the country, leaving the rest in the hands of 84-year-old Marshal Pétain who had stood at the head of the government at the worst moment of crisis. On 22 June 1940 he had concluded an armistice with the Germans and on 10 July he had become the head of the conquered state with his seat in Vichy. At the same time, in London, General Charles de Gaulle had formed a Committee of National Liberation; in a radio broadcast he told the French that 'whatever happens, the flame of French resistance must not and shall not die'. When in November 1942 the Germans occupied the whole of France, the Vichy government collaborated with the Nazis and, playing on the respect paid to the aged Marshal, demanded that all Frenchmen should recognize it.

Apart from these two political centres, each of which had their supporters, the territory of France was a matter of interest to other forces taking part in the war or backing one of the combatant sides. For the British the land of their recent ally was of great importance; for from it might come the German invasion, and it was the nearest territory on which, with American help, their counter-attack could be launched. It was for this reason that the French section of SOE was set up; but the situation was complicated by the fact that de Gaulle forced SOE to give him the right to his own section, with the code-name RF.[5] At the same time, Stalin too was keeping an eye on

France, for he was still thinking of world revolution and a march to the West and knew that he could count on the French Communist Party.

All these centres realized that when the decisive moment of the war in the West should come, it would be played out on French soil. So it was there that they sent their agents, and they even attempted to build up their own cadres of an underground army. The French section of SOE dropped parachutists, conveyed saboteurs in submarines or sent them by a roundabout route through Portugal, Spain and the Pyrenees; de Gaulle did the same. But all these agents were ultimately subordinate to London, and they had to report there after carrying out their appointed missions. These, then, were isolated operations, and they could not in themselves lead to the build-up of an extensive underground organization in France.

Apart from these operations directed from outside, there were spontaneous attempts to create an underground resistance movement on the spot. At first these attempts did not meet with great success, for a general apathy reigned, an unwillingness to take risks or make an effort;[6] but this state of mind changed under the influence of the German occupation. It is true that in some respects the occupation in the West was much milder than in Poland, for example: schools, universities, museums, libraries, newspapers and publishing firms were allowed to remain open. But the arrogance of the conquering Germans eventually provoked in the French a passionate desire to fight back.

These underground operations were often the initiative of individuals, and they took the form of sabotage groups, intelligence networks or partisan units. Although led by patriots, the groups often competed against each other, for they lacked a common leadership in a country torn between different factions. Part of the population recognized the legal government in Vichy, part obeyed the call to arms of de Gaulle (whom the legalists considered a rebel and who had been sentenced to death by Pétain), and part supported the political parties, including the fairly strong Communist Party. Communist supporters at first lay low, while Stalin made a pact with Hitler; later they began to collaborate with the Germans, until 22 June 1941, when the Third *Reich* fell on Russia; then they became noisily active, outdoing all the others in patriotic slogans. By the latter half of 1943, however, underground activities in France were widespread, and they were to a large extent united in recognition of de Gaulle's authority (thanks to his emissary, Jean Moulin, who had been dropped into France at the beginning of 1942).[7]

Colonel Wachtel was right to do his utmost to cover up the erecting of the V-1 launching-pads and everything connected with them; but he could not hide them from the eyes of the local population, many of whom were actually engaged in working on them.

3

Reserve Captain Michel Hollard, a well-built man of about 40, had left Paris with his firm just before the Germans entered the capital; but a few weeks later he returned, in order to go to earth in the city and see what would happen. The capital was a sad sight. Many Parisians had left their homes and made for the south, taking only a small part of their possessions. Those who remained, walked the unswept streets in a daze. All around German soldiers and huge army lorries were to be seen; the statues had been taken down and only the plinths remained; sandbags still rose high around the walls of government buildings.

First of all he had to find a means of living, and of legalizing his residence; so he took a job with a firm making gas engines, and thus acquired documents allowing him to reside in Paris and move around the neighbourhood fairly freely as their agent. During the first months of the occupation, France seemed to experience such shock from the invasion that it was difficult to begin any underground work; so the captain just looked around and considered what ought to be done. He listened, of course, to the radio and knew that Great Britain would fight on and that in London a French Committee of National Liberation had been set up. He had heard General de Gaulle's speech and his thoughts ran in the direction of establishing contact with London. He had also heard of the proclamation issued by Marshal Pétain's government in Vichy, but collaboration was not to his taste: he felt the necessity for further struggle.

After several months of observation, cautious contacts and consideration, and after learning that in Great Britain a special organization was in operation to bring help to the underground movements in occupied Europe*, Hollard came to the conclusion that the most useful work would be in intelligence. Information must be gathered concerning German operations, the locations of their military units, the concerns working for military production and transport—in short everything that increased German strength—and these details must be sent to London. People for the work would certainly be found; the Germans were in that sense only making things easier.

The first contacts were difficult, but the Battle of Britain had just come to an end, bringing the first German defeat, and at once the mood changed. Everyone understood that the war would be long and hard, but now it might end in victory. Captain Hollard, circulating in the neighbourhood of Paris and around northern France with his catalogues, more and more often met people who were willing to listen to his cautious remarks on the necessity for action. He had several trustworthy acquaintances and slowly began to set up a provincial network and gather information. A small intelligence group grew up, to which the captain gave the code-name *Agir*.[8]

But gathering information was not in itself enough. The problem of passing it on to London had still to be solved. The captain knew that in the unoccupied south there were several routes for sending people across the Pyrenees into Spain and then on to Portugal and Great Britain; but this was a long and dangerous road. Spain, although neutral, sympathized with Hitler, and any crossing of her territory was fraught with difficulty. Fortunately there was an alternative, more promising in that it was a matter of sending not a man but only an intelligence report. Unoccupied France bordered on Switzerland, and Michel Hollard looked in this direction. He made his way south, crossed into the so-called 'Red Zone'[9] and there, in the vicinity of Dôle, made the necessary contacts. It appeared that in spite of the German guards there was fairly regular traffic between France and Switzerland. As well as secret agents, numerous smugglers made the crossing, carrying various goods,

* The SOE.

above all jewellery, for the huge Swiss market.[10] One night the captain set off with a guide towards the frontier, and the next morning he was in Switzerland. He reached the British Embassy in Berne and there, after difficulties connected with establishing his *bona fides*, made contact with a British intelligence agent, to whom he gave the code-name *OP* and with whom he settled the details of further co-operation. It was in January 1942 that the intelligence network *Agir* was ready for active operation.[11]

For over a year nothing special happened and the reports Hollard took to Switzerland were similar to each other, until in the latter half of 1942 one of his agents, named Dandemard, a railway engineer in Rouen, sent an interesting report that the Germans were erecting some new sort of building in the department Seine Intérieure. The captain went there at once and, pretending to be a workman pushing a barrow, got on to the building site. This was not especially difficult, for about 40,000 men worked on these sites. They had been rounded up by force, and most of them were French. A quick look at the German works was enough to establish that launching-pads were being built and that they were directed to the north, towards London.

Captain Hollard had already heard of the German secret weapons; now it seemed that he had actually found them. The discovery was important, so the captain mobilized his best agents and gave each one a bicycle and a map of northern France, covering an area of about forty kilometres inland from the English Channel: within three weeks this group had found out that the Germans were building sixty launching-pads in the districts Auffay, Tôtes, Yerville, Le Bose, Malet, Brauquetuit, Abbémount and St Vaast-du-Val.[12]

This was information of great significance, but incomplete, so Hollard began to look around for men who could help him to obtain more details. He fairly quickly hit on Robert Rubenach, who had a friend, a young engineering draughtsman, André Comps. They both agreed to take the necessary risks to uncover further aspects of the German preparations.

The first step was to send them to the German contractor, who was looking for qualified men. They were both taken on. André, as a draughtsman, was sent to an office in Bois Carré, where work on the plans of the different sites was being carried out. He was not given any important blueprints, but he soon found the individual who prepared them, and through a window he was able to observe him working on them. The man sometimes went out of his room, but he always hid the blueprint in the pocket of his coat on a hanger. André kept watch and when the German again went out, he ran into his room, took out the blueprint and within a few minutes had made a copy.* The next day he pretended to be ill, got four days' sick leave and took the blueprint to Paris. It was a construction plan of one of the launching-pads with all its installations.[13]

Captain Hollard immediately set out for the south and got to Switzerland. His contact there was greatly pleased with the report and at once sent a long radio despatch to London. The report itself, together with the blueprint, went to England in a diplomatic bag carried from Berne by a neutral courier, whose way led through countries occupied by the Germans. All this took place in October 1943.[14]

After this great success, there was pressure from London for further information. Hollard gathered a great deal, not only about launching-pads but also about the transport of the flying bombs. He was helped in this by the station-master in Rouen, Pierre Bouquet, a friend of Dandemard.

Captain Hollard's network was not, of course, the only source of information about the German preparations on French territory to send off thousands of V-1s against London (the title of George Martelli's book on him, *The Man who saved London*, is rather an exaggeration). Around the northern coasts of France circulated the agents of other French underground formations, such as the groups connected with General de Gaulle, *Résistance de l'Armée, Agence Immobilière* and *Eleuthère*, which, with the support of SOE, had their own landing-grounds and dropping-zones. The secret network *Alliance*, built up in co-operation with the English, was also very active and towards the end of August and beginning of September 1943 it sent a very important despatch to London, composed by Georges Lamarque (*Petrel*), concerning Peeneumünde and the experiments being carried out there.[15] Underground soldiers of the

* See illustrations.

Polish Continental Action (*Akcja Kontynentalna*) and members of
a Polish intelligence organization in France, code-named *F2*, also
operated there.[16] And agents of the Belgian Resistance Movement,
who had received precise instructions from their Government in
London on what to look for, were also circulating in the same
region. Towards the end of 1943 they were asked for particulars of
the 'flying bombs'.[17] Finally there were the resident agents of the
British Intelligence Service, who had been living in the area for
years.

A decisive role was played by British air-reconnaissance, whose
aircraft flew time and again over France, Belgium, Holland and
northern Germany taking thousands of photographs.* These were
sent, as always, to the Central Interpretation Unit in Medmenham.
Meanwhile in London, where discussions between the British
Command and the American Air Force were laying detailed plans
for the bombing of the V-1 installations, the *Crossbow* committee
went on deliberating.

On 24 December 1943 the U.S. Eighth Air Fleet, stationed in
Britain, carried out the first major attack on the V-1 launching-
pads in France, dropping over 1,700 tons of bombs from 300
aircraft. Allied intelligence had identified 83 'ski-jumps', but only
three were destroyed and there were no casualties in Colonel
Wachtel's unit.[18] This was probably because the Americans flew by
day and dropped their bombs from a great height. After this first
attack there were others, both American and British, carried out
from a very low height, and the precision of the attacks increased
considerably. These operations against the launching-pads of the
V-1 were given the code-name *Noball*.

It is interesting that the results of these bombings, summed up in
figures, are given as more or less the same by both sides. According
to the reports sent by Captain Hollard's men, up to the middle of
January 1944, 79 launching-pads were bombed and 52 of them hit.
From the *War Diary* of Wachtel's *Flak* Regiment 155(W), it
appears that up to 31 March 1944, nine launching-pads were

*    Altogether 1,250,000 photographs were taken over these four countries
     and 4,000,000 prints made from them (P. Joubert de la Ferte, op. cit.,
     p. 100).

completely destroyed, 35 badly damaged, 29 partly and 20 lightly, out of a total number of 104. In addition, soldiers working on them sustained casualties. Here there are no means of comparing the two sources and one can only quote the German figures. In the above-mentioned *War Diary* there is an entry for 1 July 1944, from which it appears that during the air-raids 146 soldiers were killed, 240 wounded and 39 reported missing.[19]

There were also heavy losses on the Allied side. The Germans shot down 154 aircraft and 771 air crew were killed. The American losses amounted to 79 aircraft and 610 airmen, the British 75 aircraft and 161 airmen.[20]

The damage to the launching-pads was very considerable and for practical purposes put the 'ski-jumps' out of action before the attack on London had even begun. This forced the Germans to change their plans and to go over to a more modest solution, which also turned out to be more practical. The parts of the launching-pads were made in Germany and sent to France at the last moment to be assembled. They were set up in highly camouflaged places, on farms, next to churches, in parks, or in narrow gorges, so that they were virtually invisible from the air.[21] These were also attacked by Allied bombers, but much less effectively.

Unfortunately Captain Hollard was no longer operational by this time, nor was he free at the great moment of the Allied landing on French soil. In February 1944 he was arrested and, after interrogation, sent to the German concentration camp at Neuengamme outside Hamburg. Just before the end of the war the camp command transported the prisoners to Lübeck and loaded 9,000 of them on to three ships: *Cap Arcona, Thielbeck* and *Athen*, which set out to sea. Probably the intention of the *SS* was to carry out Himmler's order of 14 April 1945[22] and scuttle the ships with all prisoners on board. The captain of the *Athen* resisted pressure by the *SS* men, and in obedience to a British radio command that all ships were to remain in port, turned back; thanks to this, about 2,000 prisoners' lives were saved. Before the *SS* had carried out its task, British aircraft flew in on 3 May and, seeing German ships which had not obeyed the command, dropped bombs on them. Fires broke out, the ships began to sink. The scenes as the prisoners perished were terrible. Captain Hollard managed to save himself by swimming to the shore with about 400 other prisoners.[23]

4

Two young men nodded drowsily inside the uncomfortable fuselage of a Halifax, sneaking through the clouds over the Channel. The flight was to be a short one, from the secret airfield in Tempsford near Cambridge to northern France, but the bitter cold made itself painfully felt, so the parachutists sat back to back and covered themselves with the one blanket. Their clothes and light overcoats, such as were worn at that time in France, gave little warmth. It was 3 March 1944, and at night, especially at a height, the frost was still sometimes severe.

The young men were flying from England but they talked to each others in Polish. They were 38-year-old Lieutenant Władysław Ważny (*Tygrys*) and Sergeant Edward Bomba (*Toreador*) from the Polish Armed Forces in the West, who had both volunteered for special duties and were starting out on them with this flight to France. During the dropping operation they came under the Polish sub-section EU/P of the French section of SOE, but officially they were also closely attached to the Polish political and military authorities, at that time based in Great Britain.

This double service arose from the peculiar situation in which the governments or national committees of the countries occupied by the Nazis found themselves in London. Each of them rightly considered that their nationals were under their command, wherever they might be; on the other hand, when SOE was established and when it initiated the dropping of men and equipment into the occupied territories, it also demanded that these operations should be carried out under its sole command. As a result the general principle was adopted that every man in each national section of SOE was, when working within its framework, wholly subordinate to it; his duty to the authorities of his own country was more or less symbolic, expressed in formal contact between the leaders of SOE with these authorities. All radio liaison, the codes, and the secret air-, sea- and land-routes belonged to SOE and were known only to it. The saboteur, dropped from an aeroplane or landed secretly from a submarine on the coast of an occupied country, sent radio despatches straight to London, was always under its orders and after carrying out his mission was to return there to his section of SOE.[24]

The one exception was made for Poles, who had special privileges. The Polish section of SOE, which was set up in the late summer of 1940, was subordinate to the British authorities, but it maintained links as far into the Polish system as the VIth Bureau of the Polish General Staff. All the parachutists, emissaries and couriers who reached Poland by various routes, were chosen by the Polish authorities, and each one of them, when in his own country, ceased to be subordinate to SOE and became a soldier of the Home Army or joined the political underground. Poles alone retained the right to independent radio liaison and their own codes, even immediately before the invasion of the Continent, when very strict censorship was brought in.[25]

The Polish sub-section (EU/P) within the French section of SOE operated on more or less the same principles. Almost immediately after its arrival in Great Britain, the Polish Government began to consider the possibilities of using the numerous Polish communities outside Poland in the struggle against the Germans; at first this would be underground, but later, when the Allies landed in Europe, it would be open. This applied above all to the half-million Poles, mostly miners, who were settled in northern France, in the vicinity of Lille and St Etienne. In November 1940 it was decided to set in motion the so-called *Akcja Kontynentalna* (Continental Action). In the same month the Polish sub-section EU/P was set up.*

The two parachutists flying across the Channel had in their pockets excellently-forged French identity papers and various small items intended to prove that they were permanent residents of France. Their clothes had all either been brought across the Channel or made in Great Britain in the French manner. Even the smallest article in their possession had been thoroughly checked. Their French was correct but spoken with a noticeable foreign accent, which made their false personalities even more authentic, for they were to pass as Polish miners settled in northern France.

Lieutenant Ważny looked at his watch and at the same moment the head of the despatcher, responsible for the jump, appeared

---

* For more information about Continental Action see Appendix II, item 3.

through the small door: 'We have crossed the Channel, get ready.'

The young men threw off the blanket and automatically felt their pockets for the steely cold of their guns. The sergeant stretched out his arm and pulled towards him an old, scratched suitcase in which there was a radio transmitter. They both got up and checked the hooks to which they attached the cords of their parachutes by special clips. This small procedure required attention, for their lives depended on it.*

The aircraft must have descended and made a turn for the noise of the engine died down and the fuselage leaned over hard to one side. After a moment the propellers began to snarl more loudly and the whole machine shook with vibrations as the pilot climbed up again, describing wide circles while he looked for the dropping-zone.

Above the door a small red signal-light went on. The parachutists took a deep breath and once again, with hasty movements, checked their equipment. The despatcher came in, threw a quick, expert glance, ran his hands over the cords of the parachutes and pulled up a trap door in the floor. An ice-cold stream of air hit all three of them and threw them back a step. Ważny pushed himself forward, sat on the floor and, holding tight to the edge of the opening, put his legs through it. A megaphone gave instructions and the despatcher listened hard to catch the words above the roar of the engines and the hiss of air. The red light changed to green and the airman's hand came violently down.

In the first moment Ważny lost his breath and, caught in the icy draught, he fell like a stone. A moment later he felt a sharp tug and at once his taut nerves relaxed. The cord had done its task and in a moment the great canopy of the parachute would open out over him. He ceased to drop, the cold grew less, he began his slow float to earth. The night was dark; the pilots, flying by instruments and radar, had carried out their mission and carried it out well, for below could be seen the twinkling direction lights of the dropping-zone.

* The parachutes used by SOE were opened automatically by the tug on a cord tied at one end to the parachute and at the other to a fastening inside the aircraft. After the jump the weight of the parachutist broke the cord. The parachutists had nothing with which to open the parachute if the automatic equipment failed to work.

The Lieutenant was dropping backwards, so he manoeuvred the cords, pulled with his body and after several jerky movements had changed his position by 180°. He looked upwards and between the clouds saw the canopy of a second parachute. He was quite relaxed and his thoughts were concentrated only on one problem: to land as well as possible and to find the reception team.

5

The jump was successful and Lieutenant Ważny arrived at the Northern Group of *POWN* where he was appointed head of Intelligence. He was well prepared for this post, since in England he had undergone several months of training. He knew how to move around in strange territory, how to plot all the important points on a map, how to describe a map reference; and he knew the codes and signals to be used by Sergeant Bomba's radio transmitter. In accordance with SOE principles the transmitter was tuned to London, but there was an order for radio silence until the alert, which would arouse all intelligence cells to sudden action.[26] Preparations for the invasion of the Continent were afoot, and an assurance of quick and varied information about the German rearguard was essential.

It might perhaps have been better if the Lieutenant had originated from the Polish community in northern France, for he could have settled in the area with relatively little difficulty. On the other hand, if nobody knew him, nobody could recognize him or give away his real name—and there were spying eyes everywhere. Thanks to the reception committee he had been passed on at once into the right hands and given his preliminary contacts. He slowly began to build them up and to supplement the intelligence network which already existed and had been handed over to him. He was greatly helped by the cipher clerk, Maria Kosko (*Nounou*), who had been born in the area, knew many local people and understood conditions under the occupation; and Sergeant Leon Zapała (*Owidiusz*), detailed to him after Bomba was arrested, proved to be a good worker. Having got to know his soldiers, Ważny assigned positions to them and appointed several as his seconds-in-command. An older local Pole, Piotr Ukleja (*Grom*), turned out to be one of his best and most efficient colleagues.[27]

The period during which Wazny was on French territory was exceptionally feverish, for there were many signs that the Allies would effect a landing very shortly and that the war would move into the decisive phase. The Germans were prepared for this and had mustered large armies in northern France. Every road, every railway line, crossing and bridge was constantly patrolled, and moving round the countryside required courage, precision and initiative. Without the help of the local Polish population the lieutenant would not have achieved much. He was forced to change his place of residence frequently; he had to check his provincial network and the accuracy of the reports he received, and he had to enlarge the scope of his contacts and look for new people further and further afield. Everywhere that he appeared with the predetermined password, he found shelter, food, and help in moving around the locality which he had to reconnoitre.

On 6 June 1944 the long-awaited landing of the Allies on the French coast took place, and seven days later the first flying bombs, V-1, fell on London. That same day the Polish Ministry of Defence, with the agreement of SHAEF,* sent the following despatch to Ważny:

> 'I recommend that your chief attention should be directed to locating the emplacement of the launching-pads of the flying bombs. Their position to be given by map reference in the pre-arranged way. Report on the method of function, the bomb depots, the method of transportation. Report later on results of air-raids.'[28]

From the moment this order was received Sergeant Zapała's radio transmitter, so far silent, could begin to operate. In addition to him there were three other radio operators: Sergeant Jan Grudziak (*Nikanor II*), Sergeant Zygmunt Nowak (*Selim*) and Sergeant Stefan Lewandowski (*Alamant*). All three had been dropped from Britain.[29]

Even before this Ważny's network had brought in several reports concerning the launching-pads, but now all its efforts were directed

* Supreme Headquarters, Allied Expeditionary Force.

to this end. During the latter half of June the first radio reports reached London. When all details about the launching-pads had been checked against the map, every report was coded and sent by courier to the radio transmitters (which had to be constantly on the move to keep ahead of the Germans, whose special detector vans went round and round the area to track them down). Emplacement of launching-pads was reported in farm buildings in Bonnières, in the forest to the north of Auxi-le-Château, on the northern edge of Proville in the direction of Abbeville, in a wood beside the road from Trevent to St Pol and in many other places. Several stores of flying bombs were also located. During less than three months Lieutenant Ważny's network sent 62 reports to London giving the position of 173 launching-pads,* 17 reports of transports, 2 of garrison quarters and 15 on the results of bombing.[30]

As well as using his own network, Ważny also looked for contacts among the Poles from western Poland, now incorporated into Germany, who had been mobilized into the *Wehrmacht*. This gave good results. One of them, an NCO from Pomerania, supplied the important information that whenever there was a cross-roads signpost that was $50 \times 15$ cm large and yellow with a black edging, it indicated a launching-pad; when above it there was another sign, black with white figures, that meant a grouping of several 'ski-jumps'.[31] Poles serving in the *Wehrmacht* were also encouraged to acts of sabotage in these areas, and several underground patrols were set up for this purpose. It was one of these groups that succeeded in cutting a main cable running through Doulens from Amiens to St Pol.[32] Up to the moment of the invasion sabotage had been forbidden in that section of the Polish underground movement, in order to keep the network secret to the last minute and avoid reprisals against the local population.

These enterprises were effective, but London, under constant fire from the V-1s and fearing that the success of the invasion would be jeopardized, demanded still greater activity. This was carried out at the expense of security and the consequences were soon felt. On 9 July, Sergeant Grudziak fell into German hands with his

---

* Naturally in these reports, which were sent in great haste, the same launching-pads appeared more than once. There were only 104 of them altogether, whereas the total number identified was 173.

transmitter; on 30 July Sergeant Nowak and on 3 August Sergeant Zapała were captured. Lieutenant Ważny, knowing that the loss of the transmitters would greatly hamper his operations and that they must have been located by the German detector vans, decided to immobilize the vans' operating centre. It was situated in Amiens on the Boulevard de Chateaudun. Ważny's report, sent by the only remaining transmitter, *Alamant*, brought on an air-raid by British aircraft which seriously damaged the building and destroyed a good number of vans.[33]

Unfortunately on 19 August the Germans found Ważny. He was then hiding in Montigny-en-Ostrevent, not far from Donai, when a local *Volksdeutsch* woman noticed him. He was a stranger and seemed suspicious, so she informed on him to the commander of a unit of the *Wehrmacht* stationed in the town. The Germans knocked on the front door and Ważny leapt into the garden with a pistol in his hand. He meant to defend himself, but before he had taken a few steps he was noticed and brought down by a burst of fire from a machine-gun. The dying man was stripped of his clothes in a search for papers and other suspicious objects and handed over to the French police.*

6

In all the bigger German concentration camps there existed a resistance movement organized by a small group of those political prisoners who had managed to survive the appalling conditions of the early days, and obtain safer positions in the camp. If they had not found work in the hospital, one of the offices, the kitchen, one of the storehouses, or with a group of prisoners working indoors, they would never have survived the ever-present hunger, the cold, and the beatings; and they would not have been capable of any resistance activity.

Up to 30 October 1944, when it became independent, the camp *Dora* was a sub-camp of Buchenwald and all the transports of prisoners came from there. For several years in Buchenwald there had existed an underground movement in which German political

---

*   See illustrations.

prisoners played an important part. Some of its members had found themselves in *Dora* from the very beginning, so they were the first to undertake underground activities in the new and difficult territory. A small German group was set up with a Communist, Albert Kuntz, at the head,* to whom the *SS* entrusted the most important position of overseeing the building of the whole, new camp.[34]

In addition to the Germans, several Czechs in Buchenwald came to an agreement. They were probably led by Jan Pisala, who, from the very beginning worked in the hospital. There was also Dr Jan Češpiva,[35] who claims to have been the leader, and some Czech Communists who maintained contact with German sympathizers.**

The Poles were organized by Jan Bolesław Krokowski, a young officer in Polish intelligence and the French underground, who came from Buchenwald in January 1944. After a bad start he became *Schreiber* of barrack No.124. His knowledge of French helped him to make contacts among the French, which turned out to be useful. He contacted some Poles, who already had good jobs in the camp. Some of them, like Krokowski, before their arrest, had been members of the French underground.†

The French, as numerous in the camp as the Poles, also organized themselves. The great majority had been in the French resistance, and were followers of General de Gaulle and members of the *Organisation de Résistance de l'Armée* (ORA); there was a high percentage of intellectuals, officers and parachutists trained in Britain, and a small number of Communists. At the head of the French stood Colonel Dejussieu-Poncarral.[36] In this group there were also a number of Poles from the French *Resistance*, who had been given the letter 'F' in the camp. Besides this was a second, very small group of French Communists with Armand Bertele at its head.[37] Krokowski maintained contact with both groups.††

Citizens of the Soviet Union, the most numerous in *Dora,* also formed a strong underground group. Among them were officers, military and political, whom the camp Gestapo had not managed to uncover. From amongst them came their resistance leaders, with

* The list of other Germans in this group is in Appendix II, item 4.
** The list of other Czechs in the group is in Appendix II, item 5.
† The list of other Poles is in Appendix II, item 6.
†† The list of other French in this group is in Appendix II, item 7.

Lieutenant-Colonel Aleksander Manko and *NKVD* Captain Michail Piskunov* at the top.[38]

Some Belgians, Danes, Spaniards, Dutchmen and Yugoslavs also belonged to the underground through co-operation with the French or the Poles. The Italian prisoners of war kept apart, as did the workers of the industrial firm *Wifo*, among whom there were the nuclei of small resistance groups.

Sources which have been published in Communist countries maintain that the above groups united and that at the head of the whole stood the German communist, Albert Kuntz. This is almost certainly not accurate; there never was complete unity, and it was neither necessary nor desirable in view of the constant penetration by German counter-intelligence and the spies of the camp Gestapo. Moreover only the German group would have agreed to the leadership of a German and a Communist: the others had had more than enough of the hated supremacy of the *SS*, and Communists were by no means the most numerous in the underground.

In other camps the underground movement was chiefly occupied in making survival easier, and with preparations for self-defence if the *SS* were to carry out the mass-murder of prisoners as the war came to an end. In *Dora*, however, two other problems took priority: getting reports out and sabotaging production. Everyone understood this perfectly, both Germans and prisoners. The former did all they could to cut off the camp from the outside world and make the prisoners afraid of errors of workmanship; the latter tried to find loopholes in the tight security network surrounding the camp and the factory, and to hold back as best they could the assembly of the weapons.

Krokowski, who made friends with many of the French, had more scope than others since he could make use of contacts in two national groups. That was why, in the middle of 1944, he had an opportunity which was decisive for sending the first important report to the outside world. A Frenchman, Henri Chayot, who worked in a garage just outside the camp, told him in secret that he had become friendly with a civilian workman there, who was questioning him cautiously about the production in the underground factory. Krokowski prepared a number of questions

* The list of other Russians in this group is in Appendix II, item 8.

meant to clarify the intentions of the workman, and when he considered the replies to be satisfactory, he gave the Frenchman details and supplied him with sketches of the flying bomb and the rocket. Some weeks later another civilian worker, with a recommendation from the first, also contacted the Frenchman and also received vital details.[39] It seems that they must have been in contact with an agent of one of the Intelligence Services, for on the last day of August 1944 London received the first authoritative news of the production of the V-1 and the V-2 in the underground factory in the Kohnstein mountain. This time the information was not in the form of deduction and conjecture, nor through a chain of intermediaries, but straight from the area itself.[40]

Another Pole from this group, Stanisław Ponikiewski also had opportunities of sending news to the outside world; for while he was in the POW camp near Cologne he had made contact with Allied Intelligence, and for that reason he had been arrested and sent to Buchenwald, and then to *Dora*. He knew well two *SS*-men of Polish descent who visited him occasionally whenever he got hold of some vodka. They both agreed to send a few letters which would avoid the camp censorship. Later they also undertook to take letters and deliver them to Cologne during their short leaves. When an answer arrived, coded reports began to be sent by the same route.[41]

Other underground groups sought similar contacts. The Germans and Czechs, through the lorries circulating between *Dora* and Buchenwald, maintained liaison with the underground movement there, chiefly with the hospital.[42] The French had acquaintances among the civilian workers. Twice attempts were even made to erect a radio transmitter, but it was never finished; it seems that this was impossible in *Dora*.

Thanks to the information received, allied aircraft could commence reconnaissance flights and photograph the terrain around the underground factory. Since, however, even the heaviest six-ton bombs were unable to destroy it, protected as it was by the great mountain, the attacks were directed solely at the lines of communication. Road and rail transport was seriously disorganized, and this was reflected in the delays in production; but the bombs also fell on numerous sub-camps where prisoners were killed: unfortunately such sacrifices were inevitable.

Much has been written of sabotage in the underground factory; many statements have been made on this subject and some authors have come to the conclusion that it was this sabotage that brought about the collapse of the German V-1 and V-2 offensive in 1944 against England, and that it had a great influence on the course of the war.[43] This is an exaggeration, fairly typical when underground activity is in question; but there was indeed sabotage in *Mittelwerk*, although there is not enough information to assess it precisely.

To the extent that in the Kohnstein mountain, as in every German camp, the prisoners held fast to the principle of working as little as possible, it could be said that they sabotaged German military production. Apart from this, however, there were some deliberate acts of sabotage carried out by individual prisoners strictly on their own, without telling others and without directions from the leaders of the resistance groups. These took various forms: welders made small mistakes and the pieces of metal welded came apart sooner than they should have done; electricians caused short circuits; precision-tool craftsmen made minute mistakes in their reckonings.[44] The underground did direct small groups of prisoners, who did more serious damage to the fully—or almost fully—assembled weapons. The possibilities were great, and historians are generally agreed that in every national group—but above all among the Soviets—there were prisoners who engaged in sabotage.

The Germans knew that production was being deliberately slowed down and disorganized, and they made every attempt to prevent it. The prisoners working on the assembly of the V-1 and V-2 were divided into small working parties among which, as well as the *Kapos* and *Vorarbeiters** (usually German criminals terrified of any suspicion of sabotage), there were also civilian craftsmen. Among these men, German military counter-intelligence had placed agents to observe the work. Besides this, engineers and *SS*- men walked round the factory keeping an eye on what was going on. Finally, a prisoner's every movement was watched continually by his fellows, amidst whom were many informers. Even otherwise honest men reported on any signs of sabotage they noticed, in fear of the penalty for 'collective responsibility'.

* Foremen.

However, this was not enough for the camp and factory authorities, for they suspected that an underground movement was operating in the camp. They resorted to an unorthodox tactic: they themselves set up a provocative resistance group. This role was undertaken by a man, who in the camp bore the letter 'F' and was registered as a Frenchman, but no one seemed to know who he was. He spoke Russian, and was thought by some to be a Russian emigré; others considered him to be of Italian descent; yet others a German. There is now no absolute certainty as to his name: in books and statements he is called variously Grozzo, Groizof and André Grozdoff.[45] Probably this last is his real name.* In the second half of 1944 he began to set up a French resistance group, into which he also drew Czech, German and Soviet prisoners. His main argument was the necessity of preparing for self-defence at the end of the war. In November a large number of prisoners from the camp underground were suddenly arrested and shut up in the bunker. For the sake of appearances Grozdoff also was arrested. Confessions forced by torture brought about further arrests,** and these took in a large number of Soviet citizens, and also Kuntz. The questioning dragged on, and because there was no hope of deliverance a group of Soviet and Polish prisoners made a desperate attempt to get out of the bunker and escape. The attempt failed, hastening the executions. Almost all were hanged, some died during questioning; a few, among them Dr Češpiva, were left alive and regained their freedom at the end of the war. All the French were released from the bunker.[46]

There is no sure way of estimating the extent of sabotage carried out by the prisoners in the underground factory. As has been mentioned previously, many misfires and unsuccessful flights of the V-1 and V-2 were caused by errors in the prototypes, which were put into mass production too soon; drawing the dividing line between this cause and sabotage is quite impossible. Some idea of its degree may, however, be judged from the German reactions, which grew more forcible with every month.

In the beginning errors at work on the assembly of the secret

* It appears in the records of the *International Tracing Service* at Arolsen, West Germany.
** The list of some arrested prisoners is in Appendix II, item 9.

weapons were punished by flogging, but when they began to multiply General *SS* Gerhard Maurer of the *WVHA* (*Wirtschafts und Verwaltungshauptamt*) issued an order decreeing the penalty for sabotage to be death by public hanging.[47] At first the executions were carried out on individual prisoners and these were hanged in the underground corridors or on the roll-call ground; later there were mass executions. (Some of these executions were the subject of a trial of the *SS* men responsible, which took place in Essen during the years 1959-61.) On 12 March 1945, 50 Soviet citizens, 5 Poles, 2 Czechs and 1 Lithuanian were hanged; on 20 March of that year, 24 Soviet citizens and 6 Poles, and on 23 March 25 Soviet citizens and 5 Poles died.[48] There were further executions and about 300 prisoners in all were killed, among these about 200 for alleged sabotage. Some were murdered in the bunker by a shot in the back of the head.

In this way died some of the soldiers of the Second World War, on a silent, unknown front.

7

During his first visit to Peenemünde in April 1943, Himmler took von Braun by the arm, led him aside for a moment and politely asked if the engineer would care to work for him, since the *SS* were also carrying out experiments with rockets and could offer him excellent conditions. Von Braun refused tactfully,* and Himmler did not press him nor indicate the slightest annoyance at the time.

That short conversation had no immediate results and outwardly nothing was changed, but the head of the *SS* did not forget the incident. It was only a few months later, when British bombs had destroyed Peenemünde-East, that Himmler persuaded Hitler to hand over everything connected with the rockets to the *SS*.**

On 26 August Albert Speer, who had been present at the conference with Hitler when this decision was taken, called a confidential meeting of some of the more important men concerned: Dornberger, Degenkolb, Saur and Kammler. This was

* See Chapter Four, section 3.
** See Chapter Six, section 3.

the first time Kammler had attended such a meeting, and he was invited to take part even though he was not yet formally connected with the rockets. A few days later he was to be detailed to work on them on Himmler's personal orders; Speer had called him in because he knew that this would happen.

Kammler was unappealing, too sure of himself, arrogant and brutal, but he was bursting with almost boundless energy. He worked day and night himself, and wore out all those under him; for him nothing was too difficult, let alone impossible.[49] He rapidly put forward a number of ideas, along the lines of the decisions taken by Hitler on 22 August, but with executive details. The experts at Speer's meeting accepted these plans and Kammler, immediately he had been nominated, set about putting them into operation; they were intended to give the *SS* the utmost control.

The decision that the testing of the rockets should be transferred to Poland and their mass-production to the Harz mountains, meant that Peenemünde-East would be greatly diminished in size; but the Development Works, in which von Braun and other experts worked, were to remain. Kammler intended to move them to caves near the Traunsee, in Austria, but this plan did not come off and it was found necessary to rebuild the factories from the ruins on their old site. According to the principle adopted earlier, the ruins were left untouched; special camouflage was used and the re-building commenced from inside.

Kammler was not pleased by this solution, for, although the *SS* had considerably extended its control, Peenemünde was still under the *Luftwaffe* and the Army. Himmler had not yet tried to get the V-1 into his own hands, for Göring was in charge of it, and Göring was still Hitler's confidant and the second most powerful person in the state. But the rockets had been handed over to the *SS* and the time had come for everything connected with them to be grasped very firmly. This applied above all to the inventors, engineers and eminent scientists with von Braun at their head.

At the moment the only means of control was for Kammler to appear as often as possible on the site of the rebuilt works and to infiltrate his own men who would watch every step of the experts in whom the *SS* were interested. Kammler did this without difficulty and time and again turned up on the island of Usedom for long conferences with Dornberger. Relations between the two were bad;

it could not be otherwise, for, apart from Kammler's aggressive behaviour, Dornberger knew that he was talking to the man who meant to oust him from the job to which he was wholly devoted. Von Braun's position was different, for as an eminent specialist he could regard himself as indispensable. He tried to remain neutral and not to betray his opinions and feelings, and common-sense dictated caution. Did he know that he was constantly spied upon? Absorbed in his work, so far greatly privileged and still inexperienced, he may not have noticed.

Several months passed; the firings at Blizna went full steam ahead, and the underground factory in Nordhausen had sent over the first three rockets. The grip of the SS in this respect had become stronger and Himmler decided that the time had come to return to the problem of von Braun. He sent for him to come to his field quarters in Hochwald, not far from Hitler's 'Wolf's Lair'. Von Braun came alone, for Dornberger had not been summoned, and on the evening of 21 February 1944 he reported to Himmler's official train. The head of the SS was exceedingly polite, but without much introduction proposed that he should transfer from the jurisdiction of the army to the guardian wing of the SS. The young inventor was in difficulty, for he knew that nobody could offer him greater freedom than he then had. For the second time he mustered up the courage to refuse, giving as the reason his feeling of loyalty to the army.[50] Once again Himmler gave no signs of how he had been affected by this refusal, but his icy politeness did not augur well. Von Braun went out feeling very disquieted.

General Dornberger was on official business in Schwedt on the Oder, when, very early in the morning of 15 March he was awakened by a telephone call from Berchtesgaden.* General Walter Buhle was ringing, and Dornberger was to come as quickly as possible and report to Field-Marshal Wilhelm Keitel. The distance was over 600 kilometres, so the general put everything aside and set off. He apparently did not know why he had been summoned so urgently. When he arrived, General Buhle was non-committal; he said only that just before his telephone call the Gestapo had arrived at Peenemünde and arrested the three most

---

* The place in the Bavarian Alps where on the top of the mountain, cut out of the rock, Hitler's 'Eagle's Nest' was situated.

eminent rocket experts: von Braun, Klaus Riedel II and Hellmuth Gröttrup. They were now in the prison in Szczecin.[51]

The following morning Dornberger reported to Keitel. He was quite calm, hoping that military solidarity would cause the Field-Marshal to do everything possible in the way of effective intervention. He was greatly mistaken. Keitel was an opportunist and had no thought of risking his own head; he only shrugged and repeated the accusations made against the three engineers. The Gestapo was in possession of information that they had been sabotaging the war effort, that they had talked aloud of defeat and that they were thinking of creating not an instrument of warfare, but an interplanetary airship. Moreover, in Riedl and Gröttrup sympathy for pacifism and communism had also been discovered. The counter-intelligence *Abwehr* had come to the same conclusions and the order for their arrest had been given by Himmler himself.

Nothing remained for Dornberger but to try to save these valuable men himself. He first went to the head of the *SS*, but Himmler refused to receive him. The General travelled to Berlin to see the Reich's Chief of Security General Ernst Kaltenbrunner, but finally he talked only to his right-hand man, *SS* General Heinrich Müller. It was a far from pleasant conversation, for the *SS*-man informed the general that he himself was under constant observation and that his sarcastic remarks about Hitler's dream concerning the rockets were well known.*

It was necessary to turn for help to the *Abwehr*, which competed with the security forces. Unfortunately this channel also failed, for the struggle between Himmler and Admiral Canaris was in its final stages: Himmler was winning and the *Abwehr* was on the eve of dissolution;** its influence now was practically nil. Dornberger looked for other means. He solicited various people, and one of them, equally interested in freeing the engineers, resolved the difficulty. This was Albert Speer, who was in Klessheim, laid low by a severe illness. By a fortunate chance, Hitler, who was still very fond of his former court architect, came to visit him unexpectedly. This was a proof of exceptional favour, for the leader of the Third *Reich* never had a free moment. Speer took advantage of the

* See Chapter Four, section 1.
** It was dissolved on 1 June 1944.

occasion, put in a plea for the arrested men, and Hitler promised that they would be released. He also added that von Braun would be free from all persecution for as long as he was indispensable.

Nobody in Germany dared to oppose the will of the *Führer* and not even Himmler could risk this. Within two weeks von Braun was out of prison and had returned to his work in Peenemünde; a few days later he was joined by the other two experts. Dornberger, however, had to swear on oath that the future behaviour of the engineers would be above reproach.[52]

This incident was typical of the situation in the Third *Reich* towards the end of the war. The war-worn nation was making the maximum effort in order to win, and yet the most highly-placed men in the state were busy wresting power from each other and wasting their energies on ambitions.

# CHAPTER EIGHT

## The pursuit of the V-2 in Poland; the beginning of the invasion of the Continent; the sending of the report on the rocket to London

1

Day was breaking on a beautiful May morning in 1944 when General Eisenhower, Commander-in-Chief of the Allied Invasion Forces, returned to his caravan on the south coast of England. After a long, difficult and stubborn discussion he felt utterly exhausted. He wanted to forget his problems and rest for a few hours, but his thoughts returned to the recent briefing.

General Montgomery always annoyed Eisenhower, who with his talent for smoothing over divergences of opinion usually managed to disguise his feelings; today, however, he had nearly exploded. They had been discussing the approaching landings on the north coast of France—weighing up the meteorological forecasts and trying to guess what the Germans might know of their plans. Everyone was tired of waiting, but they understood the importance of the decision. Montgomery alone seemed to make light of it and was pushing for immediate action. At this last briefing he had been quite impossible; he had harped on the reports that on the French coast the Germans were building launching-pads for flying bombs, and insisted that, since London was in danger, the Germans must be thrown out of France as soon as possible. But Eisenhower, who was responsible for the whole operation, simply could not allow the invasion to be precipitated in this way—what would happen if through impetuosity and oversight it failed?

To make matters worse, Eisenhower was also being pressurized from the American side, not from his military entourage but from Washington itself. The President wanted the war in Europe to end quickly so that he could throw all his forces against the Japanese. There was also now the belief that the Germans already possessed multi-stage rockets which could reach the United States. Was such

great technical progress possible? He didn't know. What he did
know was that an over-hasty invasion might be disastrous.

The General took his sleeping pills. But he doubted that he would
get to sleep quickly. He pulled back the curtain and looked out. It
was perfectly quiet, not the slightest breeze moved the branches of
the trees. Beyond the horizon a tiny fragment of the rising sun
began to appear.

2

The same sun was rising slowly over the small Polish village of
Klimczyce, a thousand miles to the east of England.

The war had reached these parts long ago. Since the autumn of
1939 the area had been occupied by the Germans, with their then
ally, the Russians, who were based on the eastern bank of the river
Bug. In June 1941 the Germans had attacked the Russians and
pushed them far back to the east. Now, three years later, they had
them back again, but still some distance away, so they continued to
rule the conquered territory as their own undisputed property.
They imposed large food quotas on the villages, rounded up young
people for forced labour in the heart of Germany, and mercilessly
shot partisans and underground soldiers. This had been going on
for almost five years; it was everyday routine, and it was not for
these reasons that the bright morning of 20 May 1944 turned out to
be so important.

When the first German experimental rockets fell in Poland, and
the race began between the Germans and the patrols of the Polish
underground army to collect the fragments,* it became clear
immediately that the Germans had the advantage in this contest.
They had enormous technological superiority over the Poles, and
they could terrorize the local population with impunity. The Home
Army authorities realized this and wondered how they could
compete. They eventually decided to concentrate on two
possibilities.

The first plan was devised locally and depended on assembling a
large number of partisans, who would storm the artillery garrison

* See Chapter Six, section 6.

at Blizna and hold it for at least a few hours, during which the Germans' secrets could be discovered. After some consideration this idea had to be rejected. The Blizna garrison was too strong and it was not difficult to envisage the bloody reprisals that would fall on the local inhabitants.

The second plan, which had been conceived in Warsaw, seemed to have a greater chance of success. The command of the underground diversionary units (*Kedyw*) received orders to organize an armed operation to capture one of the trains carrying rockets to Blizna. This plan appeared quite feasible, so preparations were put in hand. The attack was to take place not far from Blizna, on the Brzesko-Tarnów line. After the guards had been killed, the whole line of waggons was to be rolled into the small station nearby and there the rocket would be re-loaded onto a large lorry. Under cover of darkness and with an armed escort the lorry would then make for a place prepared in the Lower Carpathians.[1]

In spite of various delays, everything was finally made ready, when a fortunate accident made the whole operation unnecessary. On 20 May an urgent message arrived in Warsaw: that day, at dawn, near the village of Klimczyce, not far from Sarnaki, on the swampy left bank of the river Bug, a rocket had fallen and had failed to explode. A local Home Army patrol had managed to conceal it before the Germans turned up, and there was a chance that they would not find it.[2]

3

After the resignation from the *Crossbow* Committee of Sandys, who, together with a number of eminent scientists, in particular Dr Reginald Jones, had considered the rockets to be Germany's most dangerous secret weapon, interest in London turned to the V-1. There were a number of reasons for this. Firstly, the attack on Peenemünde in August 1943\* had destroyed facilities for work on the rockets and had without doubt greatly slowed down experiments with them; secondly, intelligence on the Continent

\* See Chapter Five.

spoke continually of trial launchings of flying bombs and of a great many launching-pads built in northern France, and this was confirmed by numerous aerial photographs; thirdly, important information had been received from Danish underground intelligence, together with a diagram and photographs, of a V-1 which had fallen on the island of Bornholm.* Assembling all the accumulated details, comparing them and analysing them, British intelligence managed, fairly accurately, to visualize a V-1, estimate its range and power and calculate more or less what sort of danger would threaten London when this weapon came into mass-production. It was known that the German Air Force, experimenting with the V-1, was in competition with the Army which was interested in rocketry, and the British could see that in this race the *Luftwaffe* had now taken a slight lead. London could be in great danger within the next few months.[3]

The first reports from Poland at the beginning of 1944, about the experiments with flying objects, interested the *Crossbow* Committee. Instructions were issued to the Air Force to photograph the area of Blizna. Two reconnaissance flights were made, in mid-April and on 5 May,** and photographs were brought back which were quite adequate for interpretation purposes; but the Committee put them temporarily to one side. The main focus of attention continued to be the V-1, and there was still a great deal of scepticism about the rockets and doubt as to whether these experiments in Poland were really with them.

Suddenly, towards the end of May, the Polish staff in London passed on to the intelligence Service an urgent radio message which it had just received. A rocket had crashed near the river Bug, failed to disintegrate and had been hidden by the Poles. A special team was examining it and preparing a report.

There was no longer any time to be lost. Dr Jones shut himself up in his office through the night of 2/3 June and sat down to examine methodically all the photographs of Blizna. He wanted at all costs to find out whether there really were any rockets there.

After many hours, as dawn was breaking, Dr Jones found what

----

*   See Chapter Six, section 2.
**  See illustrations.

he was looking for: in a far corner of the area, on a loop of the narrow-guage railway, he could just distinguish a faint white line.

He immediately told Lord Cherwell of this and within 48 hours Churchill was in possession of this information. One could have been forgiven for expecting Dr Jones's important discovery, brought about by the reports and additional information from Poland,[4] to arouse the *Crossbow* Committee to decisive action. However, it became clear that personal animosities were stronger than reason. Dr Jones came under a volley of criticism from many sides, from the War Cabinet and from people who preferred not to believe that the Germans already possessed rockets; while the Allied Central Interpretation Unit protested about the 'amateur interpretation' of the photograph, which showed, they claimed, not a rocket but a railway engine. Dr Jones was not very popular with this unit, for earlier, in 1943, he had been the first to realize from the photographs of Peenemünde that there were flying bomb launching-pads there.

4

The capture near the Bug of a complete, nearly undamaged rocket, aroused the Polish Home Army intelligence to rapid action. Its head requested the commander of the Warsaw district of the Home Army to order the local commander to put at its disposal a covering force and to provide men for technical assistance. At the same time the new Research Committee, whose only task was the study of German secret weapons, was hastily alerted. This committee had been formed in March of the same year and had developed in step with the Study Bureau and the Economic Council; it was directly responsible to the head of intelligence;[5] since it was hoped that this would simplify the chain of command and expedite the transmission of information to the West. At its head stood Jerzy Chmielewski, whose fortunes require closer attention.

In September 1942, while he was engaged in setting up the Study Bureau, Chmielewski was arrested by the Gestapo.[6] Fortunately his arrest was quite by chance: the Germans did not know that he was a member of the resistance movement. After several months in *Pawiak* prison he was sent to Auschwitz, where he arrived on 13

May 1943.* Since the Germans were unaware of his role his family began to make efforts to obtain his release, helped by the sum of 150,000 złotys provided by the Home Army. These efforts were successful; in the autumn of 1943 Chmielewski was returned to the jail in Warsaw, and he was released on the 4th March of the following year. This was a remarkably rare occurrence, and it is quite extraordinary that engineer Antoni Kocjan, who was brought on to his Committee, had also been in Auschwitz and had also been quite unexpectedly freed.** The two men who were instrumental in discovering the details of the German secret weapons had therefore both been in German hands and both been released by them.

The information about the rocket electrified the Committee, and Kocjan immediately formed two teams of experts, who prepared to leave for the Bug. The first team was briefed only to acquaint itself with conditions on the spot, while the second team, with all the necessary equipment, was to dismantle the rocket, extract from it all the most important parts, take photographs, make drawings and prepare a detailed report.

After a few days, when the Germans seemed to have given up looking for the rocket, underground soldiers from the twenty-second Home Army regiment came during the night and, after struggling for several hours, pulled their trophy out of the bog with the help of three pairs of horses. It was loaded onto two carts joined together and was transported to a barn in the village of Hołowczyce-Kolonia.

When the preliminary examination of the missile was completed, Kocjan arrived from Warsaw accompanied by his closest colleague, Stefan Waciórski, and several other specialists. Two scientists and members of the Research Committee, Professor Janusz Groszkowski, a radio expert, and Professor Marceli Struszyński, a specialist in propellants, were waiting in Warsaw for the results of

* The author arrived in Auschwitz in the same transport and was given the camp number 121421, while Chmielewski's was 121390. Together with several dozen other prisoners from this transport they were both sent after a few days to the Penal Company, where they got to know each other better. Chmielewski stood out because of a certain tendency towards exhibitionism, which could be very dangerous.
** See Chapter Three.

the examination and the rocket parts.

The team got down to the slow and difficult job of dismantling the complicated mechanism, which consisted of more than 25,000 parts. The work had to be done quickly but carefully, for it was not known whether the rocket was carrying a warhead or any corrosive fluids. It was also hard to forget that everything was taking place in an area closely patrolled by the Germans.

The work of dismantling and describing the rocket slowly proceeded, and in the meantime urgent dispatches concerning this Polish find went back and forth between London and Warsaw.[7] In England this was a time of great activity; although it was a secret, the Allies were readying themselves for a landing on the coast of northern France. There was much speculation as to how the Germans were preparing themselves. The initiated knew that launching-pads for the V-1 flying bombs had already been constructed in Normandy, and that, despite bombing, some of them would be operational. There were fears that the enemy also had the V-2 rockets ready, and that, after the Allied landing had begun, the rockets would be used to destroy the ports in the south of England and cut off the invasion forces from their supplies and reinforcements.

Kocjan's team eventually succeeded in dismantling, photographing and describing the rocket. Many undamaged parts of its mechanism were removed, among them a radio-transmitter numbered 0984. Waciórski at once hit on the idea of constructing equipment to override the Germans' radio control and actually steer the rocket.[8] British specialists had similar ideas, but their thinking took a more realistic direction: they believed that even with a special piece of radio equipment they would be able only to divert the rocket from its course.[9] The German radio was sent to Warsaw where it found its way into the hands of Professor Groszkowski. Some of the corrosive fluid was collected and sent to Professor Struszyński. After analysis he declared that it was extremely highly-concentrated hydrogen peroxide. This information was then sent straight to London.[10]

The work on the recovered rocket was going well and had reached a critical stage. Engineer Kocjan went backwards and forwards between the Bug and Warsaw and only once a week did he spend the night in his small flat in the capital, where he could take a rest. He was at the height of his underground success; he was doing what interested him most and he knew that what he was doing was important and necessary. But ill-fortune intervened.

On the last day of May 1944, a Wednesday (the day he used to get home to see his wife and spend the night under his own roof), he arrived at the flat just before curfew, kissed his wife, washed, had a quick supper, went to bed early to read, and fell asleep. Suddenly he was woken by a noise. Someone was pounding at the door, shouting in German. There was no way of escaping: the door had to be opened. Two armed soldiers and two civilians came into the flat: 'Antoni Kocjan?' 'Yes.' 'Get dressed, both of you!'

The soldiers stood by the door while the civilians flashed their torches into every corner, pulled out drawers, threw the contents of the cupboard onto the floor and made a thorough search of the bed. Dawn was breaking by the time the police van brought them to the *Pawiak* prison.

At the first interrogation it appeared that the case was not hopeless. The Gestapo had uncovered a Home Army printing-press in the basement of an experimental glider factory which Kocjan had directed before the war. His connection with the place had been swiftly established, his address discovered and the raid carried out.

It was already the fifth year of the war and the Eastern front, which was advancing quickly westwards, was by now not far from the Polish capital. Kocjan was easily able to prove that he had nothing to do with the printing-press, so the Gestapo, less zealous than formerly and seeing the chance of a ransom, behaved correctly. Discreet intervention from outside, backed by money, brought about his wife's release, and he had been promised the same himself when ill-luck struck again. Kocjan had unfortunately failed to observe the basic rules of resistance work; instead of concentrating solely on secret German aerial weapons, and later the V-2, which was work of the utmost importance, he was also engaged in the secret production of hand grenades. While he was waiting for interrogation in a transit cell at Gestapo H.Q. he was seen by a liaison-girl from the same team, who had also been arrested. She was tortured to reveal her contacts and, knowing hardly anyone and seeing the engineer, she grasped at this chance. Under great pressure she named him and said what it was he did.

Instead of being released, he was cruelly interrogated. He was beaten so badly that he was taken back to the prison on a stretcher; his fingers were broken and he was burned with hot irons. When he lost consciousness from the pain, freezing water was poured over him and he was revived by electric shocks. Yet he managed to keep silent, so the work on the recovered rocket continued uninterrupted.[11]

5

The gigantic operation of the invasion of the Continent—the largest and probably most complicated in history, involving the army, navy and air forces, and troops from many different countries—depended to a great degree on accurate weather reports.

Precise and laborious preparations had been planned and effected long ago, all the instructions had been issued, every possible contingency been foreseen, every misunderstanding between the multi-lingual forces ironed out, every personal ambition appeased; but there remained one problem which human ingenuity had not yet learned to control: the weather.

General Eisenhower, whose desk was cluttered with various coloured telephones, was continually picking up one or another of them, but most frequently he reached for the set linking him with his meteorological officers. They had promised good weather for the beginning of June, but errors and unexpected changes had crept into their calculations; it was raining, a strong wind was blowing, the sea was rough and low cloud made precise air operations impossible. Several times a day the senior commanders met, considered, discussed and made suggestions. Eisenhower, thought by many to be more of a political than a military figure, a pre-war colonel raised to the highest position of Commander-in-Chief by President Roosevelt for his great qualities as a mediator, preferred to listen to others rather than to press on them his own opinions. He had, of course, to issue the final order himself, but he manoeuvred so that this should be the unanimous decision of the other Commanders, or at least of a decisive majority and not just his alone.

The south coast of England was packed to capacity with

transport, guns, tanks, every kind of armament and crowds of soldiers, who, in the tension, did not seem to know how to pass the time. They filled every available bar and café waiting, lost their last pounds and dollars at cards, and roamed around in gangs assaulting girls, fighting each other, looking for unusual uniforms and attacking intruders speaking another language, or even their own with a different accent. The military police had never a dull moment and the detention areas were overflowing.

The invasion preparations were surrounded by the strictest security and only a handful of people knew all the details; even though everyone was aware that the attack would take place any day now, no-one knew the actual day. Everything was done to keep the Germans guessing. The second surprise was to be the direction of the assault. The Germans were trying to read the thoughts of the Allies crouching on the other side of the Channel, and they had to be outwitted: the assault had to take place where the enemy least expected it.

It was cloudy at daybreak on the 5th of June; the sea was rough and visibility was poor. General Eisenhower had hardly slept all night; he crashed about his caravan in a bad mood and every few minutes went outside to look at the sky and examine the grey horizon. The meteorologists did not promise much, but they had provided one piece of information that had stuck in the General's thoughts and was slowly making up his mind for him: there might be a sudden change in the weather. Yesterday's conferences had shown that everyone had had enought of waiting and that they would easily accept any decision to act. The General also knew that the soldiers on the coast could not take much more. And the Germans? The bad weather could only cause them to relax their vigilance. He called yet another conference.

Several hours passed and, under cover of the last hours of darkness, the huge armada slowly drew away from the English coast. It had already once before been recalled, but this time there was no turning back. The ships carried vast amounts of the most up-to-date military equipment, and behind them came landing-craft. On thick steel ropes they towed artificial harbours and break-waters, and along the Channel bottom they were dragging rubber hosepipes, through which, within a few·hours, petrol was to flow. On the decks, in the cabins, in the passageways teemed a human mass in uniform, protected by metal helmets, criss-crossed by straps and laden down with weapons. Cigarette ends glowed, hearts beat more quickly. The sky was filled with the ceaseless roar of countless squadrons bearing great payloads of bombs, on their way to crush the German bunkers and open the way for the assault units.

During the preceding weeks Allied bombers had ceaselessly attacked the area around Boulogne, Calais and Dunkirk, the shortest distance from the British Isles and within artillery range.[12] But the invasion was moving in another direction. It was heading for an area to the east of the Cherbourg peninsula, over 100 kilometres away from England, where the cliffs were high, steep and inaccessible, where there were no natural harbours and where no-one expected it.

6

In Poland the Soviet/German front had already rolled across the eastern part of the country, and in Warsaw the Home Army Research Committee, together with the Economic Council, was busy collating the information gathered from the river Bug. After urgent requests for haste from London,[13] it had been settled that the details of this find should be sent to Britain by the speediest route, so work was now in progress on a clear, concise resumé. A report was drawn up called 'Special Report 1/R, no. 242'. It consisted of a text of 4,000 words, supplemented by 80 photographs and 12 drawings, a sketch-map of the artillery range at Blizna and a list of rocket firings. There were three appendices with additional information. The whole report was supported by first-class material evidence: eight parts from the original rocket.

The report, together with the bag containing the V-2 parts, had to be carried to London by someone who not only had worked on its preparation but had a technical background and was well acquainted with the whole question of German secret weapons, and in particular the V-2. The only candidate who fulfilled all the requirements (and he was ideally suited in other ways too) was Engineer Kocjan; but he was in the hands of the Gestapo. Many other candidates were considered for the task and the choice finally fell on Chmielewski. He had no technical training, and for more than a year had been away from underground work in a German camp and prison, but he had taken part in the preparation of the report, had acquainted himself with the details of the recovered rocket and was enterprising and confident.[14]

7

Among the most technically difficult and most secret operations of the last war was the air link to enemy-occupied territory. This link required not only aircraft capable of coping with improvised landing-grounds, but well-trained crews, reception committees familiar with the use of landing-lights, and finally an airstrip itself on territory occupied and patrolled by the enemy. Furthermore, there had to be faultless radio communications between the aircraft's home base and its destination.

Where the distances involved were small and the destination was France or Holland, the RAF used the Lysander, a slow, single-engined machine with a range of barely 650 kilometres, but weighing only 4½ tons and capable of taking off within about 400 metres. For longer-range missions Hudsons were used; and when after the capture of southern Italy in 1944 it became possible to make flights from there to Poland, unarmed two-engined Dakotas were introduced. These planes needed a landing-ground of about one square kilometre, since the direction of the wind governed landings and take-offs. The surface had to be hard enough for the wheels not to sink further than a few inches (experience showed that the best top surface was a field sown with clover).

The reception committee had to contain not only experts on night lighting, radio and the speedy evacuation of incoming passengers and equipment, but very often also partisans, covering the airstrip in case of German attack. This was vital in Poland, and there was one case where a secret night operation was guarded by 800 underground solders.[15]

The landings could take place only at night, and the difficult business of guiding the aircraft onto these primitive airfields was done by lights laid out on the ground. Sometimes this was inadequate, so in 1943 two pieces of radio equipment were introduced. One of these, called *Eureka,* was used on the actual landing-ground. It was a VHF (ultra-short wave) transmitter with a range of about 60 kilometres. In the aircraft a receiving device called *Rebecca* was installed. Nevertheless the system of lights sometimes turned out to be more effective, and in Poland it was the only system used. *Eureka* was heavy, weighing about 50 kg, and furthermore required trained users, which the underground soldiers, recruited in the local villages, could not always provide.

The communications link between Britain and the secret landing-grounds on the Continent (each of which had to have a radio receiver) was organized by the BBC using its normal programmes with a system of codes, which were 'reserved' tunes, known only to a few people in BBC head-quarters and to those gathered at the secret airfields. The playing of a particular tune was the signal for an operation, an aircraft departure or its recall. This radio link with Poland was code-named *Iodoform.*[16]

Of all the countries to which aircraft flew from the British Isles, Poland was the farthest away, so although parachutists and supplies were dropped there, no attempts at landing had been made before 1944, since the heavy Halifax and Liberator bombers were incapable of landing on rough strips. Only at the end of 1943, when the operational bases for these missions were transferred to southern Italy did secret landings in Poland become feasible. The first one was carried out on the night of 15/16 April 1944 and the second on 29/30 May; preparations were now underway for the third. This was to be the most important, since the aircraft was to bring back information on the V-2 rockets for London. In Poland the whole operation was code-named *Most* (which means 'bridge'), and in London *Wildhorn.* This third landing, now being set up, was called *Wildhorn III.*

On 12 July the commander of the Home Army signed 'Special Report I/R no.242' about the V-2; the bag of parts was packed and Chmielewski, under the new code-name of *Rafał,* was ready to leave. But he was not the only passenger to fly from Poland. The aircraft had still to take Tomasz Arciszewski (*Tom*), a veteran of the Polish Socialist Party, nominated by the underground Council of National Unity as the successor to the President of the Polish Republic; Józef Retinger (*Salamander*)—a special emissary from Prime Minister Churchill and the Polish Government—who, at the age of 56, had parachuted into Poland during the night of 3/4 April 1944 on a secret political mission; and with him his inseparable aide, political courier Tadeusz Chciuk (*Celt*), and Second Lieutenant Czesław Miciński, who was in command of the whole group.

Under normal conditions the Dakota could take them without any difficulty, but problems had to be foreseen and so an order of priority in which the westbound group was to board the aircraft had been laid down in advance. If for any reason the aircraft could not take them all, this order of priority would decide who was to leave. First of all came the bag with the V-2 parts together with Chmielewski, since he carried the report and had memorized a great many other details; after him came Retinger, then Arciszewski and finally Miciński and Chciuk.[17] In fact, Retinger had hurt his leg badly on landing after his jump and, later, on the way to the secret landing-ground, had fallen into some water and had become partially paralysed, so Chciuk in the end had to stay with him to carry him.

The airfield chosen for this operation was one abandoned by the Germans, near the town of Tarnów in southern Poland. It had been given the code-name *Motyl* (Butterfly), and the second landing had taken place there successfully. All the passengers gathered during the last half of July in secret quarters not far from *Motyl*. The operation was important and had been given top priority, but the flight could not be fixed beforehand for any definite night, since everything depended on the weather.

On 25 July, the weather report at eight o'clock in the evening was good enough for a Dakota to take off from Brindisi carrying 4 officers and 19 suitcases of various equipment. The crew was British, but the aircraft was piloted by Stanley George Culliford, a New Zealander, while the co-pilot and interpreter was a Pole, Flight Lieutenant Kazimierz Szrajer.

The weather was favourable and the flight uneventful, yet the whole operation was very nearly called off. The Eastern front now ran through the very centre of Poland, and the territory still in German hands was crowded with units retreating westwards: the *Motyl* landing-ground was threatened. A detachment of German airmen moved in not far away and two German Storch reconnaissance planes landed on the airstrip. They took off again shortly afterwards, but there could be no certainty that they would not return and only the optimism of the despatch officer Captain Włodzimierz Gedymin (*Włodek*), kept him from sending an urgent message cancelling the whole operation. The Blizna area, after being held for a few days by Polish partisans, was already in Soviet hands,[18] while in Warsaw Home Army units daily expected the order to rise against the Germans.

The night landing went off efficiently, although it far from fulfilled all the conditions of secrecy which a stranger to these operations might have expected. Twice the Dakota had to overfly the landing-ground which it lit up with the sharp glare of its twin searchlights and, when it climbed after its first unsuccessful run, the roar of its engines shattered the night silence. When it finally landed it was surrounded by a crowd of underground soldiers, local boys from the neighbouring villages, some of them barefoot, strangely dressed, variously armed, friendly but noisy. The landing was, of course, covered by a partisan unit, and it was a success; but if it had taken place a few years earlier it could easily have been a disaster.

Haste was necessary. The incoming passengers climbed out and vanished into the night with their luggage, and then the westbound group began to get on board. The order of priority was not observed, for it hardly seemed to matter. Arciszewski climbed in followed by Chmielewski with the bag. Chciuk carried in the helpless Retinger on his back and Miciński got aboard last. Flight Lieutenant Szrajer counted them, slammed the door and gave the pilot the signal to take off.

The engines roared, the aircraft vibrated, moved forward a few inches and stopped. It had been raining for the last few days and the ground was soft; the wheels had sunk in and made take-off impossible.

Flight Lieutenant Szrajer, the link between the crew and passengers, climbed out with the pilot and together they carefully examined the undercarriage. The wheels had sunk further into the soft grass than had been expected. After discussing the matter with the despatch officer they ordered all the passengers to get out and the baggage to be unloaded to decrease the weight of the aircraft, and the soldiers of the reception team were ordered to dig small trenches in front of the aircraft's wheels and fill them with straw.

Once this was done, Retinger was again carried aboard, the bag of V-2 parts was loaded on, the remaining passengers climbed in and the luggage was thrown on behind them. The shrieking engines rang out over the slumbering fields and must have awakened every German for miles around—but the enemy was completely exhausted by hundreds of miles of retreat from the ruthless Eastern front, and only extreme danger could have aroused them now. Unfortunately the plane still refused to move and once more the door was opened and everyone ordered to get out.[19]

The crew was now faced with the prospect of following instructions which required them to set fire to the aircraft if take-off should prove impossible; but this was a final resort to be used when there was no other way out. Flight Lieutenant Szrajer together with the despatch officer once again walked round the aircraft, examined the wheels and the ground beneath them and decided to make just one more attempt. The soldiers ran to the carts, brought over boards and laid them under the wheels. For the third time the wretched passengers were told to board. This time the order of priority might have been important. Only two people knew it: Flight Lieutenant Szrajer and Captain Gedymin, but they both stayed silent. Retinger was once again carried aboard, the rest of the passengers clambered in and the luggage was loaded on. Eighty minutes had passed since the aircraft had landed and the short July night was beginning to brighten into dawn.

This time, at last, the Dakota began to move, and its take-off was accompanied by the joyful shouts of the underground soldiers who ran alongside waving their weapons and caps.

The flight to Brindisi was without incident, although they had trouble raising the undercarriage. On take-off, believing the brakes to have jammed, they had cut the connecting cables and drained off the brake-fluid. They landed in Brindisi without brakes.[20]

After a night's rest while the Dakota was overhauled, the passengers flew on down to Rabat in north Africa. There the Polish premier, Stanisław Mikołajczyk, was to touch down briefly on his way to Moscow for talks with Stalin, so Arciszewski, Retinger and Chciuk left the plane, while Miciński and Chmielewski, with his bag, flew on to London.

They landed on 28 July, and British officers immediately tried to claim the precious bag. But Chmielewski told them that he had been ordered to hand it over only to authorized representatives of the Polish Staff.* That same day the bag and the report were in the hands of the VIth Bureau. Its head, Lieutenant-Colonel Marian Utnik, ordered the document to be deciphered immediately and brought to him in instalments. From him it went, also in instalments, to the IInd Bureau (Intelligence), which immediately handed over everything to British intelligence, including the bag. With relatively little delay the fruits of the Polish efforts reached their proper destination, the *Crossbow* Committee, in whose hands lay the threads of all information on German secret weapons.[21]

---

* In his account written after the war (M. Wojewódzki, op,cit., pp.463-473) — an account containing many errors and misinterpretations—Chmielewski relates a series of dramatic details about the flight to London and the delivery of the bag and accompanying report into the right hands. According to him, two English officers approached him on the airfield and asked for the bag; he answered by producing a knife. Then he says they drove him to a farm and threatened to shoot him if he did not hand over the bag with the V-2 parts, for Churchill had been waiting for it for several days. Chmielewski claims to have replied: 'That Mr Churchill had been waiting for this package several days does not concern me. In Poland we have been waiting four years for Mr Churchill, so he can wait a few hours for us.' Whether or not he made this remark, it must be remembered that Chmielewski had been sent to London on an extremely important mission with instructions to hand over the report and bag to an authorized Polish officer. He was thus justified in acting as he did. But he had not been authorized to express his own views in such an arrogant fashion. The contribution of Polish intelligence to the Allied war effort depended on their getting their findings to the West as soon as possible. Not only was London threatened, but also the invasion, and the British officers' impatience was perfectly understandable.

# CHAPTER NINE

## First V-1 against England; the attempt on Hitler's life; V-2 in British hands; *SS* and V weapons; first V-2 on London; Arnhem; the last offensive in Ardennes.

1

From 6 June 1944, for several days, fierce fighting went on along the French coast and the outcome fluctuated from hour to hour. The Allies had a great technical advantage and the surprise had been complete, but forcing a landing on the rocky coast was difficult, and it was defended by well-trained, courageous and disciplined German soldiers, aware of the importance of the landing. The first attack might have ended differently, if there had not been one decisive German weakness: lack of air support. By the middle of 1944 the Germans were short of petrol and their air force had dwindled. Young pilots, forced into other duties, including even the guarding of concentration camps, looked up into the skies in frustration while British and American bombers flew with impunity over the coastal fortifications reducing them to rubble.

The invasion was successful. The Allies held fast on the beaches and each day enlarged their modest gains, but the Command was very cautious in its assessment of these first successes. German resistance was still far from broken; every newly-won kilometre of land was paid for by heavy losses and intelligence agents were reporting that the enemy would any day bring into the conflict his secret weapon, the flying bomb. It was hard to estimate the real strength of this threat, let alone guess where the bomb might fall. It might be aimed at London or it might be destined for the ports in the south of England, which harboured the ships sailing with supplies for the invasion armies.

On the German side Colonel Wachtel was working feverishly at preparing his V-1 sites for a concentrated attack, but frequent bombings hindered and delayed these preparations. Of more than 100 launching-pads, less than 20 remained. This number later rose to 55, thanks to good camouflage and last-minute assembly, but the difficulties were enormous. All the railway lines and the main roads came under a constant avalanche of bombs; the quality of the weapons that did arrive left much to be desired, and Wachtel himself was given no peace by his superiors, who accused him of being slow and careless, and even threatened him with a court-martial. No-one understood the technical difficulties, or wanted to hear of them. The objective of the attack was to be London: Hitler was frantic for revenge and had put the capital higher on the list than any strategic target.[1]

At last, at about four o'clock in the morning of 13 June, the moment came for which the German Command had been waiting for months: with a roar, ten flying bombs left their 'ski-jumps'. Three exploded at once; one fell not far away and never went off; and six glided in the direction of London. Of these, four fell on English soil—one near Gravesend, the second near Cuckfield, the third in Bethnal Green and the fourth in Sevenoaks.[2]

Casualties were small, only six people died, and the precision of range appeared to be poor: but that did not alter the fact that the fabled secret weapon had at last been used. And these first bombs were believed to be only the beginning, a foretaste of something far more dangerous.

Great Britain had been preparing for this attack for many months and it came as no surprise. Intelligence reports had indicated London as the almost certain target, so the city was protected by three lines of defence. The nearest to the city, just over the southern suburbs, was 500 (later 2,000) barrage balloons; the next, further to the south, consisted of 400 batteries of anti-craft artillery; the last, fighter squadrons of Spitfires, Tempests and Typhoons. Thirteen squadrons of one-man, and nine of two-man aircraft were deployed, from which everything non-essential had been removed, and which had been specially painted to increase the speed. In spite of these improvements, the planes still had to get above the V-1s and dive in order to overtake them. When this was successful, the flying bomb could be destroyed either by gunfire, or by tipping its wings with the wings of the aircraft and thus forcing it to crash-land before reaching its target.[3]

A race began between Wachtel's launching-pads, which operated more efficiently every day, and the defences of London, which also improved as time went on. Barely a week had passed and Wachtel, commanding from a bunker in Sâleux, near Amiens, 24 metres underground, had already fired his five-hundredth bomb. Many of them exploded immediately after launching, and many were destroyed on the way, but some of them attained their objective and caused considerable damage. One of them hit the Guards' Chapel of the Wellington Barracks and killed 121 people, including 63 officers and servicemen. On 29 June the number of V-1s fired reached 2,000; on 22 July, 5,000. But the invasion of the Continent was going steadily forward, so Colonel Wachtel's soldiers were forced to leave their launching-pads at intervals and retreat eastwards. On 23 August, Wachtel had to leave his bunker in Sâleux and set up a new command post in Roubaix, near the Belgian frontier. As the Germans lost territory in France they started to attack London from the east, dropping flying bombs from Heinkel aircraft; but their own losses were heavy.

At first the British had serious problems with their defences, especially with the anti-craft artillery stationed in the southern suburbs of London. It was getting good results, but every flying bomb shot down fell all the same on the capital and caused damage. Therefore in the middle of July all the batteries were redeployed on the coast. According to the Hill Report these defences achieved the following results: fighter planes shot down 1,847 bombs, the artillery 1,878 and the barrage balloons 232.

Besides defending the city, the Allies attacked launching-pads in France and later in Holland. But the invasion of the Continent was still in progress, and air support was much needed; so some of the commanders, especially the Americans, disapproved of the bombing of targets not related to the invasion at that time. However, they were persuaded and about 40% of the bombing raids were directed at objectives indicated by the *Crossbow* Committee.

The casualties resulting from the V-1 attacks were grave. 5,864 people were killed; 17,197 seriously and 23,174 slightly injured; 24,491 buildings were totally destroyed and 52,293 so badly damaged that the inhabitants were forced to leave.[4]

The V-1 bombing had two further consequences. On the one hand, Churchill decided that his son-in-law, Duncan Sandys, should once again take over the investigation of the V-1 and V-2

and become Chairman of the *Crossbow* Committee charged with
the responsibility for reporting to the War Cabinet the effects of
the German offensive and the progress of counter-measures. On
the other, Hitler decided to restrict production of the rockets to 150
a month and channel the surplus work-force and materials into
rapid mass-production of the V-1.[5] This weapon was already
causing deaths and destruction in London, and the leader of the
Third *Reich* saw in it a factor which might tip the balance of the
fortunes of the war. Not everyone in Germany, however, shared his
hopes and enthusiasm.

2

Colonel Claus Schenk von Stauffenberg, in spite of the black patch
over his right eye and the lack of one arm, which he lost in the war
in the desert, was still a fine-looking man. It was 20 July 1944, and
he and his adjutant had just got out of a car and for the second time
shown their papers to an *SS* guard inside the 'Wolf's Lair', Hitler's
field-quarters in East Prussia. It was only 10 am and the daily staff
briefing began at 12.30 pm, so there was still time to eat breakfast
in the Officers Mess and report to the Chief of Headquarters, Field
Marshal Keitel.

Von Stauffenberg behaved quite normally, talked and joked,
and nobody would have suspected that his nerves were stretched
almost to breaking-point. The Colonel was a member of a
conspiracy, together with a number of military commanders and
politicians, and in his brief-case he was carrying a high-explosive
bomb, meant for Hitler.[6]

Twelve o'clock struck and the colonel had to pass the third
guard-post, this time manned by officers, to reach Zone A. Only
the most trusted men were allowed in since it was from here that
Hitler ruled Germany and personally commanded operations on
the Eastern front. Permits, a different one for each guard, had to
be shown by everyone, but the colonel's silhouette was so
impressive and his war wounds so obvious that the *SS*-men quickly
glanced at his papers and saluted respectfully.

Generally the daily briefing took place in a concrete bunker with
stout walls and arches, but it was such a hot day that at the last

moment everything had been moved out to a neighbouring wooden barrack, which was sometimes used as a tea-room. Around a large oak table on which was a map 24 men were gathered, among them Hitler, Field Marshal Keitel, Generals Alfred Jodl, Karl Bodenschatz, Adolf Heusinger, Günter Korten, Rudolf Schmundt, Walter Warlimont and others. Punctually at 12.30 pm, General Heusinger began to read a report on the situation at the Eastern front. A few minutes later von Stauffenberg came in and Keitel presented him to Hitler as Chief of Staff of the reserve army. For a moment the Colonel found himself standing next to the *Führer*, at his right hand. He tucked his lethal brief case under the table: a few minutes earlier, with three fingers of his crippled left hand, he had set the time-fuse. Then he was suddenly called to the telephone. He went out quickly, met his adjutant and they both made for the first inside guard post. They should have passed through it at once, but the Colonel preferred to wait a moment. He was worried by the fact that the briefing had been moved from the bunker. In the bunker the bomb's explosion would have been bound to kill all those present; but the result might be different in the wooden barrack.

At 12.43 pm the explosion was heard; the roof of the barrack was blown off and the bodies of the officers assembled there, among them Hitler's, were seen flying through the air. Two minutes later, amidst the immediate bewilderment, von Stauffenberg passed the sentries and drove to the airport. He flew off to Berlin in the Heinkel 111 waiting for him, quite convinced that his mission had been successful.[7]

Unfortunately this was not so. One of the officers had felt the brief case under his legs, and had pushed it behind the thick table leg. This shielded Hitler, who was blown out of the barrack by the explosion and escaped with burns and a wounded right hand. At the moment that the high-level conspirators in Berlin were awaiting the arrival of von Stauffenberg to confirm the telephone message they had received of Hitler's death, wounds were being dressed at 'Wolf's Lair'. Four officers died in the explosion. Hitler, after the first shock and some medical attention, concentrated all his efforts on taking control of the situation, above all in Berlin. He also had to hide his pain and fury, for in the afternoon he was to see Mussolini, who had arrived at his quarters that same day.[8] At half-past five the first telephone call between the *Führer* and the

Minister of Propaganda, Goebbels, took place. In Berlin the latter was proving to be energetic and resourceful. Shortly afterwards Hitler spoke by telephone to Major Remer, the commander of the Berlin duty battalion, and the search for the conspirators intensified.

It turned out that the conspirators, although possessing a wide-spread network and supporters in the highest military ranks in Paris, Vienna, Prague and Kassel, were unable to show the decisiveness and energy which might have gained them victory in the first few hours during which it was supposed that Hitler was dead. A number of the officers in the plot drew back at the last moment, and the duty battalion and the *SS* units soon had the situation under control. Within twenty hours of the explosion the bodies of the more prominent conspirators, among them that of von Stauffenberg, lay in the yard of a military building in Berlin.[9]

3

The end of July was hot and uncomfortable for London too. Flying-bombs were falling on the city, from the northern coasts of France came the rumble of heavy fighting, and the *Crossbow* Committee was working feverishly on the riddle of the second German secret weapon, the V-2. The results of investigation to date showed that the rockets could be more dangerous than the V-1 and, worse still, there appeared to be no defence against them. The Committee therefore tried to re-construct a prototype of this dangerous weapon and collect every possible scrap of information about it.

On 28 July, when Jerzy Chmielewski arrived in London with his sack and the report concerning the rocket acquired in Poland, the *Crossbow* Committee was at once informed and showed great interest; but it was not as enthusiastic as might have been expected, for it so happened that several days earlier a similar trophy had arrived from another source.

Although the ballistic tests had been transferred to Poland, the Germans had re-built Peenemünde East, chiefly the Research Establishment, and had resumed test flights of the V-2, although on a much smaller scale. On 13 June a rocket was fired from there, which, quite exceptionally, was equipped with a radio mechanism allowing it to be steered by remote control. This was a test of a mechanism designed not for the V-2 but for an anti-aircraft missile called *Wasserfall*. The test was a failure; the rocket flew too far and came down near Malmö in southern Sweden. The local authorities put the fragments under guard and informed Stockholm. A few days later everything that could be gathered up was in the care of the Swedish Air Force. The British heard about the rocket and towards the end of June two experts travelled to Stockholm. Sweden was a neutral country but sympathetic towards the Western Allies, so she agreed to give up two tons of the fragments collected. An American, Lieutenant-Colonel Keith N. Allen, flew to fetch them in a Dakota C-47; he brought most of the fragments to London on 16 July, and the rest came over at the end of the month.[10]

At last the scientists had got what they had been waiting for for so long. In Farnborough, near London, a huge tent was hastily put up, all the fragments of the Swedish rocket were taken there and a group of experts got down to work. Within two weeks the missile had been reconstructed and the answers found to several important questions.

Above all the pyrotechnical experts discovered to their great relief that the explosive load could not exceed one ton, so fears of five or even ten ton loads were allayed. The steering mechanism was reconstructed and to their astonishment it was established that the rocket was propelled by liquid fuel—alcohol and oxygen.[11] This was an important discovery, for so far Dr Jones, on the basis of the despatch from Poland of 12 June, had been of the opinion that the rocket's fuel was based on highly-concentrated hydrogen peroxide.

Some light was also thrown on a further problem, and here the fragments brought from Poland were very valuable, although they came into the experts' hands only at the very end of their examination. A radio apparatus, adapted to remote control, had been found in the rocket from Sweden, and the British scientists came to the conclusion that the Germans had already solved the problem of remote control and that all the V-2s would have such an apparatus. The radio No.0984 brought from Poland, was, however, simply an apparatus for receiving and transmitting signals, without any means of remote control. The experts breathed more freely: the terrible German weapon was not as dangerous as had appeared at first.

The comparison between the Swedish and Polish finds had now brought home to the British the true nature of the V-2,[12] and the threat was taken very seriously in London. Churchill attended several meetings of the *Crossbow* Committee and the War Cabinet decided that preparations should be put in hand for the evacuation of a million inhabitants, and that all the city's hospitals should be emptied to make room for the victims of the expected attack. The gravity of the situation was intensified by reports from Intelligence which, by the observation of transports, had come to the conclusion that the Germans already possessed about a thousand rockets and with each day would have more. Unlike the V-1, there was no defence against the new weapon, and bombing the launching-pads would be almost impossible since they were invisible from the air. Only the great bunkers in Watten and Wizernes and the lines of communication could be attacked.

At the beginning of July the Eastern front was approaching Blizna and Polish partisan units decided to take the testing-ground which was being evacuated. This was achieved, and for several days it was in Polish hands; but on 20 July the Germans managed to recapture it. They did not gain much by this, for a week later they were pushed out for good by the Red Army.[13]

The British discovered this through reconnaissance flights, and on 28 July the *Crossbow* Committee decided that a military mission should be sent as quickly as possible to examine things on the spot.[14] Churchill had been in contact with Stalin since June on this matter and had obtained his consent, so two days later an Anglo-American group left for Teheran under the command of Colonel T.R.B. Sanders. With them as interpreter went a young Russian-speaking reporter, David Floyd. The Soviet authorities themselves wished to collect any material left on the testing-ground after the hasty German evacuation, so the Allied mission was held up by one pretext after another and did not get to the place until 2 September. There it collected only about one-and-a-half tons of materials and a small number of documents. The mission confirmed that the rockets were propelled by alcohol and liquid oxygen, and was able to estimate exactly the capacity of the tanks,[15] but in the light of the information recieved in London from Sweden and Poland it was too late to be useful.*

## 4

After the unsuccessful attempt on Hitler's life the SS took over everything connected with the rockets. Several high-ranking officers had been involved in the plot and Hitler had lost confidence in the army as a result. Hans Kammler, Himmler's right-hand man in charge of the V-2, immediately doubled his activities.

The Germans were still faced with three problems: further ballistic experiments, mass production and the long-awaited operational use of the weapon. After the evacuation of Blizna the ballistic tests had been transferred to the testing-ground *Heidekraut,* in the Tucholska Forest in Polish Pomerania. There, on 8 September, firings began and it was at last discovered why so many of the rockets were exploding in the air. It appeared that the fuel-tanks were not standing up to the great heat and vibration and were bursting. In the underground factory in Nordhausen they now strengthened the tanks with steel reinforcing sleeves, and the number of 'air-bursts' fell considerably.[16]

Work went on constantly on these problems under Kammler's direction, and the day was approaching when the rockets were to become operational. Up to then the preparations had been made by the LXV Army Corps, to which Colonel Wachtel and his V-1 catapults were subordinate.[17] Now, when the work had reached its climax, Himmler could not allow any one but himself to be in charge of the first rocket attack against London.

For the last day of August Hans Kammler called a special meeting in Brussels, at which the final decisions of the planned attack were to be taken. The command of the LXV Corps heard

---

* The mission had to return to London via Moscow. The crates were to be freighted by the Russian authorities to the Air Ministry in London. When they arrived they were found to contain, not rocket specimens, but worthless parts of crashed aircraft (D. Irving, op.cit, p.285).

about this'and immediatèly protested, for on their behalf General Richard Metz was supposed to direct the rocket offensive. Telephones started to ring, the matter was referred to Hitler himself, and victory went to the *SS*. The Corps was still to be responsible for the technical preparations for the attack and for its outcome, but Kammler was to have overall authority, subordinate not to the High Command but to Himmler. This arrangement was nothing exceptional in Hitler's Germany.

Preparations for the offensive against London had been set in train long ago with the construction of the two huge bunkers in Watten and in Wizernes; but the Allied air forces had reduced them to rubble. Now, thanks to the successful invasion, the whole of northern France was lost in any case. There was no help for it: the forty-five sites planned between Cherbourg and Calais had to be forgotten and attention turned to Belgium. In that country a number of convenient positions between Tournai and Ghent were chosen, but the Allies were advancing so fast that only Holland remained. On 3 September Brussels fell and Kammler retreated to Wassenaar, near The Hague. He had at his disposal two artillery groups: Group North, comprising the first and second batteries of 485 Artillery Detachment; and Group South, comprising the second and third batteries of 836 Artillery Detachment and the long-established 444 battery. Group North was to bombard London; Group South would concentrate on Paris and other objectives on the European continent.

When the V-1 was put into action a few months earlier, many valuable lessons had been learned. Every attempt now had to be made to avoid the murderous attacks from the air. The V-1 'ski-jumps' had been set up in woods, at small farms and in narrow gorges: Kammler decided to do things differently, and for his V-2 launching-pads he chose The Hague itself and its near surroundings, which were densely populated. The Hague woods, the Duindigt estate on the edge of the city, the Beukenhorst park and the crossroads at Beuken Avenue were designated. Nearby places like Bloemandaal, Wassenaar, Loosduinen and Rijswijk were further chosen. Other launching-pads were envisaged at the Hook of Holland[18] and in Serooskerke on the Walcheren peninsula.[19] Battery 444 was sent to Euskirchen in Germany,to the west of Bonn.

The Hague was in grave danger, for there was no doubt that the Allies would have to attack the launching-pads as soon as they had pin-pointed them. Representatives of the civilian population tried to get the decision changed, but Kammler, designer of the gas chambers in Auschwitz, never for one moment thought of backing down.

Everything was now being done in great haste, for Hitler was getting impatient. The launching-pads themselves did not present any difficulty—a smallish metal or concrete slab sufficed—but the V-2 was a much bigger weapon than the V-1 and it took a convey of motor vehicles to transport them to the launching sites. Each battery consisted of three special tractors, each carrying a rocket and drawn by a half-track which also carried the firing-crew; behind them came three tankers, one for alcohol, one for liquid oxygen and the third for auxiliary fuels; then there was one generator truck for electric power and a truck which was the equivalent of a 'gun-director'; finally staff cars for the officers.[20]

Although the launching-pads were invisible from the air, the long convoy of vehicles, especially with such a load, was easily noticeable. So, in relevant places, the Germans ordered the evacuation of the inhabitants in an attempt to conceal the actual sites. Moreover, besides the very careful camouflage, they adopted the principle of constantly changing the firing-sites. They used to set up two or three rockets side by side, aim them at London or some other objective and then, immediately after firing, load up the vehicles again and set off elsewhere. Sometimes they returned and used the same site a few days later.[21]

The first operational firing took place on 6 September, but in the direction of Paris not London. It was carried out by Battery 444 which was probably given priority because it was ready first. The Germans would certainly have preferred an immediate attack on London, but the distance from Euskirchen was too great. The firing was only a partial success: of the two rockets only one reached the French capital. German propaganda wanted to keep this secret, to avoid losing the element of surprise.[22] London was the main objective of the long preparations.

Two days later, at about 6.30 pm, Hitler's dream finally came true: from the suburbs of The Hague the first two rockets glided away in the direction of London.

5

The Intelligence Service had warned several times that rockets would fall on London any day, but this was known only to the initiated; so the inhabitants of the sprawling city were greatly astonished when on 8 September, a few minutes before seven o'clock in the evening, they suddenly heard what sounded like two claps of thunder in the clear sky.* Then an explosion was heard in West London; the earth shook and several houses in Staveley Road in Chiswick disintegrated. From the rubble three dead bodies and seventeen seriously injured persons were dug out. Several seconds later two more thunder-claps were heard, an explosion followed at once and a great crater appeared in the ground near Epping, luckily without causing casualties.[23]

All the immediate witnesses maintained that these were not flying bombs, for the explosions had not been preceded by the characteristic 'putt-putt' (like the noise of a badly-silenced motorcycle engine) that they were all used to. But the experts knew; these were the first rockets.

Duncan Sandys, in constant contact with Civil Defence headquarters, received the news at once and drove to the scene of the explosion in Chiswick. The following day Dr Jones arrived. A quick inspection of the 30-foot crater allowed them to state with relief that the warhead was no bigger than one ton; so it seemed that the *Crossbow* Committee forecasts had been right. Strict censorship on the subject of these first explosions was ordered, and the experts urgently began considering preventive measures. It was already known that there was no defence possible against the rockets, so there remained only two possibilities: an attack from the air on the launching-pads or the speedy occupation of Holland, which would put London out of reach of the rockets.

Kammler's idea of firing the rockets from The Hague and other densely populated areas was ingenious, but it did not save him from air-raids. The Allies knew that there would be heavy casualties among the civilian population, so they did not employ 'carpet' bombing (saturating a wide area with bombs), but they could not

---

\* The same bang is heard to-day when a supersonic aircraft breaks the sound barrier.

renounce bombing altogether. Since there was no question of photographing the invisible launching-pads from the air, they had to rely on ground reports, to a great extent supplied by the Dutch Resistance Movement.

Holland, like other countries, fought on. The Royal family was in Great Britain as was the Dutch Government; the large merchant fleet crossed the ocean with supplies for the Allied armies; a great part of the Navy fought under British command; several squadrons of the Air Force had been reformed, and in Holland an underground movement operated, assisted by the Dutch section of SOE. The Dutch had suffered a terrible blow; the Germans had managed to get hold of the code which London used to communicate with the underground, and over fifty SOE agents, dropped by parachute in Holland, had fallen into the hands of the *Gestapo*.[24] The subsequent arrests had embraced thousands of men and women. Yet the underground movement recovered enough to rebuild part of its wrecked cadres, and it was still operating.

Immediately after the firing of the first two rockets from Koekoekslaan, the local underground unit sent a radio despatch to London, giving the exact position of the launching-pad.[25] The next despatch, sent by courier through underground channels, came from Serooskerke on the peninsula of Walcheren, and it was the more interesting in that it also contained two photographs of the rocket taken from behind a curtain by a young girl, Jos de Ligny. They proved to be very valuable, for they showed the rocket on a motor tractor; until then it had been assumed by London that the V-2s were transported only by rail. Thanks to this information, attacks on the railway lines stopped and they concentrated on roads and bridges.[26] Further reports were received in London and the air operations became more precise and less damaging to the Dutch population.[27]

The work of the local, underground intelligence was valued highly by London, but endeavours were made to supplement it by other means. In September, four small groups of parachutists were dropped into Holland behind the front. Two of them, commanded by Captains Gilbert Sadi-Kirschen and Emile Debèfve, with radio-telegraphists and transmitters, were to concentrate on the launching-pads of the V-2, on their means of transport, storage depots and fuel tankers. They made contact with the Dutch underground movement and operated for several months. The Belgian intelligence network, code-name *Boucle*, led by Albert Krott, was still active on German territory and also sent despatches concerning the rockets or flying bombs.[28]

The air-raids, however, were only limited in effect and it was known in advance that they would not hold up the rocket-offensive. What was necessary was to occupy Holland as quickly as possible and throw back the enemy from the coast to a distance of over 320 kilometres, so that the rockets could no longer reach London. The Commander-in-Chief of the invading armies was General Eisenhower, whose strategic plans envisaged an attack on the Rhine on a wide front and a speedy occupation of the Ruhr and Saar basins; but the northern flank was commanded by Field-Marshal Montgomery* who, putting British interests first, had a different strategic conception. He wanted to concentrate the attack on the Ruhr, and then drive farther north, which would mean that Holland would also be included in this advance.

On 9 September, 24 hours after the first rockets exploded in London, Montgomery received an urgent message from there asking how soon Holland could be liberated. This confirmed his views, and in conversation with General Eisenhower on 10 September he presented his case very forcibly, adding the information about the rockets. Eisenhower allowed himself to be convinced and the following day Montgomery was able to start putting his plans into action. They envisaged an airborne landing of the First Allied Parachute Corps under the command of General Browning, who was to seize a number of bridges over the numerous water-ways of Holland, from Eindhoven through Nijmegen up to Arnhem. The corps consisted of two American divisions, the 82nd and the 101st, one British division and the Polish Independent Parachute Brigade. The British and the Poles were to take the important bridge over the Rhine near Arnhem, the most northerly point of the whole operation; the Americans were to be dropped farther to the south. At the same time the Second Army, of which the Air Corps was a part, had to make use of the surprise and in a

---

* Promoted on 1 September 1944.

swift drive from the south take Eindhoven, Nijmegen and finally Arnhem.[29]

The operation began on 17 September, but bad weather caused the drops to be put off for a further two days. The British division and the Polish brigade were dropped thirteen kilometres from the important bridge, for fear of too strong and immediate a defence.

The mere fact of the unexpected airborne landing took some of the pressure off London, for the German Command ordered the artillery units firing the rockets to withdraw to the north and east. Those that were in The Hague moved back, some to Overveen near Haarlem, some to Germany; those that had been bombarding London from the Walcheren peninsula moved to Zwolle, 50 kilometres north of Arnhem.[30]

But in the end this airborne operation, the last of the Second World War, was a failure. Such fierce German defence as there was had not been expected, nor had Intelligence reported that two *SS* Panzer divisions had appeared in the area. In spite of much help from the Dutch population, the bridge over the Rhine was not captured. Moreover bad weather made it impossible to drop reinforcements. Before the land armies could make contact, a retreat had to be called which lasted from 25-30 September. 1,200 soldiers fell and 3,000, predominantly the wounded, were taken prisoners. Once more it was proved that parachutists could operate successfully as an advance guard but only if the main force was advancing rapidly. As an independent force against armoured divisions, artillery and infantry they were doomed to destruction.[31]

While the fighting in Arnhem was still going on, Kammler's batteries had again started to bombard London. At the same time, on 25 September they had been given a new objective. This was Norwich, 80 kilometres north of the capital. It was to be bombarded by Battery 444, which had been moved north from Euskirchen to the Walcheren peninsula, then after the attack on Arnhem to Zwolle, and finally to Staveren in northern Holland; Norwich was the obvious target-city. When the airborne attack failed, Kammler immediately ordered a return to The Hague. This took place on 3 October and that same day rockets flew towards London, fired by one of the batteries of 485 artillery unit. During the latter part of October it was joined by Battery 444, which fired 43 rockets at Norwich and one at Ipswich. Only this last one reached its objective. However these two towns were not fired at again, for Hitler now gave the order that only London and the stragetic port of Antwerp were to be bombarded. The costly secret weapon, so long awaited, was now to be fired by the Germans at a city which had been in their hands since May 1940.

6

On 30 October, Marshal Göring came to Peenemünde, and although the western side of the headland, where the experiments on the V-1 were being carried out, was under his authority, he turned up in the eastern part, to listen to a lecture given by General Dornberger on the anti-aircraft rocket, called *Wasserfall*. He was dressed in the light-grey uniform of the *Luftwaffe* with all his decorations and a great Iron Cross; over it was thrown carelessly a heavy fur of Australian opossum; his legs were encased in high red boots of soft Morocco leather, fitted with silver spurs; a white cap covered his head, and his ringed fingers idly toyed with a full-dress marshal's baton. His eyes were tired, his face puffy and the lecture was of no interest to him. From time to time he swallowed a pill and finally he pulled out a large pistol and began to throw it up into the air, until his aide-de-camp very courteously took it away from him. After the lecture he was shown a very successful firing of the V-2. Only then did he become animated enough to speak. '. . . that's terrific,' he said. 'We must have that at the first Party Rally after the war.'[32]

This almost unbelievable scene was a perfect example of how out of touch with reality the rulers of the Third *Reich* were by now. The invasion had been successful, the Allied armies were advancing, France and Belgium were partly liberated; Soviet divisions stood on the Vistula, Italy was virtually lost, German towns were in ruins, the air force had no fuel, industry was destroyed by Allied bombs—and the second most powerful man in the country after Hitler was talking about party rallies after the war had been won. Hitler must have already understood that his secret weapons had failed, that they had come too late, that production of them was inadequate. Yet he still maintained that he would win and demanded from the nation obedience and uncritical execution of his orders. Propaganda upheld the belief in a miracle, a radical change to be brought about by the secret weapons. Even some high-ranking officers,[33] who otherwise would have seen no sense in further fighting, shared or tried to share in this belief.

After the loss of northern France, further attacks on London by the V-1 were only possible by ejecting flying bombs from aeroplanes. In the meantime Colonel Wachtel had withdrawn part of his unit to Holland, and part to Germany. His regiment, which had lost half its strength, began to organize in Holland in the triangle Zwollen-Enschede-Zutphen[34] and in Germany in Eifel.

On 21 October Wachtel received the order to launch an attack on the capital of Belgium and a few days later on Antwerp. Whereas the bombardment of Brussels was an act of terrorism, the attack on Antwerp, besides Le Havre the only large port in the hands of the invasion armies, was of great military importance. Now the true menace of the flying bombs could be seen and how powerful they would have been if brought into action a few years earlier, when the Germans were still a power in the air. The new launching-pads, erected within a few days by the technique perfected in France, were operational before the Allied bombers discovered them, and the proximity of the supply bases decreased the risk of destruction of roads and bridges. The production of the V-1 improved considerably in quality and quantity, several faults were corrected and air-bursts were becoming less frequent. It is enough to say that the number of flying bombs which fell on Antwerp, causing great destruction, was higher than the similar figures for London, although the attack on the capital of Great Britain began in June and the attack on Antwerp only towards the end of October of 1944.[35] The flying bombs proved to be of such operational value that Hans Kammler, whose ambitions soared high, tried to get control of them; but Hitler, well pleased with the achievements of the V-1, refused emphatically.

The retaliatory attacks on London, carried out by the V-1, had dwindled, but there still remained the rockets, which had a greater range. Retaliation accorded well with Hitler's temperament, but once he had used the new weapons operationally, he realised how important they could be strategically on a small front. This was why in the middle of October he ordered Kammler to aim the V-2 not only at London but at other towns on the Continent already occupied by the Allies, particularly Antwerp. It would have been hard to find a better executive than the ambitious and highly efficient *SS* General, yet once again it turned out that wrong decisions taken earlier were now to have disastrous results. Hitler, excited by the early successes of the V-1, had in the latter half of June 1944 ordered production of the rockets to be held up in favour of the flying bombs, and the underground factory in Nordhausen had obeyed. While in May 437 rockets had come off the assembly lines there, in June there were only 132 and in July barely 86. To step the production rate up again would be difficult, since the plant had received a new large order for the V-1 and there was an even greater lack of raw materials and manpower. All the same, the production rate of the V-2 began to rise slowly, as witness the number of rockets fired against London from the area of The Hague and its vicinity: in September, 24; in October, 85; in November, 154.[36]

London, which had begun to breathe more freely after the V-1 offensive stopped, again found herself in great danger. Not all the rockets reached the capital, but up to the end of November over 100 had exploded there and the casualties were serious. One explosion killed 160 people in a Woolworth's store, another went off in an underground tunnel beneath the Thames and also caused great damage. The scientists tried to find a means of diverting the rocket's flight by influencing its radio equipment, but in vain. There was no means of defence other than air-raids on the launching-pads.

The British authorities were in contact with the Dutch Government in London and were also in secret liaison with occupied Holland. Although they were told that the inhabitants of The Hague realized that there would have to be casualties, the bombing was careful and limited. It was chiefly directed against transport, woods and bridges, and also rocket depots, pin-pointed by Dutch Intelligence. All the same, some of the inhabitants of The Hague and the area around had to fall victim to the Allied bombs: these were necessary sacrifices, compounding the gravity of the rocket operations.

Suddenly, in the middle of December, the rocket offensive against London died down. Something must have happened, for Intelligence reported that the rockets were now falling on Antwerp in great numbers and that the Germans were firing them mostly from the area of Zwolle and Almelo. The number of V-1s launched at the Belgian port had also greatly increased.

Before further information could be gathered, German propaganda raised a great outcry: on 16 December Hitler launched, in the Ardennes, his last offensive.


7


Towards the end of November Albert Speer met a prominent industrialist, Albert Vögler, in order to discuss the desperate situation in the Ruhr, brought about by Allied bombing. Vögler asked quite openly: 'When are we going to call it quits?' Speer, who had already learnt of the planned offensive from Hitler, mentioned it in very general terms, adding that the *Führer* intended to stake everything on one, all-out effort. Vögler considered this and began to think aloud: '. . . Naturally on the Eastern front. Nobody could be so crazy as to strip the East in order to try to hold back the enemy in the West.'[37]

This was perfectly correct reasoning, and probably the great majority of the German population at that time regarded matters in the same way, still believing that their leaders would in the end come out with a political plan along these lines. In fact it would have had small chance of success, for Roosevelt and Churchill, at the Conference of Casablanca in January 1943, had taken the decision that the Germans must surrender unconditionally. But even if there had been any prospects of its succeeding, such a plan never entered Hitler's mind. The Eastern Front had remained static for several months while the Allied offensive in the West was advancing. So the leader of the Third *Reich* decided to fight to the last soldier and, believing in a sudden, miraculous change of fortune, switched his interest to the western theatre of war. Since his field headquarters in East Prussia were being seriously threatened by the Red Army, he moved to new ones, at the other side of the country. These were powerful, underground, concrete bunkers in a lonely valley, not far from Bad Nauheim, a mile to the north-west of Ziegenberg, hidden in the forest and well camouflaged.

There, still in September, Hitler conceived the idea of a sudden offensive, which, taking the Allies by surprise, would allow their front to be broken and Antwerp recaptured. The first to learn of this was the Commander of the Western front, Field-Marshal Gerd von Rundstedt; later, other high-ranking officers heard and they all protested. But Hitler refused to give way and ordered considerable forces to be transferred from the Eastern front so that the offensive would have every chance of success.

On 16 December fog enveloped the low but wild mountains of the Ardennes, when 1,000 German tanks moved forward and took the unprepared Allies completely by surprise. Their Intelligence, normally efficient and accurate, had this time failed. The bad weather grounded the Allied aircraft and enabled the offensive to advance quickly; within three days it had covered 70 km and reached Ciney, to the south-east of Namur.[38]

At the same time Antwerp was under constant fire from the V-1 and the V-2. Kammler and Wachtel, carrying out Hitler's explicit orders, expended all their forces to execute them. Their stragetic objective was the port, but neither weapon was sufficiently precise to concentrate solely on it. In practice the rocket-and-bomb offensive turned into a terrorist attack, in which civilians suffered most. On the first day of the German thrust in the Ardennes a rocket hit the Rex Cinema and killed 567 people; [39] other rockets also found their target. Up to the end of December Hans Kammler launched 924 rockets at Antwerp and only 447 at London. Colonel Max Wachtel, at last free from aerial attacks, set up sixteen launching-pads in Central Holland and during the last ten days of December fired 1,488 flying bombs of which half fell on Antwerp and half on Liège.[40] These last were meant to impede the XXX British Corps, concentrated there.

Four days later, however, the sun appeared and with it the Allied aircraft, against which the Germans could put nothing into the air. An avalanche of bombs rained down on the narrow mountain roads and the German advance came almost completely to a halt. The Allied forces re-organized; two American armies, the First and the Ninth, placed temporarily under Field-Marshal Montgomery's command, thrust from the North with the XXX British Corps, the Third American army moved from the south, and on 24 December the Germans were brought to a standstill. It was not that they had

no heart for the fight, but the tanks and cars had stopped for lack
of petrol, and the guns and machine-guns had fallen silent, because
supplies of ammunition had failed; in the air the Allies did as they
liked. The fighting dragged on to the middle of January, but before
it had died down completely Hitler ordered that part of the Panzer
divisions should be transferred back to the East.

Before this could be effected, on 12 January, the last great Soviet
offensive was launched.

# CHAPTER TEN

## The Soviet offensive and the Yalta Conference; the last V-1 and V-2 in action; the Alpine 'redoubt'; Hitler's death; von Braun and others surrender to Americans; the end of Peenemünde.

### 1

By the beginning of 1945 the German armies in the east were no more than a collection of broken and depleted divisions, without adequate transport, artillery or armour. The air force had lost more than half of its strength and was low on fuel; the soldiers were exhausted by the hundreds of kilometres they had retreated; and the commanders did not know what to do with the pitiful remains of their once splendid forces. It was hardly surprising therefore that, despite the winter and the difficult terrain, the Soviet advance was proceeding rapidly. On 17 January the Red Army occupied the ruins of Warsaw, which had been devastated during the uprising,* and on 23 January it reached the Oder, deep inside pre-war Germany. To the north-east, Prussia continued to defend itself; in the south the advance continued, and on 13 February Budapest fell.

A day earlier the Yalta conference, at which Roosevelt and Churchill confirmed the decisions already taken in Teheran, had come to an end; they had divided Europe into spheres of influence, giving the Russians Poland, Czechoslovakia, Hungary, Rumania, Bulgaria, Austria and the Baltic countries. The conference had only accelerated the Soviet offensive: Stalin had obtained everything he had wanted in Teheran, but he did not trust the Western Allies and had preferred to sit down at the Yalta negotiating-table with the promised countries already in his grasp.

Meanwhile the Allies adhered strictly to their side of the bargain. After the failure of the airborne operations at Arnhem and the repulse of the attack in the Ardennes, they abandoned further operations for the winter. They could probably have crossed the

* See Appendix II, item 10.

Rhine several months sooner and headed for Berlin, but they had promised the German capital to the Russians; so they did not undertake an offensive during the difficult period of the winter months. And this in spite of the urgent need to bring the war in Europe to an end and turn all attention to the Far East, where Japan was still undefeated.

Germany's situation was hopeless. She too needed a quick end to the war; but Hitler refused to hear of this. He moved from his field headquarters near Bad Nauheim to the underground bunker under the Chancellery in Berlin, and from there he continued his attempts to control the running of the war. He categorically forbade retreat. *If* it was unavoidable then everything which could be of use to the enemy armies had to be destroyed. 'We will leave nothing but a desert for the Americans, English and Russians.' The fate of the German people was irrelevant, for he had come to the conclusion that if the Germans were unable to win they did not deserve to survive.[1] He thought constantly of attack, and when this was no longer possible, his thoughts turned to revenge. For this only two weapons remained: the V-1 and V-2.

The fighting in the Ardennes had not yet died down, but the aerial attack on London had increased, as had the bombardment of Antwerp. While the attack on the port had some strategic significance, the attack on the British capital was simply an act of revenge on a country which had refused to be beaten. During the final stages of the war it was difficult to avoid the feeling that the leader of the Third *Reich* harboured a greater hatred for his enemies in the West than for those in the East, although it was the latter which posed the greater threat to Germany. Possibly he felt a certain sympathy for the system which had been created by Stalin, and which differed so little from National Socialism.[2]

A few months earlier Hans Kammler had wanted to gain control over the V-1, so as to unite under his command everything to do with the revenge weapons. At that stage Hitler had refused. Now he changed his mind, and on 31 January he placed the V-1 in his hands. The one proviso was that the *Führer* alone had the right to designate the targets which were to be attacked by either weapon.[3] Thus Kammler achieved his ambitions, rising from relative obscurity as an *SS* officer to become one of the most important men within the framework of Hitler's personal command.

Full control over the revenge weapons gave Kammler the opportunity to take quick decisions. He immediately deprived Colonel Wachtel of his independence of action and disbanded his regiment (155/W), introducing the batteries which operated the 'ski-jumps' into the Vth Army Corps, which he had founded himself. The V-2 launching-pads were once again situated in The Hague and the area around it, three V-1 pads were in western Holland directed at London and a dozen or so in the triangle formed by Zwolle, Enschede and Zutphen, all aimed at Antwerp.[4]

Hitler had designated only two targets for revenge attacks: London and Antwerp. Production of missiles had increased and both cities felt the weight of this last German aerial offensive, but the Belgian port, which was a target of strategic value, suffered much the more heavily of the two.

The flying bombs posed a problem. They could no longer reach London from Holland, and launchings carried out from aircraft were abandoned on 4 January 1945 as a result of great German losses. The need arose to modify production rapidly, so that the new machines would be lighter and have a greater range. This was achieved within a very short time. There was something uncanny now in the Germans' determination and technical precision. Everything was collapsing, inevitable defeat was approaching, but the engineers, during these last weeks, managed to design new types of long-range missile. At the beginning of March Colonel Wachtel received the new V-1s, and within less than a month he had managed to fire 275 of them at London. He also continued heavy bombardment of Antwerp.

The Allied air forces were unable to keep track of the changing V-2 launching-pads and V-1 'ski-jumps', so they concentrated their attack mainly on transport: roads, railway lines and bridges. These raids were so successful that between The Hague and its supply areas there remained only one undamaged railway line, which the Dutch resistance blew up half-way through February.[5] The Hague was treated with caution, but it could not escape Allied bombs entirely, since Kammler was firing off most of his rockets from the heart of the city where he kept his supplies. On 3 March fifty-six Boston and Mitchell bombers attacked the district of Bezuidenhout, where they hoped to hit V-2 installations located in a large park; but a map-reading error caused sixty-nine tons of bombs to be dropped a few hundred metres off target. The results were tragic: 511 people killed and 344 wounded, 3,250 houses completely destroyed and 3,241 seriously damaged. This was the greatest damage done to The Hague at any stage during the war and, sadly, the Allies were responsible.[6]

The revenge attacks on the two cites greatly absorbed Kammler, but they were not his only responsibility. If he was to be able to fire rockets and launch flying bombs, he needed a supply network which could continue to carry out tests and improvements, and factories to produce the weapons. So he was kept busy issuing instructions, travelling, and making inspections. But now a new task arose, which could not have been foreseen under normal conditions.

The war was drawing to a close, and this demanded some attempt by the combatants to undertake negotiations and come to an agreement, in order to protect the civilian population from unnecessary suffering and the troops from fruitless sacrifice. This could well have been achieved, had it not been for the Allied demand for unconditional surrender and the fanaticism of dying Nazism. As it was, the young *Gruppenführer* and General of the *Waffen SS*, Hans Kammler, found himself—at the end of a war which was already lost—in a sitation about which he had probably dreamed all his life: the *Führer* personally had entrusted him with the task of continuing the war and denying the Allies a victory.


2


In December 1944 the American Press, analysing the problem of the approaching end of the war in Europe, had suggested that it might not be achieved as easily as imagined: Hitler was a fanatic and was surrounded by people of similar attitudes; none of them was thinking of surrender; they would fight to the very last soldier and would find a way to prolong the war. Defence is easiest in the mountains, so, according to the Press, Hitler was preparing his last redoubt in the Alps. His stronghold was to include part of Bavaria, Austria and northern Italy near Berchtesgaden: underground factories had already been constructed there together with supply dumps, shelters, living-quarters and tunnels, and during the last phase of the war the Nazi authorities would move there, accompanied by 200,000 *SS* veterans, ready for anything. Some commentators even suggested that the Germans might invade Switzerland in order to exploit the defence installations there.

At first these alarms were treated lightly, but their frequency in the Press began to increase and this produced additional news of a sudden threat. In Germany a secret organization called *Werwolf* was being formed in which, under the direction of the *SS*, members of the *Hitlerjugend*\* were to be trained for partisan warfare. They were to operate in areas already occupied by the Allies, carry out acts of sabotage and murder Allied soldiers and Germans collaborating with the occupiers.[7] Allied Intelligence began to collect various unrelated details and started to build up a picture, which in part corroborated the Press information. This worried General Eisenhower particularly. It was winter, and the great Allied armies were still preparing themselves for the final attack on the German homeland.

Early on the cold, misty morning of 7 March a small patrol from one of the American units on the central front reached the Rhine at the town of Remagen, to the South of Bonn, where a railway line runs east-west. To his astonishment one of the soldiers noticed that the railway bridge was intact and that no special defences were apparent. He immediately informed the patrol commander and, within a few minutes, the American soldiers were on the bridge; they crossed it, took up defensive positions and were the first to find themselves on the eastern bank of the Rhine.[8]

Hitler was furious. This was proof that his orders to destroy everything which could help the enemy were being ignored. Four German officers were sentenced to death and shot, and Field-Marshal Model was ordered to recover the bridge immediately. But it was already too late. The Allied offensive had begun, the Rhine was crossed in several other places and the Third *Reich,* with its enemies now on its soil both in the east and the west, entered the

---

\*   The Hitler Youth Movement.

final phase of the war.

Although in Teheran and Yalta Stalin had been promised that Berlin would lie within the Soviet zone of occupation, it was widely felt that the West's armies, since they had already crossed the Siegfried Line and the Rhine, would head first of all for the German capital. This was believed by politicians, senior commanders, officers and most of the soldiers. There was even a plan to drop 20,000 paratroopers on Berlin and seize the city. After all, the war was not over yet, and whatever the promises, the deeper its thrust into German territory the stronger would be the West's position in the ensuing political manoeuvering.

This line of reasoning was logical, but it was not to be followed by General Eisenhower. To the surprise of his subordinates and the anger of Churchill, he ordered Field-Marshal Montgomery to halt his armies on the Elbe, and General Omar Bradley's armies to turn south and to head for Erfurt, Leipzig and Dresden, rather than Berlin. This plan had originated with Bradley himself, who felt that Germany should be split in two in order to stop still-intact German units from moving south to Hitler's 'Alpine redoubt'.[9] Eisenhower took the idea of a 'redoubt' very seriously; he believed that the Germans would try to prolong the war in the hope of sparking off disagreements between the Allies which might lead to better terms than unconditional surrender. He was reinforced in his thinking by the view of General George Marshal, the US Chief Staff, who also held that a southern line of advance was required, towards Karlsruhe, Munich and Linz, to prevent the formation of a mountain redoubt for a final stand.[10]

Several weeks later it transpired that the 'Alpine redoubt' was a myth, created by Goebbels' astute propaganda, to encourage the Germans to resist to the last. There was no redoubt, for it would have had to have been planned several years earlier for there to have been time to build, in rock, the necessary underground installations and construct appropriate services and supplies. Nevertheless this myth influenced the decisions of the highest Western commander, and it contributed to the conditions of postwar Europe, which for the peoples of the Central and Eastern European countries turned out to be so unfavourable.

And yet there was an element of truth in those American press reports.

3

In London and Antwerp the start of the offensive in the West was received with relief. Both cities were by then exhausted by the continuous bombardment by V-1s and V-2s; in London's case it had been going on for months. Now it was expected that Holland would be speedily liberated, and that the Germans would be thrown back so far to the east that neither weapon could be effective. That is in fact what happened. On 27 March the last two rockets fell on Great Britain: the first one in the London district of Stepney, where it killed 130 people, and the second one on Orpington, without any serious damage. The same day the attack on Antwerp ceased and Kammler ordered an evacuation.*

Colonel Wachtel, whose launching-pads were located in central Holland, further east, was able to fire off his V-1s for a little longer, and the last flying bombs fell on London on 29 March and on Antwerp on the 30th; but he too was forced to retreat, destroying the installations and taking with him as many unused missiles as possible.[11]

For Kammler, withdrawal from Holland was a defeat; but his zeal and vitality did not desert him, and for some weeks now he had already been very active on a new assignment. Before he could concentrate his whole attention and efforts on it, he had first to settle the problem of the V-2 range, which had been moved from Blizna to the Tucholska Forest. In the middle of January, as a result of the pressure of the Soviet winter offensive, it had to be moved again, this time to the forests to the south of Wolgast, not far from Peenemünde. Not a single firing was made there and in mid-February it moved once more, to the area of Rethen on the Weser, to the west of Hannover. Again no new trials were carried out there.[12] However, this was no longer of any great importance for Kammler. His thoughts were concentrated on the new task, which was of the utmost importance and had to be clothed in the greatest secrecy. The 'Alpine redoubt' was a propaganda myth; but a plan, based on a similar idea, did exist and its execution had been entrusted to Kammler. The project was centred not on the Alps,

* For all figures relating to the use of the V-1 and V-2 during the war, see Appendix III.

but on the Harz Mountains and the already existing underground factory at Nordhausen.

At the beginning of 1945 the Central Works in the Kohnstein mountain was well developed. More than 40,000 political prisoners and civilians worked there, and the camp *Dora* was expanding with every day, as were the numerous sub-camps in the area, which were all engaged in similar work. The production of the V-1 and V-2 was proceeding at full speed; underground passageways were being enlarged and the number of people employed was growing. In the newly-built areas the construction of four new factories was being undertaken: two for Junkers jet-engines, one for liquid oxygen, and a refinery.

From the end of August 1944 London had been aware of these underground works, and there had been some debate as to how they should be destroyed. The Americans had suggested a very complex aerial attack, which consisted of pouring over the Kohnstein mountain thousands of gallons of an extremely inflammable mixture of petrol and soap, which would seep in through the ventilation system, then burst into flames and burn out the interior. Bombers would simultaneously attack all the exits, so that help would be impossible. Fortunately this idea was never put into practice, since it would have meant the dreadful death of several thousand political prisoners and civilian workers. The Allies contented themselves with conventional bombing raids on roads, railway lines and bridges.[13] Many prisoners died as a result of these raids, since, although camp *Dora* was not hit, bombs fell on some of the sub-camps. In one of these alone, Boelke-Kaserne, several hundred people died.

The last redoubt began to develop around these underground factories; here the already humbled Nazis were preparing a final defence. Production of the last offensive weapon left to Hitler continued; there were already great reserves of fuel, and trains with food and other supplies began to arrive. Furthermore, Kammler was not content with the existing facilities at Nordhausen, but began to build something similar close by. In the town of Bleicherode, about twenty kilometres from the Kohnstein mountain, there was a potassium mine where the Germans began to bore new tunnels, galleries and accommodation at a depth of 700 metres, with the idea of reaching a distance of sixteen kilometres.

The plan was to tunnel through to another potassium mine nearby in Neubleicherode. It was planned to install several factories for work on the V-2 and smaller anti-aircraft rockets of the *Wasserfall* type. Not far away, in a cliff-face near the town of Lehestein, a tunnel was bored with a large cave at the end in which it was decided to install a liquid oxygen plant and quarters for rocket crews. A suitable place for V-2 firings was found at the top of the cliff-face, under which opened out a wide entrance to a slate-quarry.[14]

The Soviet offensive was moving so rapidly that in mid-February it was threatening Peenemünde, and Kammler gave the order for evacuation to the Harz mountains. A new research station was already being built in the Bleicherode mine and accommodation was being prepared for the technicians and their families in the surrounding villages. The move was difficult, since transport in Germany was completely disorganized as a result of the constant air-raids; but it was made easier by the combined eagerness and determination of the people around von Braun who preferred to be captured by the Americans than by the swiftly approaching Russians. Every kind of vehicle was used: trains, trucks, private cars, even barges. It was a question of moving not only 5,000 people, but important installations, documents and specialized equipment as well. [15]

The construction of the last redoubt was proceeding rapidly, and the military authorities had great faith in it. At the beginning of April Kammler received the order to defend it by every means and to hold it at all costs. However, this order arrived too late. The Americans were so close that Kammler had to evacuate even before receipt of this final order.[16]

4

A fine spring rain whipped up by the wind slanted down and covered the lorry's windscreen with streaks of water and they had to stop every few minutes to wipe the screen with a wet cloth. The lorry was an old model driven by wood gas, its windscreen wipers did not work and the brakes could at any moment fail. It was still only evening on 4 April, but it was already dark and lights were forbidden, so they had to drive very slowly and stop at each bend to ensure that they were still on the road: they were driving from Bleicherode to the disused iron-ore mine near the village of Dörnten.

Apart from the driver there were two silent men in the lorry. They were engineers Dieter Huzel and Bernard Tessman,[17] both from von Braun's closest team who, several weeks earlier, had come with him from Peenemünde to the Harz mountains. Now they were travelling by night to carry out their last wartime mission. Behind them under a tarpaulin were several tons of particularly valuable documents; the rest, weighing fourteen tons, were being carried on several other trucks. These were the archives of the research station at Peenemünde: graphs, sketches, diagrams, columns of figures, complicated calculations, the minutes of meetings, discussions and decisions. The sound of artillery was drawing nearer; the Americans could overrun the whole area within a few days, and everything had to be hidden as quickly as possible. The old disused mine was ideal for this purpose.

On the same night the last prisoners were leaving camp *Dora* and the numerous sub-camps as part of the evacuation. It had begun on 1 April, since it was clear that there was no hope of carrying on with the underground factories threatened by the Western offensive and cut of by the ceaseless bombing from supplies of semi-manufactured goods and raw materials. There was a moment when Kammler considered Himmler's order to liquidate all prisoners before the end of the war, but he decided not to carry it out. Everywhere there were groups of ragged people moving with difficulty or painfully gasping for breath in crowded goods-waggons. They were sent to Bergen-Belsen, Neuengamme, Ravensbrück, to smaller camps around Brunswick and to similar camps near Hannover. They were transported or driven on foot, usually without food and water; the corpses were unloaded in the forests and buried there, while those who lacked the strength to go on were killed by the roadside; those who tried to escape were caught and shot. They passed frequent transports of prisoners going in the opposite direction. Allied aircraft flew over the roads and railway lines bombing them and reducing the chaos to the last stage of madness.[18]

Hans Kammler, still full of energy, had ceased to think of the defence of the final redoubt and about the opportunities for using the V-1 and the V-2; he turned his attention to saving the people under him and safeguarding his own position at the end of the war. He well knew that the enemy, coming from both east and west, was interested in the secret weapons, particularly the rockets, and that there remained a chance of using this to his advantage when the moment for surrender arose. Conversations with von Braun had strengthened his conviction that the greatest hope lay with the Americans, partly because it would be easiest to come to some agreement with them since the war had not 'directly' affected them. He also knew that he himself would be of little value to them unless he had with him a team of many first-rate minds, with von Braun at the top of the list. On 2 April Kammler's special train, together with its sleeping-cars and dining-car, took about 500 V-2 experts and carried them to the Bavarian Alps in the region of Oberammergau. There they were housed in army barracks, behind wire and under an *SS* guard. Von Braun, who several days earlier had broken his arm in a car accident, arrived separately.[19]

The fanaticism of the *SS* men, however, could not be underestimated; they might well obey their orders to destroy everything which could be of use to their enemies. Von Braun was well aware of the danger to the scientists. When he saw that the officers and soldiers guarding them were less determined than before, he managed to convince them that it was risky to keep them all together in small barracks which could be an easy target for American aircraft. They were therefore allowed to disperse amonst the local villages. Several days later General Dornberger arrived with a small staff of *Wehrmacht* officers and put up in the village of Oberjoch. Von Braun immediately joined him.[20]

Events now moved with great speed. On 20 April, Soviet forces reached the suburbs of Berlin; on the 23rd, the first meeting between American and Russian units took place on the Elbe at Torgau; and on the 28th, the Allies crossed to its eastern bank. Finally on 30 April, a whole era of bloodshed, lawlessness, brutality and death came to an end: in his underground bunker in Berlin, Hitler killed himself.

Kammler was no longer around*, so General Dornberger sent

* His fate has never been clarified. Some think he was shot by an *SS* officer on 9 May in Prague, while fighting partisans.

out von Braun's brother Magnus, who spoke English, to reconnoitre, reach the American posts and inform ·their commander that 150 German rocket experts wanted to surrender. Magnus carried out his task and on 2 May in the town of Reutte, in the Austrian Tyrol, von Braun, General Dornberger and the remaining specialists found themselves in the area occupied by the American 44th Infantry Division.[21]

Three days later units of the Second Byelorussian Front, under the command of Marshal Rokossovsky, occupied Peenemünde. All that was left were ruins, broken parts of machines and smouldering ashes.[22]

# EPILOGUE

At the same time as the Allied divisions were marching across the *Reich* from the west, and the Red Army was approaching Berlin, the Intelligence Services of the victorious Allies were trying to locate the prominent German experts to whom Hitler owed the creation of his last secret weapons. A formal alliance between the Western Powers and Soviet Russia did exist, but there were grave doubts as to its duration. Both sides were already carrying out their own experiments with new weapons, and German expertise was vital. Unseen, an intelligence war was being waged, on the outcome of which might depend the balance of power in the post-war world.

Towards the end of 1944, when it was obvious that the Germans were bound to lose, the governments of the United States and Great Britain had begun to deliberate on the problem of the post-war administration of the conquered country. A plan called *Eclipse* evolved. Besides other matters it comprised a project, earlier studied by the State Department and given the code-name *Safehaven,* which envisaged 'the control of German individuals who might contribute to the revival of the German war potential by subversive activities in foreign countries after the war'.[1] This was far and away the main concern at this stage; but the wider issues were not ignored, and both the difficulties of further war with Japan (the atom bomb was still in the experimental stage)[2] and the question of the balance of power after final victory also came under discussion.

It was clear that finding the German experts was only half the problem, so the Joint Chiefs of Staff in Washington, on 24 April 1945, just before the end of the war in Europe, issued the following order to General Eisenhower: 'Preserve from destruction and take under your control records, plans, books, documents, papers, files and scientific, industrial and other information and data belonging to German organizations engaged in military research.'³ (Nothing was said specifically about equipment and machines, but presumably this was obvious.)

At Yalta the frontiers of the four zones of occupation in Germany were fixed, and the Harz mountains, with the underground factory in Nordhausen, were conceded to the Russians. But General Eisenhower's decision to direct General Bradley's armies further to the south resulted in the Americans getting there sooner, on 11 April. The Germans had evacuated all the prisoners and specialists, but the underground installations remained practically untouched, for there was nowhere to take them and Hitler's order that all was to be destroyed had not been obeyed. Way back in the tunnels, in long rows, stood almost completed rockets and flying bombs; all around were precision tools, half-completed parts, machines and various bits and pieces.

Although numerous groups of American and British specialists, representing their armies, navies and air forces, were already looking for the German secret weapons and the men connected with them, no overall plan of action had yet been made, so the exhibits were only put under guard on the spot and the engineers and scientists interrogated. In Nordhausen no staff had been found in the V-1 and V-2 factory, when it was taken, but some few days later the news came in that von Braun, General Dornberger and a number of other rocket experts were in American hands. Requests for detailed instructions were sent off at once to Washington.

Before the State Department had come to a decision, the problem of the speedy removal of the trophies from Nordhausen had arisen. The Americans were obliged to withdraw from the Harz mountains and hand them over to the Russians, who had already sent in their officers. British and French missions had also arrived at the underground factory in the hope of getting something for themselves. The completed rockets were dismantled and loaded onto trucks. The Americans took a hundred complete V-2s, over a dozen went to Great Britain and a few to France. The rest, with the machine tools and many thousands of parts ready for assembly, were left to the Russians. There was a dispute over the territory, which was to be occupied by the Red Army but was still being administered by the Americans. Churchill argued that it should be held at least until the Conference at Potsdam was over, but

President Truman thought otherwise,* and finally it was agreed that the American army would withdraw from Nordhausen on 1 July. Besides the rockets themselves there were still documents from Peenemünde, hidden in a disused coal-mine, and five cases of important papers, buried not far from Bad Sachsa by General Dornberger. This was seen to by an American intelligence officer, Major Robert Stavar, who found several rocket experts in Bleicherode—Eberhard Rees, Karl Otto Fleisher and Walter Riedel—and profited by their help. The documents were secured at the very last moment and the grasping hands of Soviet Intelligence only just avoided.[4] The race concerned the rocket, V-2, only; nobody was very interested in the flying bombs. After all these were only pilotless jet aircraft and technically had little new potential.

Besides the evacuation of the rockets and documents, the men had to be evacuated. This was more important for they alone could guarantee the continuation of the experiments in the future, and they might fall into Soviet hands within a few days. The situation was difficult, for the Americans had as yet no clear directives and could make only vague promises, while the Russians, governed by the will of one man, had a plan ready. Every day they put out messages over the radio that they were looking for men who had worked at Peenemünde, that very advantageous contracts were ready for them, that they were assured of excellent living conditions and that their families would be able to join them. Anyone interested was to contact a Dr de Pinsky in Dresden. But it appeared that the Germans were not enthusiastic to go to Russia, and the great majority of experts gathered around von Braun, who persuaded them to look to America.

In the latter part of June there was a hasty gathering-up of German scientists and their families around Nordhausen. It was intended that 4,000 people should leave, but in the end about 1,000 boarded the last train and made for a small town, Witzenhausen, in the American zone of occupation. There about 500 V-2 specialists, with von Braun at their head, were already waiting. They had been

---

\* From 17 July to 2 August 1945 a conference took place at Potsdam, near Berlin, at which Truman, Stalin and Churchill, with Deputy Prime Minister Clement Attlee, took a number of decisions concerning post-war Europe and the occupation of Germany.

brought by Hans Kammler from the Harz mountains to the neighbourhood of Oberammergau.[5] The Red Army moved into the territory abandoned by the Americans on 1 July and a trained team immediately took charge of the underground factory and the less important research workers from Peenemünde, of whom there were over 3,000. Of the prominent scientists only Helmut Gröttrup had remained there of his own will, and although only about thirty years old he was put at the head of newly-formed organization called *Institut für Raketenbetrieb Bleicherode* (RABE). Work went on there until October 1946 when, without any previous warning, the Russians took Gröttrup and 200 other rocket experts to the Soviet Union.[6]

The British and French also tried to entice German experts with promises. Great Britain had its own rocket programme (code-named *Backfire*); with the help of German technicians they fired two V-2 from Cuxhaven, and they later borrowed six scientists from the Americans, including von Braun and Dornberger. These men were taken to Wimbledon in south London, where for ten days they were shown the British achievements. They all had American contracts in their pockets; only General Dornberger stayed behind—as a prisoner of war, for the British wished him to stand trial for the rocket bombardment of London and Antwerp. The general was never brought to trial and after spending two years in a prisoner-of-war camp was released and went to the United States. In the end neither the French nor the British undertook any large rocket programme.[7]

On 19 July 1945 a decision was finally taken in Washington on the future of the German secret-weapon specialists. The plan was given the code-name *Overcast,* and it stipulated that the scientists should be treated not as prisoners of war but as free men who should be persuaded to go to the America to carry on further experiments. However, their employment was to be for six months only (at the most it might be prolonged for a further half-year), and families were to stay in Germany; the budget set aside was very modest and wages were fixed at barely $6.00 a day. Of course, these decisions were only provisional: the war with Japan was uppermost in most people's minds, and it was a matter of great urgency to consider the possibility of using German know-how to bring it to a speedy end (the men taking the decision did not yet know that the atom bomb would be used within the next couple of weeks).[8]

But it was not only the war in the Far East that produced such a deficient plan. Prominent scientists and public figures, such as Albert Einstein, Dr H. Robertson, Richard Neuberger, Philip Murray, Rabbi Stephen Wise, Norman Peale and others, raised great objection to the idea of mobilizing Germans for further experiments: it might only bring the threat of another war nearer when these men returned to their own country. This disagreement could have had alarming consequences, for the Russians were tempting the scientists with better offers. But the most eminent were already in the American zone of occupation. 127 were selected and offered contracts; all of them accepted.[9]

On 6 August the American atom bomb exploded over Hiroshima and from that moment the *Overcast* plan was no longer feasible. The terrible consequences of the atomic attack made it improbable that even the greatest fanaticism could allow Japan to carry on the war any longer. Short-term plans were now unnecessary.

The war in the Far East came violently and suddenly to an end just as the first German experts arrived in America. Within the framework of *Overcast* there was now nothing for them to do. In spite of opposition in the States, the political leaders decided that the scientists should be used in the realization of new plans, reaching far into the future. On 13 March 1946 a new name came into being: *Operation Paperclip*. It was decided to offer the German scientists and inventors very favourable, long-term contracts which would allow them to bring their families to America and eventually to become citizens.

Those who over the years settled in America within the framework of this plan, numbering 1,136 in 1948 (492 scientists and 644 dependents), represented various branches of science and responsibility for various German secret weapons. They had worked in different laboratories and often had not known each other at all before. The team of 127 engineers and inventors from Peenemünde, grouped around von Braun, stood out among them. They had been together for a long time, and had experiences and achievements in common. The V-2 rockets were their creation. Now they were to work together on developing and perfecting a missile for outer space.[10]

# SELECT BIBLIOGRAPHY

## ARCHIVAL SOURCES

### 1. Archives

— *Comité D'Histoire de la 2e Guerre Mondiale,* Paris: books, periodicals.
— *Instytut Polski i Muzeum im. gen. Sikorskiego* (General Sikorski Historical Institute), London: department of reports and statements.
— *International Tracing Service,* Arolsen, W. Germany: central records.
— *Museet for Danmarks Frihedskamp,* 1940-45, Copenhagen: department of reports, photograph department.
— *Public Record Office,* London: War Cabinet and Committee of Imperial Defence.
— *Rijksinstituut voor Oorlogsdocumentatie,* Amsterdam: department of reports.
— *Studium Polski Podziemnej* (Polish Underground Movement [1939-45] Study Trust), London: files of the VIth Bureau of the Polish General Staff.
— *Yad Vashem,* Jerusalem: department of Court Records.

### 2. Unpublished documents, reports and statements

— Cabinet and Committee of Imperial Defence, Catalogue No. E 255, War Cabinet, Crossbow Committee, C.B.C. (44): 6th Meeting, 14.7.1944; 7th Meeting, 18.7.1944; 8th Meeting, 10.8.1944; 9th Meeting, 31.8.1944 (Public Record Office).

— German Long Range Rocket Development: D. Sandys's report for War Cabinet, 27.6.1943, reference: Premier 3/110, Public Record Office.

— Iranek-Osmecki, Kazimierz: authorized statement, 11.11.75, in author's possession.

— Jones, Reginald Victor: report written in August 1944 on V-2, copy in author's possession; recorded statement for West German TV in 1963, copy of the typescript of the tape in author's possession.

— Kawałkowski, Aleksander: account written in 1954 in answer to Colonel T. Wasilewski's article published in *Bellona* in 1953-4, file: POWN, General Sikorski Historical Institute.

— Kossak, Maria: account about some problems of the Intelligence of the HQ of the Home Army, in possession of K. Iranek-Osmecki.

— Krokowski, Jan Bolesław: memoirs in French. Answers to a questionnaire of the student circle *Dora* of the German faculty of the Adam Mickiewicz University in Poznań. Description of underground activities in *Dora*. Group of French officers. La conspiration Grozdoff au camp de concentration *Dora*. Group of French officers. Execution of prisoners of *Dora*. Ponikiewski, Starzyński, Kolczyński. (All copies in author's possession.)

— Landgericht Essen, Urteil, Catalogue No. TR-10/769, Yad Vashem.

— Special Report l/R, no. 242, 12.7.44: files of the VIth Bureau of the Polish General Staff, Polish Underground Movement (1939-45) Study Trust.

— Pilecki, Witold: written account of his underground activity in the Auschwitz concentration camp, Italy, 1946. Polish Underground Movement (1939-45) Study Trust. File: Witold Pilecki.

— POWN, 'Grom's' intelligence reports. File: Grupa Północ; sub-file: intelligence reports.

— Document no. 34, file II. General Sikorski Historical Institute.

— Tuskiewicz, Otto: 'Polskie Siły Powietrzne na Obczyźnie', London, 1947, copy in author's possession.

— Zieliński, Bohdan: authorized statement, 29.7.1976, in author's possession.

Hitler's Last Weapons

## 3. Letters to the author

— Bittner, Czesław (Paris), 8.9.76.
— Celt, Marek (Chciuk Tadeusz), (Munich), 23.11.75.
— Gheysens, Roger (Brussels), 5.4.76.
— Helme, Jørgen (Copenhagen), 21.12.75 and 15.5.76.
— Hornung, Zbigniew (Vlissingen, Holland), 8.3., 9.4., and 23.6.76.
— Jones, Reginald V. (Aberdeen), 23.6. and 17.11.76, 6.1. and 19.1.77.
— Jong, L. de (Amsterdam), 17.11. and 2.12.75.
— Krokowski, Jan B. (St Avold, France), 18 letters in 1976 and verbal statement 9.9.76.
— Maurer, Bjarne (Copenhagen), 16.6. and 2.7.76.
— Protasewicz, Michał (Paris), 19.11. and 26.11.75, and 12.4.76.
— Szczęsny, Remigiusz (Lamberdart, France), 18.6. and 19.7.76.
— Winkelen, J.C. van (Serooskerke, Holland), 21.4.76.

## 4. Other letters

— Vintras, R.E., to Miss Ligny, 5.12.74, copy in author's possession.

## BOOKS AND ARTICLES

— *Armia Krajowa w dokumentach, 1939-1945*, vols I, II and III, Studium Polski Podziemnej, London, 1970, 1973 and 1976.
— Arnold, Henry H., *Global Mission*, New York, 1949.
— Bartoszewski, Władysław, *1859 dni Warszawy*, Znak, Cracow, 1974.
— Bekker, Calus, *Hitler's Naval War*, Purnell, London, 1974.
— Bernard, Henri, *Histoire de la Résistance européenne*, Marabout Université, Vervières, 1968; *La Résistance 1940-1945*, La Renaissance du Livre, Brussels, 1968.
— Bertrand, Gustave, *Enigma ou la plus grande énigme de la guerre 1939-1945*, Plon, Paris, 1973.
— Boer, J.F.A., *Raketten over den Haag*, Amsterdam.
— Bornemann, Manfred, *Geheimprojekt Mittelbau*, Munich, 1971.

— Bornemann, Manfred and Broszat, Martin, 'Das KL Dora-Mittelbau', *Schriftenreihe der Vierteljahreshefte für Zeitgeschichte,* No. 21, Stuttgart.

— Bór-Komorowski, Tadeusz, *Armia Podziemna,* Veritas, London, 1951.

— Braun, Wernher von and Frederick I. Ordway III, *History of Rocketry and Space Travel,* Nelson, London, 1966.

— Bregman Aleksander, *Najlepszy sojusznik Hitlera,* 4th edn, Odnova, London, 1974.

— Cabała, Adam, *Upiory tunelu Dora,* MON, Warsaw, 1959.

— Calvocoressi, Peter and Wint, Guy, *Total War,* Penguin, London, 1972.

— Churchill, Winston, *The Second World War,* Vol. V, Cassel, London, 1952.

— Collier, Richard, *Duce!,* Collins, London, 1971; *Eagle Day,* Dutton, New York, 1966.

— Comité International de Buchenwald-Dora at Commandos, *Dora,* Strasbourg-Paris, 1967.

— Cookridge, E.H., *Inside SOE,* Barker, London, 1966.

— Czarnecki, Wacław and Zonik, Zygmunt, *Kryptonim Dora,* Książka i Wiedza, Warsaw, 1973.

— Dornberger, Walter, *V-2,* Panther, London, 1958.

— *European Resistance Movements, 1939-1945,* Pergamon Press, Oxford, London, New York, Paris, 1960.

— Felsztyn, Tadeusz, *Rakiety i podróże międzyplanetarne,* B. Swiderski, London, 1959.

— Foot, Michael R.D., *Resistance,* Methuen, London, 1976; *SOE in France,* HMSO, London, 1966.

— Fourcade, Marie-Madeleine, *Noah's Ark,* Allen and Unwin, London, 1973.

— Garliński, Józef, *Fighting Auschwitz,* J. Friedmann, London, 1975. *Poland, SOE and the Allies,* Allen and Unwin, London, 1969.

— Haestrup, Jørgen, *From Occupied to Ally,* Ministry of Information, Copenhagen, 1963.

— Hein, Wincenty, *Zagłada więźniów obozu Mittelbau (Dora),* Główna Komisja Badania Zbrodni Niemieckich, Vol. XVI, Warsaw.

— Hill, Roderic, 'Air Operations by Air Defence of Great Britain and Fighter Command in Connection with the German Flying Bomb and Rocket Offensive, 1944-1945', Supplement to the *London Gazette,* 19.10.48.

— Hilten, D.A. van, *Van capitulatie tot capitulatie,* Leiden, 1949.
— Höss, Rudolf, *Wspomnienia komendanta obozu oświęcimskiego,* Wydawnictwo Prawnicze, Warsaw, 1956.
— Irving, David, *The Mare's Nest,* Kimber, London, 1964.
— Jacobsen, Hans-Adolf, 'The Kommisarbefehl and Mass Execution of Soviet Russian Prisoners-of-War', *Anatomy of the SS State,* (authors: H. Krausnick, H. Buchheim, M. Broszat, H.A. Jacobsen), London, 1968.
— Jokiel, Jan, *Udział Polaków w bitwie o Anglję,* PAX, Warsaw, 1968.
— Joll, James, *Europe since 1870,* Weidenfeld and Nicholson, London, 1973.
— Joubert de la Ferte, Philip, *Rocket,* Hutchinson, London, 1957.
— Kent, John, opinion about Poles, *Udział Polaków w bitwie o Anglję,* Warsaw, 1968.
— Kesselring, Albert, *The Memoirs,* Kimber, London, 1974.
— King, J.B., and Batchelor, John, 'German Secret Weapons', *History of the World Wars* (special), BPC, London, 1974.
— Kisielewski, Władysław, *W walce z V-1 i V-2,* KAG, Warsaw, 1975.
— Kokhuis, G. J. I., *Van V-1 tot ruimtavaart,* Amsterdam.
— Kozaczuk, Władysław, *Złamany szyfr,* MON, Warsaw, 1976.
— Król, Władysław, *Polskie dywizjony lotnicze w Wielkiej Brytanii, 1940-1945,* MON, Warsaw, 1976.
— 'Le Réseau F2', *Revue Historique de l'Armée,* France, 1952.
— Ley, Willy, *Rockets, Missiles and Men in Space,* Viking, New York, 1968.
— Lisicki, Tadeusz, 'Działania Enigmy', *Orzeł Biały,* London, July-August, 1975; 'Enigma i Lacida', *Przegląd łączności,* London, 1973-4; 'Pogromcy Enigmy we Francji', *Orzeł Biały,* London, Sept. 1975.
— Mader, Julius, *Geheimnis von Huntville,* Deutscher Militärverlag, Berlin, 1967.
— Martelli, George, *The Man who saved London,* Fontana, London, 1963.
— McGovern, James, *Crossbow and Overcast,* Hutchinson,

London, 1965.
— Michel, Henri, *The Shadow War,* Deutsch, London, 1972.
— Michel, Jean, *Dora,* Lattès, Paris, 1975.
— Montgomery, Bernard Law, *The Memoirs,* Fontana, London, 1958.
— Newman, Bernard, *They saved London,* London, 1957.
— *Polskie Siły Zbrojne w II-giej wojnie światowej,* vol. III, Home Army, General Sikorski Historical Institute, London, 1950.
— *Polski słownik biograficzny,* vols XIII and XIX, Wrocław-Warsaw-Cracow, 1967 and 1974.
— Price, Alfred, *Pictorial History of the Luftwaffe, 1933-1945,* London, 1969.
— Pruszyński Mieczysław, 'Wspomnienia nawigatora z lotu bojowego nad półwyspem Walcheren', *Polskie dywizjony lotnicze w Wielkiej Brytanii, 1940-1945,* MON, Warsaw, 1976.
— Royce, Hans, Zimmermann, Erich, Jacobsen, Hans-Adolf, *20. Juli 1944,* Berto-Verlag GMBH, Bonn, 1961.
— Rozhdestvensky, C., 'Tayna Nemetskikh V', *Nowoye Russkoye Slovo,* No. 23, Nov. 1975, Paris.
— Ryan, Cornelius, *The Longest Day,* Fawcett, New York, 1960.
— Snyder, Louis, *Documents of German History,* Rutgers University Press, New Brunswick, 1958.
— Speer, Albert, *Inside the Third Reich,* Weidenfeld and Nicholson, London, 1970.
— Strawson, John, *Hitler as Military Commander,* Batsford, London, 19711.
— Suchowiak, Bogdan, *Neuengamme,* MON, Warsaw, 1973.
— Szumowski, Tadeusz, 'Polska Organizacja Wojskowa we francuskim ruchu oporu', *Wojskowy Przegląd Historyczny,* MON, Warsaw, July-Sept. 1959.
— Thomas, John Oram, *The Giant-Killers,* Michael Joseph, London, 1975.
— Vader, John, 'Les V-1', *Historia* (2e Guerre Mondiale), 2nd edn, Paris, 1974.
— Wachtel, Max, 'Unternehmen Rumpelkammer', *Der Spiegel,* No. 49, West Germany, 1965.
— Wasilewski, Tadeusz, 'Polski ruch podziemny we Francji', *Bellona,* London, 1953.
— Whiting, Charles, *The Battle for Twelveland,* Cooper, London,

1975; *Werewolf,* Corgi, London, 1972.
— Williams, Neville, *Chronology of the Modern World, 1763-1965,* Penguin, London, 1975.
— Winkelen, J.C. van, 'Serooskerke en het Duitse oorlogstuig', *P.Z.C.* (a local paper in Vlissingen, Holland), 13.9.75.
— Winterbotham, Frederick W., *The Ultra Secret,* Futura, London, 1975.
— Wojewódzki, Michał, *V-1, V-2,* 3rd edn, PAX, Warsaw, 1975.
— Zaborowski, Jan, preface to the book by Tomasz Sobański, *Ucieczki Oświęcimskie,* 3rd edn, MON, Warsaw, 1974.
— Zukov, Georgy K., *The Memoirs,* Cape, London, 1971.

**PERIODICALS**

— *After the Battle* (quarterly), London.
— *Bellona* (quarterly), London.
— *Biuletyn Głównej Komisji Badania Zbrodni Hitlerowskich w Polsce* (occasional), Warsaw.
— *De Vligende Hollander* (daily of the Allied Air Forces), Holland.
— *Historia* (weekly), Paris.
— *Historia* (monthly), Paris.
— *History of the World Wars* (monthly), London.
— *London Gazette* (daily), London.
— *Na Antenie* (monthly), Munich.
— *Novoye Russkoye Slovo* (weekly), Paris.
— *Przegląd łączności* (quarterly), London
— *P.Z.C.* (weekly), Vlissingen, Holland.
— *Schriftenreihe der Vierteljahreshefte für Zeitgeschichte* (quarterly), Stuttgart.
— *Der Spiegel* (weekly), West Germany.
— *La Voix de la Résistance* (quarterly), Paris.
— *Wojskowy Przegląd Historyczny* (quarterly), Warsaw.
— *Wrocławski Tygodnik Katolicki* (weekly), Wrocław.
— *Zeszyty Historyczne* (quarterly), Paris.

# NOTES

## CHAPTER ONE

1. Calus Bekker, *Hitler's Naval War*, pp. 40-1.
2. David Irving, *The Mare's Nest*, pp. 15 and 33.
3. Ibid, p. 14.
4. Michał Wojewódzki, *V-1, V-2*, pp. 34-6.
5. Julius Mader, *Geheimnis von Huntville*, pp. 74-6.
6. Willy Ley, *Rockets, Missiles and Men in Space*, p. 144.
7. Mader, p. 85.
8. Ibid, p. 87.
9. Ley, pp. 202-3.
10. Wojewódzki, p. 48.
11. Irving, pp. 23-4.
12. Henry H. Arnold, *Global Mission*, p. 206.
13. Ley, pp. 419-27.
14. Irving, pp. 24-5.
15. Ibid, pp. 23-4. Wojewówdzki, pp. 61-2.
16. Ley, pp. 206-7.
17. Wojewódzki, p. 76.
18. Ley, p. 46.
19. Ibid, pp. 150-4.
20. Ibid, pp. 194-9 and 498-9.
21. Ibid, pp. 200-1.
22. Wojewódzki, p. 73.
23. Ley, p. 185.
24. Walter Dornberger, *V-2*, pp. 35-6.
25. Wojewódzki, pp. 56-7.
26. Wojewódzki, p. 55.
27. Albert Speer, *Inside the Third Reich*, p. 129.
28. Dornberger, pp. 51-3.

29. Extract from the document 079-L, exhibit US-27 in the Nuremberg trial (Mader, p.117).

## CHAPTER TWO

1. *Polski słownik biograficzny,* pp. 229-30.
2. Witold Pilecki, report, p. 102.
3. Jan Jokiel, *Udział Polaków . . .*, p. 25.
4. John Kent (Group-Captain, a Canadian, commander of Squadron 303 during the Battle of Britain; opinion of Poles—J. Jokiel, p. 43).
5. Albert Kesselring, *The Memoirs,* p. 72.
6. Otto Tuskiewicz, *Polskie Siły . . .*, in the section 'Fighters in Great Britain', p. 4. Richard Collier, *Eagle Day,* p. 14.
7. Reginald Victor Jones, a letter to J. Mader (Mader, p. 127).
8. Michael R. D. Foot, *SOE in France,* pp. XVII-XXII.
9. Jørgen Haestrup, *From Occupied to Ally,* pp. 3-4.
10. John Oram Thomas, *The Giant-Killers,* pp. 14-15.
11. Józef Garliński, *Poland, SOE and the Allies,* p. 26. (In May 1942 Hambro was the head of the whole of SOE after its first head, Sir Frank Nelson, had resigned for health reasons. He fulfilled his function until September 1943, when he handed it over to General Colin Gubbins.)
12. Haestrup, pp. 24-5.
13. Ibid, p. 36.
14. Ley, p. 199; Irving, p. 18.
15. Dornberger, p. 54.
16. Irving, p. 18.
17. Speer, p. 374.
18. Garliński, *Fighting Auschwitz,* pp. 86-88.
19. Speer, pp. 368-70.

## CHAPTER THREE

1. John Strawson, *Hitler as Military Commander,* p. 152.
2. Bregman, p. 134 (Nikita Khruschchev, speech at the XXth Party Congress).

3. Speer, pp. 193-5.
4. James Joll, *Europe since 1870,* p. 390.
5. Hans-Adolf Jacobsen, 'The Kommissarbefehl . . .', p. 510.
6. Speer, p. 215.
7. Irving, p. 19.
8. Ibid.
9. Ibid, p. 22.
10. Wojewódzki, p. 19.
11. *Armia Krajowa w dokumentach,* vol. I, p. 262-4.
12. ZWZ (*Związek Walki Zbrojnej*—Union for Armed Struggle) was an underground, widely-spread, Polish military organization, subordinate to the Polish Government and Polish General Staff in London.
13. Kazimierz Iranek-Osmecki, conversation.
14. *Armia Krajowa . . .,* vol. II, pp. 20-1 and 58.
15. Jones, report . . ., p. 4.
16. Irving, p. 34.
17. Jones, report . . ., p. 5.
18. Ibid.
19. Speer, p. 368 (*Führer's* protocol July 8th, 1943).
20. James McGovern, *Crossbow and Overcast,* p. 8.
21. Michał Protasewicz, letter (19.11.75).
22. Protasewicz, letter (12.4.76).
23. Wojewódzki, pp. 25-6.
24. Ibid, pp. 27-8.
25. Protasewicz, letter (12.4.76). *Armia Krajowa . . .,* vol. I, map 2.
26. Ibid, letters (19.11.75 and 12.4.76).
27. Charles Whiting, *The Battle of Twelveland,* pp. 145-8; Jones, letter, 17.11.76.
28. Whiting, op. cit., pp.149-151.
29. Jones, report . . ., p. 7.
30. Irving, pp. 36-8.
31. Winston Churchill, *The Second World War,* vol. V, p. 202.
32. Irving, p. 40.
33. Jones, report . . ., p. 3.
34. Bernard Newman, *They saved London,* pp. 27-8.
35. Philip Joubert de la Ferte, *Rocket,* pp. 42-3.
36. Ibid, p. 57.

37. Duncan Sandys, *Report* . . ., reference: Premier 3/110.
38. Newman, pp. 27-8.

## CHAPTER FOUR

1. Dornberger, p. 69.
2. Ibid, pp. 66-7.
3. Irving, pp. 56-8.
4. Dornberger, p. 67; Irving, pp. 26-30.
5. Ibid.
6. Ibid, p. 77.
7. Joubert de la Ferte, p. 82.
8. Irving, p. 23.
9. Joubert de la Ferte, p. 84.
10. Ley, p. 206.
11. Dornberger, pp.71-2.
12. Ibid.
13. Ley, p. 208; Mader, p. 159.
14. Dornberger, p. 73.
15. Irving, pp. 73-4.
16. Mader, p. 161.
17. Irving, pp. 73-4.
18. Dornberger, p. 131.
19. Ibid.
20. Ibid, p. 128.
21. Ibid, pp. 75-6.
22. Ibid.
23. Ibid.
24. Speer, p. 368.

## CHAPTER FIVE

1. Ley, p. 218.
2. Sandys, 'Rocket Development . . .'.
3. Irving, p. 75.
4. Ibid, P. 75-6.
5. Ibid, p. 78.

6. C. Rozhdestvensky, 'Tayna Nemetskikh V'.
7. Wojewódzki, p. 12.
8. Jones, letter to the author; Whiting, *The Battle of Twelveland* (according to him, both Luxembourg informants survived the bombing).
9. Irving, p. 81.
10. Ibid, p. 97; McGovern, p. 15.
11. Ibid, p. 98.
12. Ibid, p. 93.
13. Ibid, p. 108.
14. Ibid, p. 109.
15. Ibid, p. 106.
16. Ibid, pp. 112-15.
17. Dornberger, p. 120.
18. Ibid, pp. 119-20.
19. Wojewódzki, pp. 143-4 (based on the memoirs of *'Fraülein X'* in *Münchener Illustrierte*, January, 1958).
20. Dornberger, p. 120.
21. Ibid.
22. Irving, pp. 117-20.
23. Ibid, p. 115.
24. Ibid, p. 117.

## CHAPTER SIX

1. Max Wachtel, 'Unternehmen Rumpelkammer', p. 104.
2. Irving, p. 25.
3. Wachtel, p. 103.
4. Ibid, p. 104.
5. Ibid, p. 99.
6. Jørgen Helme, letter to the author, 21.12.75.
7. Bjarne Maurer, letter to the author, 16.6.76.
8. Joubert de la Ferte, p. 48 ( he made an obvious error, writing about V-2 when there is no doubt that the V-1 was in question).
9. Irving, pp. 127-8.
10. Dornberger, pp. 138-40. It is probable that Dornberger was not objective in his opinion for he was afraid of Kammler and regarded him as his rival. Albert Speer had a much better

opinion of him (op. cit., p. 374) and Rudolf Höss, the commandant of Auschwitz, who knew Kammler very well, writes positively about him and says that in private life he was very straightforward and modest (op. cit., Polish version, p. 325).

11. Garliński, *Fighting Auschwitz,* pp. 84-5.
12. Manfred Bornemann and Martin Broszat, 'Das KL Dora-Mittelbau', p. 59.
13. Speer, pp. 369-70.
14. Ibid, pp. 373-4.
15. Wincenty Hein, *Zagłada więźniów* . . ., pp. 70-6; Bornemann and Broszat, p. 181 (they say that on 1.11.44 the number in *Dora* was 13,737 prisoners, made up of 4,051 Soviet citizens, 3,883 Poles, 2,375 French, 1,185 Germans, 557 Czechs and 472 Hungarian Jews and others).
16. As the result of military defeats, on 25 July 1943 the King of Italy, Victor Emanuel III, demanded the dictator Benito Mussolini's resignation. That same day Mussolini was arrested and imprisoned on the top of the Gran Sasso mountain, while Marshal Pietro Badoglio took over authority. On 3 September 1943 he signed an armistice with the Western Allies (Richard Collier, *Duce!*, pp. 224-236).
17. Hein, p. 77.
18. Ibid, pp. 76-7 and 86-7.
19. Ibid, pp. 70-1.
20. Speer, pp. 370-1.
21. Garliński, *Fighting Auschwitz*, pp. 86 and 94.
22. Bornemann and Broszat, p. 171.
23. Jan Bolesław Krokowski, answers to a questionnaire . . ., pp. 6-8; W. Czarnecki and Z. Zonik, *Kryptonim Dora*, pp. 29-35.
24. Jan Zaborowski, Preface . . ., p. 21.
25. Irving, p. 204.
26. Maria Kossak, statement.
27. Tadeusz Bór-Komorowski, *Armia Podziemna*, pp. 146-7.
28. Iranek-Osmecki, conversation.
29. Bornemann, *Geheimprojekt* . . ., p. 105.
30. Wojewódzki, pp. 160-1.
31. Iranek-Osmecki, conversation.
32. Ibid. R. Jones, Report on the V-2 . . ., p. 4 (in it he gives the

date of one of the Polish reports: 29.3.1944).
33. Tadeusz Lisicki, 'Enigma i Lacida', p. 1.
34. Paul Paillol, former head of French Counter-Espionage, says
    that he was called Hans-Thilo Schmidt and that in 1943 he was
    betrayed by a French agent with code-name *Lemoine*.
35. Lisicki, 'Działania Enigmy . . .', pp. 7-8.
36. Gustave Bertrand, *Enigma* . . ., p. 61.
37. Lisicki, 'Pogromcy Enigmy . . .', pp. 8-9.
38. Frederick W. Winterbotham, *The Ultra Secret*, pp. 31-2.
39. Lisicki, 'Pogromcy Enigmy . . .', pp. 9-10.
40. Jones, Report . . ., pp. 4-5.
41. Ibid, p. 7; Winterbotham, pp. 147-9.


## CHAPTER SEVEN

1. Ley, p. 209; Irving, p. 148.
2. In reality the V-2 weighed 12,805 kilograms, of which 8,796
   consisted of fuel (alcohol and oxygen).
3. Irving, pp. 155-8 and 173-4.
4. Ibid, pp. 175-6.
5. Foot, *SOE in France,* pp. 21-5.
6. Henri Michel, *The Shadow War,* p. 71.
7. Foot, *Resistance,* pp. 239-40.
8. George Martelli, *The Man Who Saved London,* p. 7.
9. This was eastern French territory, 80-100 kilometres across,
   temporarily annexed by Germany.
10. Rudolf Höss, *Wspomnienia* . . ., p. 195.
11. Martelli, p. 7 (Hollard is said to have crossed the Swiss frontier
    94 times).
12. John Vader, 'Les V-1', *Historia* (2e Guerre Mondiale), 2e
    édition, no. 384 (19.2.74), p. 2017; Martelli, pp. 131-41.
13. Martelli, pp. 140-50; Wachtel, p. 109.
14. There is confirmation of this, for on 20 December Lord
    Cherwell studied a plan of the V-1 launching-pad sent from
    France (Irving, p. 188).
15. Fourcade, *Noah's Ark,* pp. 257-9; Jones, a letter, 17.11.76.
16. *Le Réseau F2,* publié par le Revue Historique de l'Armée.
17. Bernard, *La Résistance* . . ., p. 76.

18. Irving, p. 188.
19. Joubert de la Ferte, pp. 96-7; Martelli, pp. 159-61.
20. Ibid, p. 112.
21. Wachtel, pp. 109-10.
22. This order concerned all the prisoners of concentration camps.
23. Bogdan Suchowiak, *Neuengamme,* pp. 194-252.
24. Foot, *SOE in France,* pp. 21-5.
25. Garliński, *Poland, SOE and the Allies,* pp. 27-8.
26. Remigiusz Szczęsny, letter to the author, 19.7.76; Tadeusz Szumowski, 'Polska Organizacja . . .', *Wojskowy Przegląd Historyczny,* p. 244.
27. Szumowski, p. 244.
28. Ibid.
29. Ibid, p. 247.
30. *The Gen. Sikorski Institute . . .,* file: POWN. Szumowski, p. 246.
31. Szumowski, p. 244.
32. *Sikorski Institute . . .,* Northern Group, document No. 34.
33. Szumowski, pp. 245-6.
34. Bornemann and Broszat, pp. 189 and 194-5.
35. Czarnecki and Zonik, p. 224; Krokowski, statement, 9.9.76.
36. Jean Michel, *Dora,* p. 241.
37. Krokowski, Organizacja konspiracyjna . . ., p. 6; letter to the author, 14.8.76; oral statement, 9.9.76. Czarnecki and Zonik, p. 228.
38. Ibid.
39. Krokowski, 'Memoirs in French . . .'
40. Irving, p. 205 (he does not give the source of this information, but stresses strongly that all the efforts of the allied intelligence agents had brought no results and that it was only a ground report that uncovered the secret of the underground factory in Nordhausen).
41. Krokowski, 'Description of underground activities . . .', pp. 3-4.
42. Czarnecki and Zonik, p. 234.
43. Czarnecki and Zonik, pp. 253-4.
44. Ibid, pp. 255-69.
45. Krokowski, 'Memoirs in French . . .', pp. 19-33; letter to the author, 14.8.76. Mader, pp. 324-7. Michel, p. 220. Czarnecki

and Zonik, pp. 245-6. Adam Cabała, *Upiory tunelu 'Dora* p. 65.

46. Czarnecki and Zonik, pp. 246-7. Mader, pp. 324-7. Krokowski, 'Egzekucje więźniów . . .', typescript.
47. Ibid (photograph of the document).
48. *Yad Vashem,* Landgericht Essen . . . , document TR-10/769.
49. Höss, p. 323.
50. Irving, pp. 205-6.
51. Ley, p. 214.
52. Speer, p. 373; Dornberger, pp. 14-15.


## CHAPTER EIGHT

1. Iranek-Osmecki.
2. Wojewódzki, p. 268.
3. Jones, recorded statement for German television . . ., pp. 7-8.
4. Irving, pp. 264-6; Wojewódzki, p. 251 (despatch No. 366/1176 of 12.6.44 about hydrogen peroxide in the rocket).
5. Iranek-Osmecki, p. 2.
6. His post was taken by Adam Mickiewicz.
7. Wojewódzki, pp. 278-80 (statement of Lieutenant-Colonel Marian Utnik who at that time took over the VI Bureau from Lieutenant-Colonel Protasewicz).
8. Iranek-Osmecki, p. 1 (this was wrong, the rockets could not be steered).
9. Wojewódzki, p. 288 (the opinion of von Braun expressed after the war).
10. Jones, p. 9; Wojewódzki, p. 251. Wojewódzki states that this information was sent in an intelligence despatch No. 366/1176. At first the experts believed that this was the rocket fuel; actually it was the liquid for driving the turbo fuel-pump).
11. Wojewódzki, pp. 282-4 (Kocjan died in the Pawiak. Some people believed that he died at the end of July in solitary confinement, others that he was executed together with some other prisoners on August 13th).
12. Cornelius Ryan, *The Longest Day,* p. 18.
13. War Cabinet, *Crossbow Committee. . .*, Catalogue No.E 255.
14. Iranek-Osmecki, pp. 3-4.

15. Garliński, *Poland, SOE and the Allies,* pp. 89-91 and 154-8.
16. Ibid, pp. 78-81.
17. This order of precedence is given in a despatch of 20 July 1944 (No. 1071/VV/222) sent by Colonel Ryszard Dorotycz-Malewicz, chief of the operational base in Brindisi, to Lieutenant-Colonel Marian Utnik, head of the VI Bureau in London (*Polish Underground Movement (1939-45) Study Trust,* archives of the VI Bureau).
18. Wojewódzki, pp. 414-418.
19. Tadeusz Chciuk, 'Trzeci Most', *Na Antenie,* No. 47, p. 6; Kazimierz Szrajer, *Zeszyty Historyczne,* No. 37, a letter, p. 238; Jan Nowak, conversation.
20. Szrajer.
21. *Studium Polski Podziemnej,* file: rockets, 'Special Report 1/R, No. 242'; R.V. Jones, pp. 8-9.

## CHAPTER NINE

1. Wachtel, pp. 113-15.
2. Roderic Hill, 'Air Operations . . .', *London Gazette,* 19.10.1948.
3. Joubert de la Ferte, pp. 117-8 and 168-9 (extracts from *The Times* of 8.9.1944).
4. Ley, p. 216.
5. Irving, pp. 237 and 240.
6. Hans Royce, Erich Zimmermann and Hans-Adolf Jacobsen, *20.Juli 1944,* pp. 118-20.
7. Ibid, p. 120.
8. On 8 September 1943, on Hitler's personal order, *SS* Captain Otto Skorzeny, at the head of 75 parachutists, had released Mussolini from confinement on the Gran Sasso mountain and taken him to North Italy, where the *Duce* had started to rule again in total subservience to the Germans (Collier, pp. 242-268).
9. General Friedrich Fromm, commander of the reserve army, arrested at first by conspirators, was released the same day and at once summoned a court martial, composed of three generals, which pronounced the death sentence on General

Friedrich Olbrycht, General Erich Hoepner, Colonel Merz von Quinheim, Colonel Claus von Stauffenberg and Lieutenant Werner Haeften. General Ludwig von Bock, the prospective head of state, committed suicide (Royce, Zimmermann and Jacobsen, pp. 122-4).

10. Ley, p. 215; Irving, pp. 263-7.
11. Wojewódzki, pp. 289-90 (the oral statement made by Engineer Wiktor Narkiewicz, who as an expert on engines took part in the examination of the rocket from Sweden).
12. *Crossbow Committee,* 10th Meeting, 28.7.44.
13. Wojewódzki, pp. 416-18.
14. *Crossbow Committee,* 10th Meeting, 28.7.44.
15. David Floyd, oral statement, 17.1.1976.
16. Irving, pp. 281-2.
17. Chapter VI, p. 122.
18. G.J.I. Kokhuis, *Van V-1 tot ruimtevaaet,* p. 57; *After the Battle,* 1974, p. 30.
19. J.C. van Winkelen, letter, 21.4.1976.
20. Ley, p. 216.
21. Kokhuis, p. 47.
22. Ley, p. 217.
23. Hill.
24. E. H. Cookridge, *Inside SOE,* pp. 290-432.
25. *After the Battle,* p. 31.
26. Winkelen, 'Serooskerke . . .', *P.Z.C.* (local paper) and letter, 21.4.76. R.E. Vintras, letter to Miss Ligny, 5.12.44.
27. Władysław Król, *Polskie dywizjony* . . ., pp. 258-9.
28. Bernard, pp. 77 and 128-9.
29. Bernard Law Montgomery, *The Memoirs,* pp. 283-308.
30. *After the Battle,* p. 31. Irving, p. 287.
31. Peter Calvocoressi and Guy Wint, *Total War,* pp. 523-25.
32. Dornberger, pp. 178-80.
33. Speer, p. 410.
34. Kokhuis, p. 49.
35. During the period from 13.6.44 to 29.3.45, 2,419 V-1 fell on London, and in the period from the end of October 1944 to the end of March 1945, 2,448 on Antwerp (Irving, p. 295).
36. Ley, p. 217.
37. Speer, p. 416.

38. Calvocoressi and Wint, p. 526; Montgomery, p. 318.
39. Kokhuis, p. 64.
40. Irving, pp. 293-4.


## CHAPTER TEN

 1. Speer, pp. 426 and 440.
 2. Ibid, p. 422.
 3. Dornberger, p. 168.
 4. Kokhuis, p. 49.
 5. Dornberger, p. 188.
 6. Kokhuis, p. 6.
 7. Charles Whiting, *Werewolf,* pp. 138-9.
 8. Calvocoressi and Wint, p. 534.
 9. Ibid, pp. 534-6; Whiting, p. 144.
10. Whiting, pp. 150-1.
11. Kokhuis, p. 57.
12. Dornberger, p. 172.
13. Irving, p. 312.
14. Ibid, pp. 300-1.
15. Von Braun and Ordway III, p. 114.
16. Hein, pp. 117-8.
17. James McGovern, *Crossbow and Overcast,* pp. 3 and 178; Wojewodzki, pp. 437-8.
18. Czarnecki and Zonik, pp. 271-5.
19. McGovern, pp. 109-12.
20. Von Braun and Ordway III, pp. 115-16.
21. Ibid, p. 116.
22. At the end of October 1944, Rokossovsky was transferred to this front as its commander (Georgy K. Zukov, *The Memoirs,* p. 553).


## EPILOGUE

 1. McGovern, p. 241.
 2. German progress in this field was investigated by a special American mission *Alsos,* led by Dr Samuel Goudsmit

(McGovern, p. 240).
3. *Documents of German History,* p. 572.
4. Von Braun and Ordway III, p. 118.
5. Ibid.
6. Ibid.
7. Ibid, pp. 116-18.
8. McGovern, pp. 243-4.
9. Ibid, pp. 190 and 247.
10. Ibid, pp 245-6.

# APPENDIX I

**Item 1 (see p. 10)**
Hanna Reitsch, at that time about 30 years old, was awarded the Iron Cross, 1st Class; she was the first German woman to receive it. Later she received diamonds to her pilot's wings. She was very close to Hitler, who valued and trusted her. Towards the end of April 1945, when the Red Army was taking Berlin and Hitler was in the underground shelter under the Chancellery of the Third *Reich,* Hanna Reitsch proposed that he should escape by aeroplane. He did not accept the proposal, but she made the flight successfully herself (Wojewódzki, op. cit., p. 64).

**Item 2 (see p. 14)**
After the Second World War the eastern territories of Germany were given to Poland in compensation for her own eastern territories which had been taken by Soviet Russia. The new Polish-German frontier runs through the island of Usedom, called in Polish Uznam, with only a small part of the island lying on the Polish side. That part of the island mentioned in this work lies wholly in the German Democratic Republic, so all the names are given in German, particularly since the events described took place either before or during the war. With the new frontier, the town of Szczecin and the mouth of the river Oder came to Poland.

**Item 3 (see p. 17)**
*Abwehr* was set up in 1925, and from 1935 it was directed by Admiral Wilhelm Canaris, who was of Greek descent. The head of the *SS*, Himmler, opposed him in every way and tried to break up and destroy his organization. On 1 June 1944 the *Abwehr* ceased to exist and the rest of its staff was incorporated into the SD (*Sicherheistdienst*). Canaris, arrested after the attempt on Hitler's life in July 1944, was finally hanged in the concentration camp in Flossenbürg.

**Item 4 (see p. 22)**
It passed into history as the 'Ribbentrop-Molotov pact', since it was signed by the foreign ministers. One of the secret clauses foresaw a new partition of Poland.

**Item 5 (see p. 24)**
They were the designers of the famous pre-war Polish light aeroplane, RWD. In 1929 engineer Wigura with Lieutenant Franciszek Żwirko flew around Europe in it; and in 1932 they were the winners of the international competition for light aircraft known as Challenge (*Challenge International des Avions de Tourism*). In the same year they were both killed during a flight to Czechoslovakia.

**Item 6 (see p. 37)**
The situation in occupied Denmark worsened from month to month and on 28 August 1943 a general strike broke out, ending the period of peaceful occupation of the country. The German authorities made many arrests and put the whole administration under German control; the Danish government ceased to exist and a formal state of war had developed between Germany and Denmark. In September of that year the secret Danish Freedom Council came into being, consisting of seven leaders of the resistance movement. The cadres were established of an underground army which by Christmas 1943 numbered 25,000 and by May 1945, when the war ended, had grown to 45,000 (J. Heastrup, op. cit. pp 28-35).

**Item 7 (see p. 54)**
This was a code-name of Władysława Macieszyna, who towards the end of 1942 undertook courier service for the Home Army and travelled to Vienna and Heidelberg. She was arrested in Vienna on 8 April 1943 and, after interrogation, brought to trial on 22 February 1945 and sentenced to death by beheading. There was no guillotine in Vienna so she was to have been taken to Germany, but she fell ill of typhus, and just before the Red Army occupied the city she was released. She died in Poland in 1967 (*Polski słownik biograficzny* . . ., pp. 79-80).

# APPENDIX II

**Item 1 (see p. 53)**

Among Poles there is widespread conviction that Polish authorities in London received despatches and reports on the subject of Peenemünde as early as 1942. Wojewódzki states this (op. cit., pp. 18 and 252) and quotes Chmielewski's statement. But this statement is untrue and tendentious, like all his other statements made after the war (see Chapter VIII). Equally untrue is the statement of Lieutenant-Colonel Marian Utnik (Protasewicz's second-in-command, and from 5 July 1944 his successor) that after the war the British authorities took away all the archives of the VIth Bureau (Wojewódzki, op. cit., p.252). They in fact remained in Polish hands and are now to be found complete in the Polish Underground Movement (1939-45) Study Trust in London. Among them there is not a single document from 1942 concerning the V-1 and the V-2, nor has any been entered in the day-book of the VIth Bureau. That there were no messages received on this subject in 1942 is confirmed by Colonel Protasewicz (letter to the author, 19.11.75) and Lieutenant-Colonel Bohdan Zielinski, head of the Bureau of Military Studies in the Home Army Intelligence in Warsaw in 1943-44 (authorized conversation with the author, 29.7.76). On the other hand, while there is not a single document on this subject from 1943, and while none has been entered in the day-book, such documents and radio despatches *were* sent from Warsaw in 1943 and reached London, for this is definitively confirmed by Colonel Protasewicz (letters to the author, 19.11.75 and 29.11.75). According to him, he made use of them during briefings at the Polish General Staff. When asked why no copies were preserved in the archives of the VIth Bureau, and why nothing was even noted in the day-book, Protasewicz explained (letter to the author, 12.4.76) that certain despatches of a strictly secret character and great urgency were forwarded to the IInd Bureau (Intelligence) *without being entered* in the day-book, but after being de-coded. Copies of them were made in the IInd Bureau and entered into their day-book. This cannot be verified, nor can the documents be examined, for after the British authorities withdrew recognition from the Polish Government in London in July 1945, the head of the IInd Bureau, Colonel Stanisław Gano, handed over all the archives of his office to the British authorities (K. Iranek-Osmecki, op. cit.). Since the archives of the British Intelligence Service are still closed, these documents are inaccessible.

**Item 2 (see p. 72)**
On 12 November 1942, Himmler issued a decree to open the first territory for German colonization in the *General Gouvernement* (central Poland). During the few months from November 1942 to January 1943, over 100,000 Poles were displaced from Zamość province and some tens of thousands of Germans settled in their place. Some of the deported perished in the Auschwitz gas chambers, and any of their children with blue eyes and fair hair were sent to Germany to be 'turned into' Germans. The Polish underground movement, with the Home Army at its head, undertook reprisal action, attacking the colonized villages and the German guard-posts. They succeeded in interrupting the settlement operation which was in fact never completed.

**Item 3 (see p. 133)** ·
The preliminary work of Continental Action was undertaken in the Spring of 1941, but it really got going only in June of that year, when, after Hitler's attack on Russia, the mood changed in France. The Polish Government concluded an agreement with the British in July 1941 and obtained a preliminary credit of £600,000. Aleksander Kawałkowski, the former consul in Lille, was nominated as head of *Action* and began to set up an underground network under the name *Polska Organizacja Walki o Niepodległość—POWN* (Polish Organization of Fight for Freedom), code-named *Monika*. It was to give support to and maintain liaison with the SOE sub-section EU/P. The first briefing of *Monika* took place in Lyons on 6 September 1941. In July 1943 Major Antoni Zdrojewski parachuted into France in the neighbourhood of St Etienne and took over the military command of *Monika*. In close agreement with the British a special plan was

drawn up for using *Monika* at the time of the invasion of the Continent. This plan was given the code-name *Bardsea*. (This is by no means a full description of the Polish underground activity in France during the last war.)

**Item 4 (see p. 139)**
Christian Beham, August Kroneberg, Fritz Lehmann, Otto Runki, Heinz Schneider, Ludwik Szymczak, Georg Thomas, Jupp Wortmann (Czarnecki and Zonik, op. cit., pp. 214-19).

**Item 5 (see p. 139)**
Lubomir Bastar, František Blaha, Jan Chaloupka, František Linhard, Václav Polak (Czarnecki and Zonik, op. cit., p. 224).

**Item 6 (see p. 139)**
Jan Bogus awski, Marek Kolczyński, Antoni Kuligowski, Bohdan Kwiatkowski, Tadeusz Patzer, Stanisław Ponikiewski, Józef Radzymiński, Jerzy Sokołowski, Michał Sołtyk, Lech Wróblewski, Andrzej Wysogota-Zakrzewski (Krokowski, op. cit.).

**Item 7 (see p. 139)**
Colonel André Cazin-d'Honnincthun, Henri Chayot, René Cogny, Charles Hauter, Gabriel Lacoste, Edouard Lambert, Charles Landy, Claude Lauth, Colonel Marian Leschi, Jean Michel, Marcel Petit, Jean Poupault, Bernard Zuber (Krokowski, op. cit.; Michel, op. cit., pp. 241-2).

**Item 8 (see p. 140)**
Lutsian Galkin, Semeon Grinko (Captain Yelovoy), Yuri Yevgorov, Yuri Nasyakin, Nikolay Petrenko, Daniel Piekarov, Misha Plaksin, Konstantin Zhuravsky (Krokowski, op. cit.; Czarnecki and Zonik, op. cit., p. 228).

**Item 9 (see p. 143)**
Lubomir Bastar, Jan Češpiva, Jan Chaloupka, Captain Yelovoy, August Kronberg, Albert Kuntz, Jean Michel, Stanisław Ponikiewski, Tadeusz Patzer, Nikolay Petrenko, Jean Poupault, Otto Runki, Heinz Schneider, Konstantin Zhuravsky.

**Item 10 (see p. 187)**
On 1 August 1944, while units of the First Byelorussian Front, commanded by Marshal Konstantin Rokossovsky, were already in the eastern suburbs of the city, the Home Army rose against the Germans. This uprising lasted until 2 October and ended in the capitulation of the insurgents and the destruction of the city. But the Russian forces did not come to Warsaw's assistance and attack the Germans, and Stalin did not agree to allow Allied aircraft, carrying supplies for the struggling city, to land on Soviet airfields to the east of the the Vistula.

# APPENDIX III

**Figures concerning the V-1 and V-2 during the Second World War**

|  | V-1 | V-2 |
|---|---|---|
| *Produced* | 30,000-32,000 | c. 6,000 (half for trials) |
| *Fired operationally* | 20,000 | c. 3,000 |
| *Against London* | 10,492 (7,488 reached England; 2,420 fell on target) | c. 1,300 (517 fell on target) |
| *Against other cities in Great Britain* | 3,132 | 537 (61 fell into the sea) |
| *Against Antwerp* | 2,448 (not all exploded) | 1,265 (some fell in the vicinity) |
| *Against Brussels and other towns* | not known | 447 |
| *Against the whole of Belgium* | 6,585 (RAF and A-A shot down 2,455) | as above |
| *Against Paris* | none | 19 |
| *Against other cities* | Antwerp 1,800 Liège 1,096 | Norwich 43, Liège 27, Lille 25, Tourcoing 19, Maastricht 19, Hasselt 13, Tournai 9, Arras 6, Cambrai 4, Mons 3, Diest 2, Ipswich 1 |
| *Number of people killed in Great Britain* | 5,864 | London 2,511 other places 213 |
| *Wounded in Great Britain* | badly 17,197 lightly 23,174 | London 5,869 other places 598 |

|                                         | V-1                                                   | V-2                          |
|-----------------------------------------|-------------------------------------------------------|------------------------------|
| *Number of people killed on the Continent* | Antwerp (V-1 and V-2 combined) The vicinity (V-1 and V-2 combined) | 2,915<br><br><br>895 |
| *Wounded on the Continent*              | Antwerp (V-1 and V-2 combined) The vicinity (V-1 and V-2 combined) | 4,810<br><br><br>1,264 |
| *Houses destroyed in Great Britain*     | 24,491                                                | 5,000                        |
| *Houses damaged in Great Britain*       | badly 52,293 lightly 50,000                           | as above                     |
| *Houses destroyed in Antwerp and the vicinity* | (V-1 and V-2 combined)                          | 3,613                        |
| *Houses damaged in Antwerp and the vicinity*   | (V-1 and V-2 combined)                          | badly 29,352 lightly 77,322  |

The V-1 offensive against London lasted from 13 June 1944 to 29 March 1945, and against Antwerp from October 1944 to 29 March 1945. The V-2 offensive against London lasted from 8 September 1944 to 27 March 1945 and against Antwerp from October 1944 to 27 March 1945.

The British and American Air Forces, between August 1943 and March 1945, carried out 68,913 individual sorties and dropped 122,133 tons of bombs on all targets directly connected with V-weapons, of which 98,000 tons fell on targets connected solely with the V-1.

The British defence against the V-1 shot down or destroyed 3,957 of them in the following manner: fighters, 1,847; A-A, 1,878; barrage balloons, 232.

The above table was prepared on the basis of the Hill Report and the books of D. Irving, W. Kisielewski, G. J. I. Kokhuis and W. Ley, quoted earlier in the text.

# PLACE AND NAME INDEX

238

# SUBJECT INDEX